The Mental Capacity Act 2005: A Guide for Practice

The Mental Capacity Act 2005: A Guide for Practice

Third Edition

ROBERT BROWN

PAUL BARBER

DEBBIE MARTIN

Series Editor: Keith Brown

Los Angeles | London | New Delhi
Singapore | Washington DC

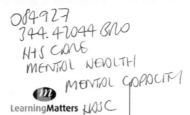

084927
344.47044 BRO
HHS CORE
MENTAL HEALTH
MENTAL CAPACITY

Learning Matters
An imprint of SAGE Publications Ltd
1 Oliver's Yard
55 City Road
London EC1Y 1SP

SAGE Publications Inc.
2455 Teller Road
Thousand Oaks, California 91320

SAGE Publications India Pvt Ltd
B 1/I 1 Mohan Cooperative Industrial Area
Mathura Road
New Delhi 110 044

SAGE Publications Asia-Pacific Pte Ltd
3 Church Street
#10-04 Samsung Hub
Singapore 049483

Editor: Kate Wharton
Development editor: Lauren Simpson
Production controller: Chris Marke
Project management: Swales & Willis Ltd,
Exeter, Devon
Marketing manager: Camille Richmond
Cover design: Wendy Scott
Typeset by: C&M Digitals (P) Ltd, Chennai, India
Printed in Great Britain by
CPI Group (UK) Ltd, Croydon, CR0 4YY

Library of Congress Control Number: 2015942765

British Library Cataloguing in Publication Data

A catalogue record for this book is available from the
British Library

MIX
Paper from
responsible sources
FSC® C013604
www.fsc.org

ISBN 978-1-4462-8726-2
ISBN 978-1-4462-9421-5 (pbk)

Contents

Foreword from the Series Editor

This third edition builds on the success of the original text by adding material to cover the implications of the recent Supreme Court judgments on what amounts to a deprivation of liberty. The Mental Capacity Act 2005 affects all mental health professionals who work with people over the age of 16 who may lack capacity in relation to any decision.

Robert Brown, Paul Barber and Debbie Martin have written this text in a style that is accessible to all professionals, and their detailed knowledge and experience of working in this field is very apparent. All professionals need to be aware of the Mental Capacity Act 2005 and its implications for their practice and this text clearly spells out these implications. Mental health professionals and other workers with adults would be wise to have a copy of this text close to hand to help inform their practice.

I warmly commend this text to all professionals, which together with the two companion texts from this series – *The Approved Mental Health Professional's Guide to Mental Health Law* and *The Approved Mental Health Professional's Guide to Psychiatry and Medication* – make a valuable contribution to the development of the best possible mental health practice in our society.

Keith Brown

Director of the National Centre for Post-Qualifying Social Work and Professional Practice

Bournemouth University

About the authors

Robert Brown is a Visiting Fellow at Bournemouth University and was a Founding Director of Edge Training and Consultancy Limited. He was a Mental Health Act Commissioner from 1992 until 2010. He provides refresher training for Approved Mental Health Professionals (AMHPs) and Best Interest Assessors (BIAs) and contributes to the training of section 12 approved doctors and Approved Clinicians in South West England and Wales. He provides consultation and supervision for the AMHPs/BIAs in the Deprivation of Liberty Team in Cornwall. Rob also provides consultation to Lead AMHPs in Hampshire, Lambeth and West Berkshire. He has published widely in the field of mental health and mental capacity law.

Paul Barber qualified as a solicitor in 1976. From 1979 until December 2003 he was a partner at Bevan Ashford (now Bevan Brittan), where for many years he led the firm's NHS Litigation Department, increasingly specialising in the field of mental health, mental capacity and human rights law, being involved in a number of leading cases. Still associated with the firm, he is now largely a freelance trainer and lecturer. He has been extensively involved in training on section 12, Approved Clinician and DOLS courses, and also provides training to AMHPs, nurses, managers and others. Among other publications he is co-author of *Mental Health Law in England and Wales* (2nd edition, 2012).

Debbie Martin is Director of the Bournemouth University Approved Mental Health Professional's course in South West England. She is also involved in the training of section 12 Approval and Approved Clinician courses, and provides training to various NHS Trusts, Health Authorities and Local Authorities. She has published in the field of mental health and mental capacity law. She is a registered social worker, and has practised as a social worker, a mental health manager and an Approved Mental Health Professional.

Preface to the 2015 edition

Welcome to this guide to the Mental Capacity Act 2005. This third edition has been revised and enlarged to include the crucial impact of the Supreme Court decisions in the 'P' and 'MIG and MEG' cases. We hope that the book will be useful for a wide range of people including health and social care professionals, service users, carers and others interested in the fields of mental health, physical health, learning disability and old age. The law as described relates to England and Wales. Note that the law is significantly different in Scotland, in Northern Ireland, in the Isle of Man and in the Channel Islands.

There are two companion texts in this series. *The Approved Mental Health Professional's Guide to Mental Health Law* is issued to many trainee and practising AMHPs. It covers mental health law in some detail, and the third edition considers the overlap between mental health and mental capacity law. There is significant potential overlap between these two areas of law. There is also the *Approved Mental Health Professional's Guide to Psychiatry and Medication*. This book contains a brief summary of current law in both areas in so far as they affect treatment for mental disorder. Readers who need a more detailed analysis of the Mental Health Act 1983, together with access to that Act and accompanying regulations, may wish to see *Mental Health Law in England and Wales* which is also published by Sage.

With the exception of the DOLS provisions the Mental Capacity Act has been operational since October 2007 in England and Wales. The DOLS provisions cover people who lack capacity to make a decision about being in hospitals, nursing homes or care homes in situations which amount to deprivation of liberty. This part of the Act came into effect in April 2009. As well as the amendments to the Act itself this volume contains new chapters to explain the procedures.

The Mental Capacity Act 2005 takes, adapts and clothes in statutory form a number of areas of common (judge made) law, in particular:

- the test for incapacity;
- the means of establishing 'best interests';
- the authority to intervene in relation to a person lacking capacity and the limits to that authority;
- the law relating to advance decisions.

Just when the common law will continue to apply in relation to dealing with those lacking capacity is an interesting issue and outside the scope of this book. What is left of the common law will depend to some extent upon how the courts construe the Mental Capacity Act, whether broadly or narrowly. Perhaps the safest advice would be to confine the use of common law powers in relation to a person lacking capacity to emergencies and short-term interventions.

This book is not just aimed at social workers because the Mental Capacity Act 2005 affects all those who are dealing with anyone over the age of 16 who may lack capacity in relation to any decisions. This long awaited Act should assist staff in these circumstances. Hopefully this book will make the law accessible and understandable to a wide range of practitioners.

At the end of each chapter we have included key points and questions, sometimes in multiple choice form, in an attempt to aid learning. Some of the most important points are then summarised in Appendices to try and help busy practitioners.

We would like to thank Tracy Gallagher and Anthony Harbour who read and commented on the original text when it was in its draft form. Their views, based on their experience and knowledge of how the law operates in practice, were very helpful to us. However, we accept responsibility for any inaccuracies which remain within the text.

Robert Brown, Visiting Fellow, Bournemouth University

Paul Barber, Consultant, Bevan Brittan, Solicitors

Debbie Martin, South West England AMHP Programme Director, Bournemouth University

Chapter 1
Background to the Mental Capacity Act 2005

Introduction

The Mental Capacity Act, as passed in 2005 and implemented in 2007, was the culmination of more than 15 years of work. Before making a detailed examination of the provisions of the Act, it is worth placing it in context by looking briefly at the events that led to the Act reaching the statute book. The amendments to the Act that resulted from the Mental Health Act 2007 will be considered in Chapter 2.

The Law Society (1989) had highlighted some difficulties in a paper published prior to the conference on 'Decision-Making and Mental Incapacity'. This led to the involvement of the Law Commission (1991), which published Consultation Paper No. 119 entitled 'Mentally Incapacitated Adults and Decision-Making: An Overview'. Paragraph 1.9 of the Law Commission paper clearly stated why new law was needed:

> The existing law relating to decision-making on behalf of mentally incapacitated adults is fragmented, complex and in many respects out of date. There is no coherent concept of their status, and there are many gaps where the law provides no effective mechanism for resolving problems. Debate, stimulated by a series of High Court decisions on sterilisation and abortion, has recently focused on the obtaining of consent to serious medical procedures, but the problems extend far beyond this issue.

The Consultation Paper identified a number of problem areas involving capacity and decision-making. These included:

- consent to medical treatment;
- disputes between relatives;
- significant life decisions. Where an adult was not capable of making decisions such as whether to continue living at home, it was not clear who had ultimate responsibility for making such a decision;
- suspicions of abuse or neglect. There were problems deciding at what stage intervention was justified and who should be responsible for taking any action;
- young people leaving care. Those with a mental incapacity might not be eligible for guardianship under the Mental Health Act 1983 and yet neither foster parents nor local authority would have any continuing legal responsibility under child care law.

Prior to the passing of the Mental Capacity Act there was a variety of legislation which was relevant to these issues but, as noted above, it was fragmented, complex and out of date.

Key issues to be resolved

There are some tensions that the law may be asked to deal with. Maximising freedom and autonomy may conflict with a need for care or control. Again, protection from abuse or exploitation may involve some invasion of a person's autonomy. Another issue is how to identify an acceptable level of risk for an individual. If a professional intervenes without a clear legal base and guidance, they lay themselves open to allegations of undue influence or misconduct. If they do not intervene, they may be accused of neglecting their duty of care. Finally, not intervening may result in other people being harmed or in suffering in some way. If the person causing the harm is seen as 'mentally incapacitated', this raises the question whether they should face the full penalty of law (e.g. through a criminal or civil action) or whether they should be dealt with differently because of their lack of understanding of the consequences of their actions.

The concept of mental capacity

There is a distinction to be drawn between a legal definition of capacity (or incapacity) and medical or psychological definitions, though on some occasions they will be the same. Paragraph 2.10 of the Law Commission's 1991 paper stated:

> *A legal incapacity arises whenever the law provides that a particular person is incapable of taking a particular decision, undertaking a particular juristic act, or engaging in a particular activity. Incapacity can arise from a variety of conditions; historically, these included being under the age of majority, or a married woman, or of unsound mind. Under the modern law, a great many different approaches have developed to the question of capacity based on mental state. Generally there is a presumption that the person is capable until proved otherwise, and capacity is judged in relation to the particular decision, transaction or activity involved. There is also a basic common law test of capacity, to the effect that the person concerned must at the relevant time understand in broad terms what he is doing and the likely effects of his action. Thus, in principle, legal capacity depends upon understanding rather than wisdom: the quality of the decision is irrelevant as long as the person understands what he is deciding.*

This approach to the definition of mental incapacity was broadly followed in the 2005 Act, as will be seen when we examine the provisions in detail.

The work of the Law Commission

There were four consultation papers before the Law Commission (1995) published its final report. This comprehensive document included a draft Mental Incapacity Bill. The proposal, which has broadly been revived by the 2005 Act, was to introduce a new Act, which would be separate from the Mental Health Act 1983, and which would provide a coherent statutory framework for decision-making for those who lacked capacity. The two key issues were capacity and best interests, and these are at the heart of the 2005 Act. A new Court of Protection would be created to provide a statutory jurisdiction for making a range of decisions on behalf of people who lacked capacity.

It is unfortunate that these proposals were stalled by the then Government's decision not to proceed. A proposed consultation on the report did not materialise. Ashton *et al.* (2006) attribute the Government's reaction to a defensive response to an attack on the Law Commission by the *Daily Mail* in support of family values. Living wills in particular came in for criticism. There were some echoes of these issues in the criticisms of the 2005 Act in its final stages as a Bill.

Who Decides?

This Green Paper was published by the Lord Chancellor (1997). It contained recommendations for defining incapacity, providing a framework for carers, giving more powers to the Court of Protection and introducing new powers of attorney. It also considered the issue of costs and whether the expense of any new legislation would be worthwhile.

Making Decisions

The Lord Chancellor's proposals were contained in this 1999 report. Many of these proposals would find their way into the 2005 Act:

- a new functional test of capacity;
- a best interests approach to decision-making;
- a reformed Court of Protection with a regional presence and powers to make single issues orders or to appoint someone to manage decisions for someone who lacked capacity;
- continuing powers of attorney.

Despite this revival of key elements of the Law Commission's proposals there was still a wait for Parliamentary time and it was another four years before a Bill was published.

The Mental Incapacity Bill

A draft Mental Incapacity Bill was published in 2003. (This was three years after Scotland passed its own Adults With Incapacity (Scotland) Act 2000. A discussion of the Scottish Act can be found in Ashton *et al.* (2006).) The draft Mental Incapacity Bill was scrutinised by a Joint Committee of both Houses of Parliament. This led to a number of changes including:

- a change in the title from 'Incapacity' to 'Capacity';
- a statement of principles to be included;

- refinements to the proposals for Lasting Powers of Attorney;

- standards of professional conduct to be included in the Codes of Practice.

The committee also considered that the Bill should receive priority and then influence mental health law. The amended Bill was introduced in Parliament in June 2004 and passed in April 2005 just before the General Election.

The Government's responses to the European Court judgment in the *HL v UK* case came too late to be included in the 2005 Act. The new Deprivation of Liberty Safeguards (DOLS) procedures were a response to the 'Bournewood Gap' and through the amending Mental Health Act 2007 they became effective in April 2009 and are included in this revised text.

Despite some late alarms the Bill just managed to complete its passage before Parliament was dissolved and at last England and Wales were to have a statutory response to difficult issues of decision-making where persons over the age of 16 lacked the capacity to make decisions for themselves. In many ways it is a radical and innovative Act and it will be of great interest to see if it is viewed as a success in terms of improving legal support for some very vulnerable individuals.

Chapter 2
The key features of the Mental Capacity Act 2005

Introduction

In this chapter we provide an overview of the main provisions of the Mental Capacity Act and consider how the Act should work in practice. This will be followed by a chapter on the Code of Practice. The rest of the book looks at the Act in more depth. The text of the main body of the Act is provided at the end of the book for reference purposes (pages 143–259). The Act was amended by the Mental Health Act 2007 to include the Deprivation of Liberty Safeguards (DOLS). The procedures and further details are set out in Schedules A1 and 1A to the Act.

This chapter can serve as a quick introduction to the essential elements of the Mental Capacity Act 2005, or it can serve as a revision tool for those who are more familiar with the Act's provisions.

The Mental Capacity Act provides a statutory framework for decision-making for persons over the age of 16 who are incapable of making certain decisions for themselves. The Act does not prescribe who the decision-maker should be in every circumstance, and the guidance on this issue in the Code of Practice is very limited, although it does provide a mechanism for resolving any disputes in this area. A significant part of the Act is devoted to setting out the procedures that should be followed in making any such decisions. It covers a broad range of decisions including personal welfare decisions, medical and healthcare decisions, as well as financial decisions. To a significant extent many well-established common law principles are enshrined within the Act.

We will now summarise the key features of the Act.

The five principles

In stark contrast with the Mental Health Act 1983 (which starts with a definition of mental disorder) the Mental Capacity Act begins by establishing five key principles to be followed whenever working within the framework of the Act. These are as follows.

1. A person must be assumed to have capacity unless it is established that he or she lacks capacity.

2. A person is not to be treated as unable to make a decision unless all practicable steps to help him or her to do so have been taken without success.

3. A person is not to be treated as unable to make a decision merely because he or she makes an unwise decision.

4. An act done, or decision made, under this Act for or on behalf of a person who lacks capacity must be done, or made, in his or her best interests.

5. Before the act is done, or the decision is made, regard must be had to whether the purpose for which it is needed can be as effectively achieved in a way that is less restrictive of the person's rights and freedom of action.

These principles will be considered in more depth in Chapter 4.

Mental incapacity defined

Section (s) 2 of the Act states that for the purposes of the Act:

> *a person lacks capacity in relation to a matter if at the material time he is unable to make a decision for himself in relation to the matter because of an impairment of, or a disturbance in the functioning of, the mind or brain.*

This is referred to as the 'diagnostic test'. This broad definition, which might catch so many people, is effectively cut down by application of the 'functional test' so that only the smallest area of decision-making necessary is identified for application of the incapacity test.

Section 3 then provides the test that should be used. It is an interesting development of tests that had been established by the courts such as in the case of C *(Adult: Refusal of Medical Treatment)* (1994). The s 3 test is that:

> *a person is unable to make a decision for himself if he is unable –*
>
> *(a) to understand the information relevant to the decision,*
>
> *(b) to retain that information,*
>
> *(c) to use or weigh that information as part of the process of making the decision, or*
>
> *(d) to communicate his decision (whether by talking, using sign language or any other means).*

An inability to satisfy any one of these four conditions would render the person incapable. Chapter 5 looks at the functional approach to defining mental incapacity, offers a checklist for assessment and considers the issue of how to record any assessments of capacity.

Best interests

Section 4(2) of the Act states that a person making a decision with regard to someone who lacks capacity must, in determining their best interests, take the following steps. These, in effect, are a checklist which is set out in s 4 of the Act. This is considered in more depth in Chapter 6 but, in summary, the decision-maker must:

- consider whether it is likely that the person will at some time have capacity in relation to the matter in question;
- permit and encourage the person to participate as fully as possible in any act done for him or her and any decision affecting him or her;
- consider the person's past and present wishes and feelings (and, in particular, any relevant written statement made by him or her when he or she had capacity);
- consider the beliefs and values that would be likely to influence his or her decision if he or she had capacity, and the other factors that he or she would be likely to consider if he or she were able to do so;
- take into account, if it is practicable and appropriate to consult them, the views of:
  - anyone named by the person as someone to be consulted on the matter in question or on matters of that kind;
  - anyone engaged in caring for the person or interested in his or her welfare;
  - any donee of a Lasting Power of Attorney granted by the person; and
  - any deputy appointed for the person by the court,

  as to what would be in the person's best interests.

It is important to note that in the case of an act done, or a decision made, by a person other than the court, there is sufficient compliance with this section if (having complied with this checklist) he or she reasonably believes that what he or she does or decides is in the best interests of the person concerned. Chapter 6 describes the Act's approach to determining best interests.

Protection for those making decisions

One of the essential features of the Mental Capacity Act is the protection it offers to anyone who makes a decision after applying the requirements of the Act. In essence, if a person does something in connection with the care or treatment of another person, they are protected if, before doing the act, they take reasonable steps to establish whether that person lacks capacity in relation to the matter in question, and, when doing the act, reasonably believe that the person lacks capacity in relation to the matter, and that it will be in their best interests for the act to be done. In many situations people will find it appropriate to make a clear record of this process and some NHS Trusts and local authorities have produced guidance for this. For ease of access the 'best interests checklist' is set out at Appendix 4. Professional staff might wish to ensure that any local proformas meet the statutory requirements by checking them against this list to ensure that all points have been covered.

If a decision-maker follows the Act's requirements it would, in effect, be as if the incapacitated person had had capacity and had made the decision themselves. This protection will be of no value, however, if the person has not followed the best interests checklist or has acted negligently. Chapter 7 looks at the relevant subsection (subs) 5–8 in some detail.

Lasting Powers of Attorney

A Lasting Power of Attorney is a power of attorney under which the donor (who must be 18 or over) confers on the donee (or donees) (sometimes referred to as an attorney) authority to make decisions about all or any of their personal welfare matters or their property and affairs, and which includes authority to make such decisions in circumstances where P no longer has capacity. ('P' is used in the Act to define the person whose capacity is in question, and 'D' is used to define the person who does an act in respect of 'P'. See s 5.) Personal welfare could include health or social matters.

This is a form of substituted decision-making. These powers are dealt with in Chapter 8. From 1 October 2007 no new Enduring Powers of Attorney (EPAs) can be made. They are replaced by Lasting Powers of Attorney (LPAs), which may be either a property and affairs LPA or a personal welfare LPA. If a person wishes to cover both areas of decision-making, separate LPAs will be required. EPAs made before 1 October 2007 will still be valid but will be limited to property and affairs.

Deputies and declarations

If a person lacks capacity in relation to a matter either of personal welfare or property and affairs, the court may make the decision on the person's behalf in relation to the matter, or the court could appoint a deputy to make decisions on the person's behalf in relation to the matter or matters. Again, this is sometimes referred to as 'substituted decision-making'. The court will start from the presumption that it will make the decision itself, but there will be some complex cases involving a series of decisions where it may be seen as more appropriate to appoint a deputy. This is considered in more detail in Chapter 9.

In addition, as a branch of the High Court of Justice the Court of Protection has power to make declarations as to whether a person has or lacks capacity to make certain decisions. It would be appropriate to ask the court for a declaration in circumstances where, despite following the procedures set out in the Act and the guidance contained in the Code of Practice, the decision-maker found it impossible to reach a conclusion as to whether the person had capacity or not. It would not be appropriate to ask for a declaration simply to give reassurance for a decision that was fairly clear.

Declarations could also be made with regard to the lawfulness or otherwise of any act done, or to be done, in relation to a person.

Advance decisions

This part of the Act only covers people aged 18 or over.

Advance decisions to refuse treatment, sometimes referred to as 'living wills', 'advance directives' or 'advance refusals', have long been recognised within common law. An adult of sound mind is entitled to refuse medical treatment, whether face to face with the healthcare professional, or in advance, anticipating a time when the person may lack capacity to refuse the treatment in question.

The Mental Capacity Act codifies this law and adds a requirement that for life-sustaining treatment issues the advance decision should be in writing and witnessed. For other treatments there is no such requirement, but the refusal needs to be seen as valid and applicable in the particular circumstances that present themselves. Chapter 10 covers this issue in some depth.

Independent Mental Capacity Advocates (IMCAs)

In England this aspect of the Act was introduced in April 2007. In Wales it was not introduced until the rest of the Act was implemented in October 2007. The IMCA scheme was piloted in a number of areas before the Act was passed.

Where serious medical treatment or a change of residence is proposed for a person who lacks capacity in relation to the decision, and where that person has no family or friends whom it is appropriate to consult, an IMCA must be appointed.

The advocate should take such steps as are necessary to support the person they have been instructed to represent so that the person may participate as fully as possible in any relevant decision. They should also:

- obtain and evaluate relevant information;
- find out what the person's wishes and feelings would be likely to be;
- ascertain the beliefs and values that would be likely to influence the person if they had capacity;
- explore what alternative courses of action are available;
- obtain a further medical opinion where treatment is proposed and the advocate thinks that one should be obtained.

The Mental Capacity Act 2005 (Independent Mental Capacity Advocates) (General) Regulations (2006, No. 1832) which accompany the Act also make provision as to circumstances in which an advocate may challenge, or provide assistance for the purpose of challenging, any relevant decision.

Staff should ensure that they know how to contact the IMCA scheme in relevant circumstances. The circumstances in which IMCAs could (as opposed to must) become involved have also been expanded. Chapter 11 looks at IMCAs.

The Court of Protection and the Public Guardian

The Court of Protection is a far more powerful and wide-ranging body in its powers and scope than the court as it was established under the Mental Health Act. Chapter 12 describes the court's structure. It will deal with all issues concerning people who lack capacity, not merely making orders in respect of their property and affairs but in addition covering issues of personal welfare, including the making of medical decisions. Most decisions will be made without recourse to the court, but some examples of when the court would be involved are:

- where the cumulative restrictions or restraints imposed upon a person who lacked capacity amounted to a deprivation of liberty and therefore could not lawfully be imposed as an s 5 act (although from April 2009 the DOLS might be appropriate);

- where there were genuine concerns about the manner in which an attorney or a deputy was acting (for example, apparently ignoring the best interests checklist);

- where there was doubt over the meaning or construction of an LPA or whether an advance decision was valid or applicable;

- where it was felt that there might be the need for a deputy to be appointed.

There are more examples set out in Chapter 12.

The gateway to the Court of Protection is a new body, the Public Guardian, appointed by the Lord Chancellor. The functions of the Public Guardian include:

- establishing and maintaining registers of LPAs and court-appointed deputies;

- supervising deputies;

- directing Court of Protection Visitors to visit and report on LPA attorneys, deputies or the person lacking capacity.

Other issues

There are a number of other aspects to the Mental Capacity Act which are summarised in the last four chapters. The introduction of new offences connected with ill-treatment or neglect of a person should help to strengthen vulnerable adults procedures.

There are some areas that are specifically excluded from the scope of the Act and these are identified in Chapter 13.

There are significant new safeguards and procedural safeguards with regard to research involving people who lack the capacity to consent to take part. These are listed in Chapter 14.

Chapter 15 considers the relationship of the Mental Capacity Act with other legislation such as the Human Rights Act 1998.

The 'Bournewood' provisions are outlined in Chapter 16. These Deprivation of Liberty Safeguards were added to the Act by the Mental Health Act 2007 to cover the situation of the person who is mentally incapable of deciding whether to be in a hospital, nursing home or care home, but who is in effect deprived of his or her liberty.

Chapter 17 looks at an area that has caused some confusion among practitioners. This is the interface between the Mental Capacity Act and the Mental Health Act. This then leads to the final difficult question, covered in Chapter 18, which is the distinction between restrictions of movement and deprivation of liberty.

The Act is reprinted at the end of the book for easy access. This now includes all of the Schedules to the Act. The book also has several other appendices, which provide some quick and easy guides to working under the Act. These also include the answers to the multiple choice questions which appear at the end of some chapters (starting with this one) to help consolidate knowledge of the material.

ACTIVITY **2.1**

Multiple choice questions
Read each question carefully and tick the appropriate box(es). Where a statement is correct, tick the box next to it; if it is incorrect, leave it blank. You may need to tick more than one box per question.

Appendix 5 (pages 279–83) gives the answers.

2.1 The Mental Capacity Act 2005:

   (a) Places advance decisions relating to treatment on a statutory footing   ☐

   (b) Defines incapacity   ☐

   (c) Retains the current common law test for capacity to consent to treatment, without change   ☐

   (d) Introduces substituted decision-making in relation to healthcare matters   ☐

   (e) Regulates research relating to incapacitated persons   ☐

   (f) Fills the 'Bournewood Gap' by allowing deputies to authorise deprivation of liberty   ☐

2.2 The Mental Capacity Act contains a checklist which determines who should be the decision-maker in any specified situation:

   (a) True   ☐

   (b) False   ☐

2.3 Under the Mental Capacity Act someone may be appointed under a Lasting Power of Attorney to make healthcare decisions for a person when he/she becomes incapacitated:

   (a) True   ☐

   (b) False   ☐

(Continued)

ACTIVITY **2.1** *continued*

2.4 *To be protected when doing anything under s 5 of the Act a person must:*

   (a) *Establish that the person lacks capacity in relation to the matter in question*

   (b) *Notify the Public Guardian of the decision if it incurs significant costs*

   (c) *Believe that the action will be in the person's best interests*

   (d) *Obtain medical evidence of mental incapacity*

   (e) *Inform the nearest relative of any action taken*

Chapter 3
The Code of Practice
(sections 42–43)

Introduction

The Code of Practice came into effect in April 2007 to coincide with those provisions of the Act which were introduced at that time, namely the Independent Mental Capacity Advocacy Service for England and the section (s) 44 criminal offence of ill-treatment or neglect of a person lacking capacity. A supplement to the Code of Practice ('the DOLS Code'), covering the Deprivation of Liberty Safeguards procedure introduced as an amendment to the Act by the Mental Health Act 2007, was issued in 2008. Both Codes are now showing their age as a result of subsequent developments in case law, in particular in relation to assessments of capacity, deprivation of liberty and the impact of Article 5(4), and currently in some respects the new Mental Health Act Code (April 2015) provides more up-to-date guidance.

What does the Code of Practice cover?

Section 42(1) sets out what the code or codes must cover, including:

- guidance for people assessing capacity;
- guidance for people performing s 5 acts (i.e. acts in connection with the care or treatment of a person lacking capacity);
- guidance for people appointed as attorneys under Lasting Powers of Attorney (LPAs);
- guidance for deputies appointed by the Court of Protection;
- guidance for people carrying out research covered by ss 30–34 of the Act;
- guidance for Independent Mental Capacity Advocates;
- guidance in relation to advance decisions covered by ss 24–26;
- guidance in relation to such other matters concerned with the Act as the Lord Chancellor sees fit.

The DOLS Code specifically focuses on providing guidance for:

- people exercising functions relating to the deprivation of liberty safeguards; and
- people acting as a relevant person's representative under the deprivation of liberty safeguards.

It would seem that those charged with drawing up the Code construed their obligations broadly, as there are substantial chapters in relation to:

- the position of children and young people, whether under this Act or the Children Act or indeed the Mental Health Act (Chapter 12);

- the informal and formal resolution of disputes, whether between health and social care professionals or health and social care professionals and others (Chapter 15);

- the interface between the Mental Capacity Act and the Mental Health Act (Chapter 13); and

- the rules governing access to information about a person who lacks capacity (Chapter 16).

The DOLS Code makes a serious attempt to distinguish between a deprivation of liberty and a restriction of movement (Chapter 2) by distilling the then existing case law, but suffers from not having been updated since.

In these chapters the Code of Practice resembles less a paraphrase of the Act (which is its tendency elsewhere) than a useful and informed commentary on its context. The Code is eminently readable, indeed almost chatty, including many examples and case studies within the text to illustrate the practice points being made. As a result it is quite long, running to some 300 pages and is rather bulky for health and social care professionals to carry around with them at work for reference. Despite its length there are parts which would justify considerable expansion, where potential problems in practice can be anticipated. An example would be the identification of the decision-maker in relation to the assessment of capacity and the determination of best interests, particularly in areas where there is a large number of different stakeholders in the decision and outcome. This is an issue on which the Act is virtually silent, and the advice in the Code of Practice is all too brief. Paragraph 5.8 identifies a few simple examples, but in practice this is an area where difficulties are often encountered.

To whom does the Code of Practice apply?

Section 42(4) sets out that a person is under a duty to have regard to the Code of Practice if acting in relation to a person who lacks capacity in one or more of the following ways:

- as an attorney under a Lasting Power of Attorney;

- as a deputy appointed by the Court of Protection;

- as a person carrying out research covered by ss 30–34;

- as an Independent Mental Capacity Advocate;

- in a professional capacity;

- for remuneration.

As the Code of Practice itself points out in its introduction, the last two categories cover a wide range of individuals. Those acting in a professional capacity would include: healthcare staff such as doctors, dentists, nurses, therapists, radiologists, paramedics, etc.; social care staff such as social workers, care managers, etc.; and others

> *who may occasionally be involved in the care of people who lack capacity to make the decision in question, such as ambulance crew, housing workers, or police officers.*

It would also include solicitors and other professionals. Those acting for remuneration would include:

> *care assistants in a care home, care workers providing domiciliary care services, and others who have been contracted to provide a service to people who lack capacity to consent to that service.*

These are the people the Act requires to 'have regard' to the Code of Practice. However, the Act itself applies to anyone who is acting in respect of or making a decision for someone who lacks capacity, including those doing so informally. So the Code urges them too to follow its guidance as far as they are aware of it.

In respect of recording assessments of capacity and best interests the Code advises:

- assessments (particularly by informal carers) of capacity to take day-to-day decisions do not require recorded documentation (4.60);
- paid carers should keep a record of steps taken (4.60);
- assessments of capacity by professionals in relation to particular decisions should be recorded (4.61) (the new Mental Health Act Code of Practice, in force from April 2015, is more prescriptive in this respect, e.g. at chapter 13.22);
- staff involved in providing care should make sure a record is kept of the process of working out best interests for each relevant decision and it would be useful for family and other carers to keep a similar record of major decisions (5.15);
- if the decision-maker is not following the written wishes of the person now lacking capacity the reasons must be recorded (5.43).

In practice, a care plan incorporating the regular day-to-day decisions and actions taken for a person assessed as lacking capacity to make them will be recorded as having been tested against the best interests checklist, thereby giving protection to staff implementing them. This is subject to the need to be aware that the person may regain capacity to make some at least of those decisions for himself or herself, and that decisions outside those recorded in the care plan will need a separate assessment. This at least is the implication of the rather sparse guidance contained in 5.11 and 4.61.

In the foreword to the Code of Practice Lord Falconer states that the Mental Capacity Act will make a real difference to the lives of people who may lack mental capacity. It will *empower people to make decisions for themselves wherever possible, and protect people who lack capacity by providing a flexible framework that places individuals at the very heart of the decision-making process. It will ensure that they participate as much as possible in any decisions made on their behalf, and that these are made in their best interests. It also allows people to plan ahead for a time in the future when they might lack the capacity, for any number of reasons, to make decisions for themselves.*

One of the problems inherent in an Act which aspires to promote a new culture in relation to decision-making for people who lack capacity is that of ensuring that its provisions are made known not simply to health and social care professionals but to all who may be involved, including those caring as best they can and with the best of intentions for a relative who lacks capacity living with them in their home. The existence of an eminently readable and sensible Code of Practice will not by itself ensure that the Act's aims and requirements reach everyone concerned. It is likely to be a number of years and to require a process of direct education of those caring for people who lack capacity by those working in the community who come into contact with them, before the full impact of the Act will be felt. This was recently confirmed by the House of Lords' Scrutiny Committee's comment inter alia about increasing general awareness of the Act and its implementation.

What is the status and effect of the Code?

As stated above, certain categories of people are required to 'have regard' to the Code of Practice when acting in relation to people who lack capacity. This includes the DOLS Code. This requirement is spelled out in s 42(4) of the Act. Section 42(5) adds that:

If it appears to a court or tribunal conducting any criminal or civil proceedings that –

(a) a provision of (the) Code, or

(b) a failure to comply with (the) Code

is relevant to a question arising in the proceedings, the provision or failure must be taken into account in deciding the question.

As the Code itself states, it focuses on those who have a duty of care to someone who lacks the capacity to agree to the care that is being provided. While there is therefore no obligation to comply with the Code, any failure to have regard to any of its guidance must, if considered relevant, be taken into account in deciding whether, for example, a health or social care professional has acted negligently or failed to comply with good practice. Although spelled out rather than implied, the legal effect is likely to be similar to a failure to follow the Mental Health Act Code of Practice guidance, and the House of Lords' judgment in the *Munjaz* case (2005), which dealt with the status of the Mental Health Act Code of Practice, is likely to apply with equal force. The guidance will have to be considered seriously and followed 'unless there are cogent reasons for not doing so', but it will be possible to depart from it without necessarily risking court proceedings; nor will adherence to its guidance determine the issue as to whether an act, omission to act or decision made in relation to a person lacking capacity constitutes a breach of that person's rights under the European Convention on Human Rights.

ACTIVITY **3.1**

Multiple choice questions

Read each question carefully and tick the appropriate box(es). Where a statement is correct, tick the box next to it; if it is incorrect, leave it blank. You may need to tick more than one box per question.

Appendix 5 (pages 279–83) gives the answers.

3.1 *The Code of Practice to the Mental Capacity Act 2005 provides guidance for:*

(a) *People assessing capacity* ☐

(b) *People appointed as attorneys under Lasting Powers of Attorney* ☐

(c) *People appointed as guardians under the Mental Health Act 1983* ☐

(d) *Deputies appointed by the Court of Protection* ☐

(e) *Independent Mental Capacity Advocates* ☐

(f) *Independent Mental Health Advocates* ☐

3.2 *Under the Mental Capacity Act a failure to follow the Code of Practice would always lead to court proceedings if reported to the relevant authority:*

(a) *True* ☐

(b) *False* ☐

3.3 *Principles for the Mental Capacity Act are set out in the Code of Practice and not in the Act itself:*

(a) *True* ☐

(b) *False* ☐

Chapter 4
Principles (section 1)

Introduction

The Parliamentary Joint Committee which examined the draft Mental Incapacity Bill was persuaded of the importance of having clear principles explicitly stated in the Act, rather than just in the Code of Practice. One of the most persuasive arguments was that, although lawyers might have been able to identify principles from the provisions of the Act, this was legislation which would be looked at and used by a wide range of people other than lawyers. It was seen as important that people should be aware of these key principles right from the outset.

The popularity of this approach was one of the reasons for a subsequent attempt to have principles inserted at the beginning of the Mental Health Act 1983 when it was reformed in 2007. Chapter 17 examines the links, similarities and differences between the two Acts.

The principles are set out in section (s) 1, right at the beginning of the Act, even before the definition of lack of capacity. There is a strong emphasis within the principles on maximising a person's ability to take part in decision-making. This is reflected throughout the Act and the Code of Practice.

The five principles

As has been noted, these are set out in s 1 of the Act. They are fairly easy to remember and they govern any actions taken within the framework of the Act.

The principles

The following principles apply for the purposes of this Act.

(1) A person must be assumed to have capacity unless it is established that he lacks capacity.

(2) A person is not to be treated as unable to make a decision unless all practicable steps to help him to do so have been taken without success.

(3) A person is not to be treated as unable to make a decision merely because he makes an unwise decision.

(4) An act done, or decision made, under this Act for or on behalf of a person who lacks capacity must be done, or made, in his best interests.

(5) *Before the act is done, or the decision is made, regard must be had to whether the purpose for which it is needed can be as effectively achieved in a way that is less restrictive of the person's rights and freedom of action.*

Each of the five principles will now be examined to see why it was seen as important to include them on the face of the Act. There will then be some discussion on how each principle should operate in practice. The Code of Practice will be cited where it helps to illustrate how the principles would apply.

A person must be assumed to have capacity

This first principle is consistent with the common law approach which existed before the Act became law. Prior to the introduction of the Mental Capacity Act, if an issue came to court, the burden of proof was on the person alleging a lack of capacity. The standard of proof was 'the balance of probabilities'. This can also be expressed as 'more likely than not'. This standard of proof is repeated in the Mental Capacity Act in s 2 (see Chapter 5) and should not present a problem to those who were used to working in this area within the common law.

Capacity must be considered in relation to a particular decision at a particular time (the 'functional' test). The starting point is then always the presumption of capacity, even if this is very quickly disproved on assessment. For practitioners working with people with severe intellectual disabilities this is sometimes easier said than done. It requires a disciplined mindset to avoid slipping into the practice of assuming incapacity in certain individuals known to the decision-maker, and a need to remind oneself of the fact that a person does not have or lack capacity in general but only in relation to the specific decision which needs to be made at the time.

Fortunately, there is no expectation that formal assessments are carried out for every decision. For day-to-day decisions or actions it is sufficient for the person acting to have a reasonable belief that the other person lacks capacity, as long as they have objective reasons for this belief.

Practicable steps to help the person make a decision

This second principle states that:

A person is not to be treated as unable to make a decision unless all practicable steps to help him to do so have been taken without success.

In justifying an intervention a person would need to show that all such practicable steps had been unsuccessful before making a final assessment that the person lacked capacity in relation to the matter in question. It represents a mandatory step to be taken between reaching the provisional conclusion that a person is unable to make a decision and proceeding to determine what is in that person's best interests.

This principle was not expressed as 'all reasonable attempts' (the original expression used by the Law Commission) because critics were concerned that this was too weak and would lead to more people being regarded as incapable than was necessary.

The Code of Practice gives some useful guidance on this issue.

> *2.7 The kind of support people might need to help them make a decision varies. It depends on personal circumstances, the kind of decision that has to be made and the time available to make the decision. It might include:*
>
> - *using a different form of communication (for example, non-verbal communication)*
>
> - *providing information in a more accessible form (for example, photographs, drawings, or tapes)*
>
> - *treating a medical condition which may be affecting the person's capacity or*
>
> - *having a structured programme to improve a person's capacity to make particular decisions (for example, helping a person with learning disabilities to learn new skills).*

The 'time available to make the decision' is of course always a relevant consideration. Chapter 3 of the Code gives more information on ways to help people make decisions for themselves. It includes a number of scenarios which illustrate how staff could provide relevant information, help with specific communication difficulties, put the person at their ease and choose the right time and place to talk to the person concerned.

Many organisations have begun to produce information in different forms to make it more accessible and therefore more likely that people will be able to make decisions for themselves.

The introduction to Chapter 3 of the Code also includes the following checklist, which is repeated at Appendix 2 in this text.

> *To help someone make a decision for themselves, check the following points:*
>
> *Providing relevant information*
>
> - *Does the person have all the relevant information they need to make a particular decision?*
>
> - *If they have a choice, have they been given information on all the alternatives?*
>
> *Communicating in an appropriate way*
>
> - *Could information be explained or presented in a way that is easier for the person to understand (for example, by using simple language or visual aids)?*
>
> - *Have different methods of communication been explored if required, including non-verbal communication?*
>
> - *Could anyone else help with communication (for example, a family member, support worker, interpreter, speech and language therapist or advocate)?*

Making the person feel at ease

- *Are there particular times of day when the person's understanding is better?*

- *Are there particular locations where they may feel more at ease?*

- *Could the decision be put off to see whether the person can make the decision at a later time when circumstances are right for them?*

Supporting the person

- *Can anyone else help or support the person to make choices or express a view?*

A case example of what is required to meet this second principle is seen in *CC v KK* (2012) EWHC (COP), where Baker J was considering the situation where there was a choice between a person going home or staying in a care home. He noted that the person should be provided with a detailed analysis of the effects of the decision either way, which in turn would necessitate identifying the best ways in which the option would be supported. In order to understand the likely consequences of returning home, KK should be given full details of the care package that would or might be available.

Unwise decisions

This third principle states that:

> *A person is not to be treated as unable to make a decision merely because he makes an unwise decision.*

This has been part of the common law since at least as early as 1850, when it was stated in *Bird v Luckie* that, although the law requires a person to be capable of understanding the nature and effect of an action, it does not require that he should behave 'in such a manner as to deserve approbation from the prudent, the wise and the good'.

The Law Commission received an overwhelming majority of opinion that this principle should be explicitly included in the Act. Some concern has been expressed, for example from those giving evidence to the Joint Committee during the pre-legislative scrutiny of the draft Bill, that a decision on its own might just appear unwise, but that a series of unwise decisions might actually indicate a lack of capacity. Ashton *et al.* (2006, page 68) say that some caution is needed when applying this principle and they give some sound advice:

> *Although as a general rule, capacity should be assessed in relation to each particular decision or specific issue, there may be circumstances where a person has an ongoing condition which affects his or her capacity to make a range of interrelated or sequential decisions. One decision on its own may make sense but the combination of decisions may raise doubts as to the person's capacity or at least prompt the need for a proper assessment. But equally, an unwise decision should not, by itself, be sufficient to indicate a lack of capacity.*

Best interests

The fourth principle states that:

> *An act done, or decision made, under this Act for or on behalf of a person who lacks capacity must be done, or made, in his best interests.*

Professionals who have worked with people who lack capacity should be familiar with this principle, as it has been well enshrined within the common law. The significant change introduced by the Mental Capacity Act is the mandatory process whereby best interests should be determined and this is explored further in Chapter 6.

Less restrictive approach

Finally, the fifth principle states that:

> *Before the act is done, or the decision is made, regard must be had to whether the purpose for which it is needed can be as effectively achieved in a way that is less restrictive of the person's rights and freedom of action.*

This is often referred to as the 'least restrictive alternative' approach, but this is at slight variance with the wording in the Act itself. One key element in applying this principle is to consider whether the purpose for which the decision is needed 'can be as effectively achieved' in a less restrictive way. There may be less restrictive interventions available, but they may not be as effective in achieving the purpose. In applying this principle the question will be asked as to whether any intervention is indeed needed at all.

As with the others, this fifth principle contributes to an overall approach of only making decisions for someone when it is really necessary and of involving them in the process as far as is possible.

ACTIVITY *4.1*

Multiple choice questions

Read each question carefully and tick the appropriate box(es). Where a statement is correct, tick the box next to it; if it is incorrect, leave it blank. You may need to tick more than one box per question.

Appendix 5 (pages 279–83) gives the answers.

4.1 Key principles of the Mental Capacity Act 2005 include:

(a) A presumption of capacity exists for all those aged 16 or over ☐

(b) All practicable steps are to be taken to help a person make the decision before they're considered incapable ☐

(c) An unwise decision implies a lack of capacity   ☐

(d) Acts done on behalf of an incapacitated person must be in his/her best interests   ☐

(e) All decisions made on behalf of an incapacitated person must be registered with the Court of Protection   ☐

(f) Decisions should be the least expensive available in terms of cost to the person   ☐

(g) Decisions should seek to be less restrictive in terms of the person's rights and freedom of action   ☐

4.2 The Court of Protection is not covered by the principles as they only apply to other decision-makers under the Act:

(a) True   ☐

(b) False   ☐

Chapter 5
What is lack of capacity? (sections 2–3)

Introduction

One of the benefits of having an Act of Parliament in this complex area is that, at last, we have a single statutory definition of what amounts to a lack of capacity to make specific decisions.

Section (s) 2 of the Act states that:

> *a person lacks capacity in relation to a matter if at the material time he is unable to make a decision for himself in relation to the matter because of an impairment of, or a disturbance in the functioning of, the mind or brain.*

As a result of the Court of Appeal decision in *PC v City of York* (2013) EWCA Civ 478 the approach to be adopted to any specific decision is to apply the s 3 'functional test' followed by the 'diagnostic test' contained within s 2.

The s 3 'functional test' is that:

> *a person is unable to make a decision for himself if he is unable –*
>
> *(a) to understand the information relevant to the decision,*
>
> *(b) to retain that information,*
>
> *(c) to use or weigh that information as part of the process of making the decision, or*
>
> *(d) to communicate his decision (whether by talking, using sign language or any other means).*

An inability to satisfy any one of these four conditions would render the person incapable.

The next test is to see if this is *because of an impairment of, or a disturbance in the functioning of, the mind or brain.*

It does not matter if this impairment or disturbance is permanent or temporary and some decisions will need to be made even though a person may regain capacity within a short space of time.

The standard of proof is outlined in s 2(4).

In proceedings under this Act or any other enactment, any question whether a person lacks capacity within the meaning of this Act must be decided on the balance of probabilities.

If the person lacks capacity, having applied the functional test, but there is no evidence that this is due to any impairment of, or disturbance in the functioning of, the mind or brain, it may be in some cases that the issue will need to be referred to the High Court to make a decision under its inherent jurisdiction, as it will not be possible to rely on the Mental Capacity Act.

It may be a very young adult with insufficient maturity to make a decision, or the person may be subject to such pressure from others that they are effectively incapacitated. In these cases they might still be seen as a vulnerable adult falling outside the provisions of the Mental Capacity Act but in need of the protection of the High Court.

The disturbance in mind or brain may well be a mental disorder as defined in the Mental Health Act 1983 as 'any disorder or disability of mind', but just because someone has a mental disorder does not mean they are incapable of making a particular decision. They could even be detained under the Mental Health Act but the relevant decision happens to fall outside the scope of that Act (e.g. treatment for a physical disorder or a social decision).

Non-discrimination

Both in this part of the Act, and in relation to determining best interests, a principle of 'equal consideration' applies.

Section 2(3) states:

A lack of capacity cannot be established merely by reference to –

(a) *a person's age or appearance, or*

(b) *a condition of his, or an aspect of his behaviour, which might lead others to make unjustified assumptions about his capacity.*

This was an amendment proposed by the Making Decisions Alliance, which was an organisation made up of a number of charities who were campaigning for the Act. The Alliance was concerned that prejudice against certain groups would disadvantage them. Rather than becoming one of the five key principles, this was included in the part of the Act defining lack of capacity and in the process of establishing best interests. The words 'appearance' and 'condition' would cover a wide range of situations such as visible disability, skin colour, dress and mental disorder.

The section 3 'functional' test

The four elements of the test will now be considered.

(a) Understanding the information relevant to the decision

Chapter 4 of the Code of Practice identifies that relevant information would need to include the nature of the decision, the reason why the decision is needed, and the likely effects of deciding one way or another or of making no decision at all.

Section 3(4) of the Act states that:

> *The information relevant to a decision includes information about the reasonably foreseeable consequences of –*
>
> *(a) deciding one way or another, or*
>
> *(b) failing to make the decision.*

Section 3(2) states that:

> *A person is not to be regarded as unable to understand the information relevant to a decision if he is able to understand an explanation of it given to him in a way that is appropriate to his circumstances (using simple language, visual aids or any other means).*

The Code of Practice gives a range of examples of how people might be helped to understand the information by presenting it in different ways, such as with sign language, visual representations or computer support.

(b) Retaining the relevant information

Section 3(3) states that:

> *The fact that a person is able to retain the information relevant to a decision for a short period only does not prevent him from being regarded as able to make the decision.*

Essentially, the person would need to retain the information long enough to reach the end of the process of decision-making, including communicating the decision. For more straightforward decisions this may just require a matter of a few minutes, but for more complex decisions there might be a risk that the person would forget some of the information before they had finalised and communicated their decision. The Code of Practice (at para 4.20) suggests that notebooks, photographs, posters, videos and voice recorders may help someone to record and retain information.

(c) Using or weighing the relevant information as part of the process of making the decision

This is based on the existing common law position that has been established through a series of cases. The Code of Practice gives two examples at para 4.22.

> *A person with the eating disorder anorexia nervosa may understand information about the consequences of not eating. But their compulsion not to eat might be too strong*

for them to ignore. Some people who have serious brain damage might make impulsive decisions regardless of information they have been given or their understanding of it.

(d) Communicating the decision (whether by talking, using sign language or any other means)

It will be unusual that a person would be unable to communicate if they have successfully completed the first three parts of the capacity test. However, there is a rare condition known as 'locked-in syndrome' where a person may be conscious but unable to speak or move in such a way as to be able to communicate. Clearly, all practicable steps should be taken to help someone to communicate. This might involve speech or language therapists. Note that the section refers to an *inability* to communicate the decision, not a *refusal* or *reluctance* to do so.

Situations requiring the capacity test

When someone suspects that a person may lack capacity to make a particular decision, and where they consider that a decision needs to be made, that person will usually be the person applying the test. For many decisions that will be an informal carer. They do not need to be experts in assessing capacity, but they do need to have reasonable grounds for believing that the person lacks capacity if they intend to intervene. There would need to be objective grounds for their opinion. The Code's checklist (set out in this book on pages 29–30 and also at Appendix 3) may be helpful as part of this process.

For a legal transaction a solicitor (or other legal practitioner) must assess a person's ability to instruct them. The information that will need to be understood will vary according to the transaction, but the test itself will be as outlined in this chapter. Where there is doubt about the effect of any impairment, expert advice should be sought.

Whenever professional opinion is sought it should be remembered that the final decision about a person's capacity rests with the person making the decision in question. The Court of Protection would be the final decision-maker in disputed cases.

For healthcare decisions the Code of Practice notes at para 4.40 that:

> *If a doctor or healthcare professional proposes treatment or an examination, they must assess the person's capacity to consent. In settings such as a hospital, this can involve the multi-disciplinary team (a team of people from different professional backgrounds who share responsibility for a patient). But ultimately, it is up to the professional responsible for the person's treatment to make sure that capacity has been assessed.*

What is a reasonable belief that someone lacks capacity?

When someone suspects that a person may lack capacity to make a particular decision, how far do they need to go in testing this? We noted in Chapter 4 that for day-to-day decisions or actions it is sufficient for the person acting to have a 'reasonable belief' that the other person lacks capacity. Carers do not have to be experts in assessing capacity. But to have protection from liability when providing care or treatment they must have this 'reasonable belief' that the other person lacks capacity to make relevant decisions about their care or treatment. This is acceptable as long as they have objective reasons for this belief.

The decision-maker must have taken reasonable steps to establish that the other person lacks capacity to make a decision or to consent to an act at the time the decision or consent is needed. They must also establish that the act or decision is in the person's best interests.

They do not usually need to follow formal processes or involve a professional to make an assessment. However, if somebody challenges their assessment they must be able to describe the steps they have taken.

Paragraph 4.45 of the Code of Practice notes that:

> *Professionals, who are qualified in their particular field, are normally expected to undertake a fuller assessment, reflecting their higher degree of knowledge and experience, than family members or other carers who have no formal qualifications.*

The same paragraph sets out a helpful list of pointers to consider. A more formal checklist follows, but this is a useful summary of some key points.

- *Start by assuming the person has capacity to make the specific decision. Is there anything to prove otherwise?*
- *Does the person have a previous diagnosis of disability or mental disorder? Does that condition now affect their capacity to make this decision? If there has been no previous diagnosis, it may be best to get a medical opinion.*
- *Make every effort to communicate with the person to explain what is happening.*
- *Make every effort to try to help the person make the decision in question.*
- *See if there is a way to explain or present information about the decision in a way that makes it easier to understand. If the person has a choice, do they have information about all the options?*
- *Can the decision be delayed to take time to help the person make the decision, or to give the person time to regain the capacity to make the decision for themselves?*
- *Does the person understand what decision they need to make and why they need to make it?*
- *Can they understand information about the decision? Can they retain it, use it and weigh it to make the decision?*
- *Be aware that the fact that a person agrees with you or assents to what is proposed does not necessarily mean that they have capacity to make the decision.*

A checklist for assessing capacity

The quick summary at the beginning of Chapter 4 of the Code of Practice provides a useful checklist for assessing capacity. This list is repeated in this book at Appendix 3.

Assessing capacity

This checklist is a summary of points to consider when assessing a person's capacity to make a specific decision.

Presuming someone has capacity

- The starting assumption must always be that a person has the capacity to make a decision, unless it can be established that they lack capacity.

Understanding what is meant by capacity and lack of capacity

- A person's capacity must be assessed specifically in terms of their capacity to make a particular decision at the time it needs to be made.

Treating everyone equally

- A person's capacity must not be judged simply on the basis of their age, appearance, condition or an aspect of their behaviour.

Supporting the person to make the decision for themselves

- It is important to take all possible steps to try to help people make a decision for themselves.

Assessing capacity

- Anyone assessing someone's capacity to make a decision for themselves should use the two-stage test of capacity.

- Does the person have an impairment of the mind or brain, or is there some sort of disturbance affecting the way their brain or mind works? (It doesn't matter whether the impairment or disturbance is temporary or permanent.)

- If so, does that impairment or disturbance mean that the person is unable to make the decision in question at the time it needs to be made?

Assessing ability to make a decision

- Does the person have a general understanding of what decision they need to make and why they need to make it?

- Does the person have a general understanding of the likely consequences of making, or not making, this decision?

- Is the person able to understand, retain, use and weigh up the information relevant to this decision?

- Can the person communicate their decision (by talking, using sign language or any other means)? Would the services of a professional (such as a speech and language therapist) be helpful?

Assessing capacity to make more complex or serious decisions

- Is there a need for a more thorough assessment (perhaps by involving a doctor or other professional expert)?

Recording by professionals

Where a professional has carried out an assessment of a person's capacity to make a particular decision, this should be recorded in the relevant professional records. Doctors and healthcare professionals would be expected to record this in the patient's clinical notes. Solicitors should keep records on their clients' files when they have assessed capacity to give instructions or carry out a legal transaction. Social care staff will keep records according to their area of work (e.g. within the Care Programme Approach or relevant assessment process) and records will need to be quickly accessible if they are to be helpful.

ACTIVITY **5 . 1**

Multiple choice questions

Read each question carefully and tick the appropriate box(es). Where a statement is correct, tick the box next to it; if it is incorrect, leave it blank. You may need to tick more than one box per question.

Appendix 5 (pages 279–83) gives the answers.

5.1 *A decision on a person's mental capacity needs to be made in relation to the particular matter at the time when the decision has to be made:*

(a) True ☐

(b) False ☐

5.2 *The test for capacity under the Mental Capacity Act is whether the person can:*

(a) Understand the relevant information ☐

(b) Retain the relevant information ☐

(c) Believe the relevant information ☐

(d) Use or weigh the relevant information as part of the decision-making process ☐

(e) Communicate the decision ☐

(f) Read and sign a consent form ☐

5.3 *The fact that a person is able to retain the information relevant to a decision for a short period only will prevent him from being regarded as able to make the decision:*

(a) True ☐

(b) False ☐

Chapter 6
Best interests (section 4)

Introduction

Many professionals will be familiar with the principle of acting in the best interests of a person who lacks capacity. This has long been established within the common law, and more recently the principle has been extended by case law to go beyond just medical decisions to include social welfare matters.

What people will need to become familiar with, though, is the Act's new requirement that certain steps will need to be followed in determining what would be in a person's best interests.

The checklist approach

The approach adopted by the Mental Capacity Act is to set out a checklist of common factors, which as a minimum should be considered on each occasion that a decision needs to be made. The Law Commission (1995, para 3.28) was aware that care should be taken not to make this approach too unwieldy when it stated:

First, a checklist must not unduly burden any decision-maker or encourage unnecessary intervention; secondly it must not be applied too rigidly and should leave room for all considerations relevant to the particular case; thirdly, it should be confined to major points, so that it can adapt to changing views and attitudes.

The principle of equal consideration

As with the definition of mental incapacity, the best interests checklist starts with this anti-discriminatory principle. Section 4(1) states:

In determining for the purposes of this Act what is in a person's best interests, the person making the determination must not make it merely on the basis of –

(a) the person's age or appearance, or

(b) a condition of his, or an aspect of his behaviour, which might lead others to make unjustified assumptions about what might be in his best interests.

In practice this means, for example, that decisions about best interests should not be made on pre-conceived ideas about the quality of life of older people or people with severe disabilities. One would hope that this would not be the case, but the

Act covers such a wide range of people and circumstances that it was considered necessary to include such a phrase.

All relevant circumstances

This is a catch-all expression which means that, as well as following the rest of the list, a person should consider all other relevant matters which affect the particular decision that is under consideration.

Subsection 11 defines 'relevant circumstances' as those:

(a) *of which the person making the determination is aware, and*

(b) *which it would be reasonable to regard as relevant.*

This allows for a degree of flexibility so that one would not have to make exhaustive enquiries in every set of circumstances.

Regaining capacity

This was added to the original list proposed by the Law Commission.

Section 4(3) requires a decision-maker to consider:

(a) *whether it is likely that the person will at some time have capacity in relation to the matter in question, and*

(b) *if it appears likely that he will, when that is likely to be.*

If it is possible to put off the decision until the person can make it for themselves, then this is what should happen. In an emergency this may not be possible. It may, however, be feasible to limit the scope of a decision so that a small intervention can be followed by the person making more significant decisions when they have regained capacity.

The Code of Practice (para 5.28) includes a list of indicators that a person might regain or develop capacity in the future:

- *the cause of the lack of capacity can be treated, either by medication or some other form of treatment or therapy*

- *the lack of capacity is likely to decrease in time (for example, where it is caused by the effects of medication or alcohol, or following a sudden shock)*

- *a person with learning disabilities may learn new skills or be subject to new experiences which increase their understanding and ability to make certain decisions*

- *the person may have a condition which causes capacity to come and go at various times (such as some forms of mental illness) so it may be possible to arrange for the decision to be made during a time when they do have capacity*

- *a person previously unable to communicate may learn a new form of communication.*

Participation of the individual

Section 4(4) requires the decision-maker, as far as is reasonably practicable,

to permit and encourage the person to participate, or to improve his ability to participate, as fully as possible in any act done for him and any decision affecting him.

The 'practicable steps' to help the person make the decision may not have been successful but they will still be relevant for this part of the checklist. Even if the person is unable to make the decision, their maximum involvement in the process should be encouraged and facilitated. As well as helping to determine what is in the person's best interests this process may gradually move the person towards a greater ability to make related or simpler decisions.

Life-sustaining treatment

Much of the debate in Parliament before the Act was passed was focused on life and death issues involving people who lacked capacity. There was some concern that the Act would lead to the introduction of euthanasia or assisted suicide. An amendment was introduced in the House of Lords. The final wording is contained in section (s) 4(5):

Where the determination relates to life-sustaining treatment he must not, in considering whether the treatment is in the best interests of the person concerned, be motivated by a desire to bring about his death.

As long as the motivation is not to bring about a person's death it will still be possible to withdraw life-sustaining treatment in the final stages of a terminal illness or for someone in a persistent vegetative state if there was no prospect of recovery. The best interests of the person might lead to this conclusion.

Similarly, a drug such as diamorphine might be known to be likely to hasten someone's death, but it may be given for pain relief if that is the motivation rather than to bring about their early death.

Paragraph 5.31 of the Code of Practice approaches the issue in this way:

All reasonable steps which are in the person's best interests should be taken to prolong their life. There will be a limited number of cases where treatment is futile, overly burdensome to the patient or where there is no prospect of recovery. In circumstances such as these, it may be that an assessment of best interests leads to the conclusion that it would be in the best interests of the patient to withdraw or withhold life-sustaining treatment, even if this may result in the person's death. The decision-maker must make a decision based on the best interests of the person who lacks capacity. They must not be motivated by a desire to bring about the person's death for whatever reason, even if this is from a sense of compassion. Healthcare and social care staff should also refer to relevant professional guidance when making decisions regarding life-sustaining treatment.

Wishes, feelings, beliefs and values

Section 4(6) requires the decision-maker, 'so far as is reasonably ascertainable', to consider:

> (a) *the person's past and present wishes and feelings (and, in particular, any relevant written statement made by him when he had capacity),*
>
> (b) *the beliefs and values that would be likely to influence his decision if he had capacity, and*
>
> (c) *the other factors that he would be likely to consider if he were able to do so.*

This requires the decision-maker to concentrate on the person in question and to make efforts to find out about any views they may have expressed in the past, including any written statements. Formal advance decisions in the Act only cover advance refusals of medical treatment (which may include psychiatric treatment subject to the limitations noted elsewhere when Part 4 of the Mental Health Act is relevant). However, this part of the Act may encourage some people to record their views, knowing that they will need to be taken into account by anyone determining their best interests at a later date in the event of their losing capacity.

Such recorded views would not be binding on later decision-makers, because they might then conflict with what is in the person's best interests. However, recording views would make them more accessible to decision-makers at a later date and a number of people may well choose to make such advance statements, knowing that they would not be binding. It is also worth noting that a person could specify people that they would like to be consulted in future on particular matters.

The Code of Practice (para 5.46) notes that a person's beliefs and values might be deduced from things such as their cultural background, religious beliefs, political convictions or past behaviour or habits.

The views of other people

This consideration includes an important change in the law. This is the first time that carers, family members and others have had a statutory right to be consulted on decisions affecting a mentally incapacitated person. People used to be asked what they knew of the person's own wishes but did not have the right to state what they thought should happen themselves.

Section 4(7) requires the decision-maker to take into account, if it is practicable and appropriate to consult them, the views of:

> (a) *anyone named by the person as someone to be consulted on the matter in question or on matters of that kind,*
>
> (b) *anyone engaged in caring for the person or interested in his welfare,*

(c) any donee of a lasting power of attorney granted by the person, and

(d) any deputy appointed for the person by the court, as to what would be in the person's best interests and, in particular, as to the matters mentioned in subsection (6).

This would not then bind the decision-maker to follow what others have said, but they must give their views due consideration. Those caring for the person could involve children, as there is no age limit set by this provision. The potential overlap with the role of the nearest relative under the Mental Health Act is explored in Chapter 16.

If the decision-maker decides that it is not practical or appropriate to consult someone on this list the Code suggests (5.51) that they should be able to explain why this was the case and that it would be good practice to record these reasons.

Best interests checklist

These key steps are from the quick summary in Chapter 5 of the Code of Practice. They are reproduced at Appendix 4 as a quick guide.

A person trying to work out the best interests of a person who lacks capacity to make a particular decision ('lacks capacity') should:

Encourage participation

- Do whatever is possible to permit and encourage the person to take part, or to improve their ability to take part, in making the decision.

Identify all relevant circumstances

- Try to identify all the things that the person who lacks capacity would take into account if they were making the decision or acting for themselves.

Find out the person's views

- Try to find out the views of the person who lacks capacity, including:
  - the person's past and present wishes and feelings – these may have been expressed verbally, in writing or through behaviour or habits;
  - any beliefs and values (e.g. religious, cultural, moral or political) that would be likely to influence the decision in question;
  - any other factors the person themselves would be likely to consider if they were making the decision or acting for themselves.

Avoid discrimination

- Not make assumptions about someone's best interests simply on the basis of the person's age, appearance, condition or behaviour.

Assess whether the person might regain capacity

- Consider whether the person is likely to regain capacity (e.g. after receiving medical treatment). If so, can the decision wait until then?

If the decision concerns life-sustaining treatment

- Not be motivated in any way by a desire to bring about the person's death. They should not make assumptions about the person's quality of life.

Consult others

- If it is practical and appropriate to do so, consult other people for their views about the person's best interests and to see if they have any information about the person's wishes and feelings, beliefs and values. In particular, try to consult:
  - anyone previously named by the person as someone to be consulted on either the decision in question or on similar issues;
  - anyone engaged in caring for the person;
  - close relatives, friends or others who take an interest in the person's welfare;
  - any attorney appointed under a Lasting Power of Attorney or Enduring Power of Attorney made by the person;
  - any deputy appointed by the Court of Protection to make decisions for the person.

- For decisions about major medical treatment or where the person should live and where there is no-one who fits into any of the above categories, an Independent Mental Capacity Advocate (IMCA) must be consulted (see Code, Chapter 10 for more information about IMCAs).

- When consulting, remember that the person who lacks the capacity to make the decision or act for themselves still has a right to keep their affairs private – so it would not be right to share every piece of information with everyone.

Avoid restricting the person's rights

- See if there are other options that may be less restrictive of the person's rights.

Take all of this into account

- Weigh up all of these factors in order to work out what is in the person's best interests.

ACTIVITY 6.1

Multiple choice questions

Read each question carefully and tick the appropriate box(es). Where a statement is correct, tick the box next to it; if it is incorrect, leave it blank. You may need to tick more than one box per question.

Appendix 5 (pages 279–83) gives the answers.

6.1 *According to the Mental Capacity Act decisions made in relation to an incapacitated person must be in that person's best interests but the list of points to consider are in the Code rather than being set out in the statute:*

(a) *True*

(b) *False*

6.2 *Following best interests could lead to the withdrawal of life-sustaining treatment:*

(a) *True*

(b) *False*

6.3 *The best interests checklist includes:*

(a) *Decisions should not be based on a person's appearance*

(b) *Waiting where possible for the person to regain capacity*

(c) *Never going against the incapacitated person's current views*

(d) *Consulting anyone who has been named by the person*

(e) *Seeking to incur minimal expense for the person themselves*

(f) *Identifying all relevant circumstances*

Chapter 7

Protection for those making decisions (sections 5–8)

Introduction

Many professionals are understandably concerned about their legal liability if they intervene and make decisions for someone, which turn out later to have negative consequences. The Mental Capacity Act approaches this issue in an interesting way. Essentially, if it can be demonstrated that the requirements of the Act have been followed by the decision-maker (D) it will be as if the person who lacked capacity (P) had made the decision themselves.

Section 5 acts

Section 5 is worded as follows:

(1) *If a person ('D') does an act in connection with the care or treatment of another person ('P'), the act is one to which this section applies if –*

  (a) *before doing the act, D takes reasonable steps to establish whether P lacks capacity in relation to the matter in question, and*

  (b) *when doing the act, D reasonably believes –*

   (i) *that P lacks capacity in relation to the matter, and*

   (ii) *that it will be in P's best interests for the act to be done.*

(2) *D does not incur any liability in relation to the act that he would not have incurred if P –*

  (a) *had had capacity to consent in relation to the matter, and*

  (b) *had consented to D's doing the act.*

So the key for the decision-maker is to clearly identify the act and why it needs to be performed, and then that they have a reasonable belief:

- that the person lacks capacity in relation to the matter at the particular time of intervention, and
- that it will be in the person's best interests.

Chapters 5 and 6 should equip people with the knowledge required for these two stages. If the person making the decision can confirm that he or she has applied these tests appropriately he or she will be safe from legal liability. Note that in most cases it will not be possible for someone to demonstrate that he or she has acted in the best interests of an incapacitated person without having applied the s 4 checklist. No checklist, no best interests, so no s 5 protection.

Four further comments are necessary at this stage.

Firstly, s 5 does not mean that staff can act recklessly or negligently.

Section 5(3) states:

(3) *Nothing in this section excludes a person's civil liability for loss or damage, or his criminal liability, resulting from his negligence in doing the act.*

The second point is that s 5 does not allow a decision-maker to override a valid and applicable advance refusal of treatment.

The third comment concerns Lasting Powers of Attorney (LPAs) and deputies. Section 6(6) states:

Section 5 does not authorise a person to do an act which conflicts with a decision made, within the scope of his authority and in accordance with this Part, by –

(a) *a donee of a lasting power of attorney granted by P, or*

(b) *a deputy appointed for P by the court.*

There will be more of an onus on people to check in certain situations as to whether there is an LPA or whether a deputy has been appointed. In cases of doubt the Office of the Public Guardian will help with this. If a person makes a decision in genuine ignorance of such a person existing or having made a conflicting decision they will be covered by s 5.

If there is any uncertainty over these last two points and where a person's life may be at risk, s 6(7) states:

But nothing in subsection (6) stops a person –

(a) *providing life-sustaining treatment, or*

(b) *doing any act which he reasonably believes to be necessary to prevent a serious deterioration in P's condition,*

while a decision as respects any relevant issue is sought from the court.

The final issue concerns restraint. If restraint is used, s 6 makes further conditions before people can rely on the protection of s 5.

Restraint

The use of restraint is controversial. It may well be that, in the past, under the common law, restraint has not been used when it would have been appropriate because the staff concerned were not sure of their legal position. There have also been a number of occasions when people have justified the use of restraint by saying it was necessary in a person's best interests when closer examination suggested that this was not the case. The hope is that the clarification of this area in the Act will lead to more consistent and positive practice.

Restraint is defined as:

(i) *the use or threat of force in any action which the person resists, or*

(ii) *any restriction of a person's liberty of movement, whether or not they resist.*

If restraint amounts to deprivation of liberty this goes beyond the scope of s 5 and is precluded by s 4A. This issue will be explored in more depth under a separate heading below.

For the person using restraint to keep the protection of s 5 there are two conditions. The position is expressed in s 6 in the following way:

(1) *If D does an act that is intended to restrain P, it is not an act to which s 5 applies unless two further conditions are satisfied.*

(2) *The first condition is that D reasonably believes that it is necessary to do the act in order to prevent harm to P.*

(3) *The second is that the act is a proportionate response to –*

   (a) *the likelihood of P's suffering harm, and*

   (b) *the seriousness of that harm.*

It is not enough to argue that restraint is necessary to prevent the person from harming someone else. Intervention in these circumstances may well be appropriate but it would not link with the protection of s 5 and would be justified, if at all, under common law. For restraint to be justified under the Mental Capacity Act there needs to be a sufficient likelihood of the person suffering harm and the potential harm needs to be serious enough to make this a proportionate response.

Deprivation of liberty

We noted above that a decision-maker does more than merely restrain a person if he or she deprives him or her of his or her liberty within the meaning of Article 5(1) of the Human Rights Convention (whether or not the decision-maker is a public authority). Article 5 states:

No one shall be deprived of their liberty except for specific cases and in accordance with procedure prescribed by law e.g. after conviction, lawful arrest on suspicion of having committed an offence, lawful detention of person of unsound mind, to prevent spread of infectious diseases. Everyone deprived of liberty by arrest or detention shall be entitled to take proceedings by which the lawfulness of the detention shall be decided speedily by a Court and release ordered if the detention is not lawful.

A procedure prescribed by law has been introduced by the Deprivation of Liberty Safeguards (DOLS) as from April 2009 (see Chapter 16).

The Mental Health Act 1983 also has a procedure to detain mentally disordered persons. In certain circumstances this would be an appropriate response where interventions under the Mental Capacity Act were involving restraint that was beginning to approach a deprivation of liberty. There is more information in Chapter 17 about links between these two Acts.

Where a person lacks the capacity to decide about being in a particular place, and is in effect deprived of their liberty, there are several options:

(i) *scale down the level of restrictions (including any restraint) to what would be seen as a restriction of movement rather than a deprivation of liberty;*

(ii) *arrange an assessment under the Mental Health Act with a view to using its powers;*

(iii) *make an application to the Court of Protection to make a personal welfare decision;*

(iv) *follow the new DOLS procedures as covered in Chapter 16;*

(v) *consider short-term or emergency use of common law powers.*

What amounts to deprivation of liberty?

This is a question that has troubled mental health professionals, especially since the Bournewood case, which is examined in more detail in Chapter 18. There is no single factor which determines deprivation of liberty. In Bournewood (*HL v UK*, 2005) the European Court of Human Rights stated that the difference was one of degree or intensity rather than nature or substance. It may depend on the type of care being provided, how long the situation lasts, what the effects are and how the situation came about. There is some guidance in the Code of Practice (para 6.52) as to what factors contribute to deprivation of liberty. These have been drawn from European case law.

The European Court of Human Rights has identified the following as factors contributing to deprivation of liberty in its judgments on cases to date:

- *restraint was used, including sedation, to admit a person who is resisting*

- *professionals exercised complete and effective control over care and movement for a significant period*

- *professionals exercised control over assessments, treatment, contacts and residence*

- *the person would be prevented from leaving if they made a meaningful attempt to do so*

- *a request by carers for the person to be discharged to their care was refused*

- *the person was unable to maintain social contacts because of restrictions placed on access to other people*

- *the person lost autonomy because they were under continuous supervision and control.*

These pointers are repeated in the DOLS Code, where there is further advice on deprivation of liberty in Chapter 2.

In 2014, the bar which sets the level for a deprivation of liberty came down to a much lower level as the result of the Supreme Court decision in the cases of 'P' and 'MIG and MEG'. Where the confinement is attributable to the state and the person is under continuous supervision and control and is not free to leave, they will be deprived of their liberty unless they have the capacity to give valid consent. This has led to a dramatic increase in referrals for DOLS assessments or applications for detention under the Mental Health Act. There are, as yet, no new codes of practice for the MCA but the revised Code of Practice to the Mental Health Act sets out the position clearly and briefly:

> *13.44 The precise scope of the term 'deprivation of liberty' is not fixed. In its 19 March judgment P v Cheshire West and Chester Council and another and P and Q v Surrey County Council ('Cheshire West'), the Supreme Court clarified that there is a deprivation of liberty in circumstances where a person is under continuous control and supervision, is not free to leave and lacks capacity to consent to these arrangements.*

> *13.45 The Supreme Court also noted that factors which are not relevant in determining whether there is a deprivation of liberty include the person's compliance or lack of objection and the reason or purpose behind a particular placement. The relative normality of the placement (whatever the comparison made) is also not relevant.*

> *13.46 A deprivation of liberty can occur in domestic settings where the state is responsible for such arrangements. In such cases, an order should be sought from the Court of Protection.*

Chapter 17 looks at the current overlaps with mental health law in this area.

Financial implications of section 5 decisions

Another area of concern for those making decisions on someone else's behalf is where the money will come from if there are any financial implications of the decision. Paying for goods and services provided is covered by s 7, which states that:

(1) *If necessary goods or services are supplied to a person who lacks capacity to contract for the supply, he must pay a reasonable price for them.*

(2) *'Necessary' means suitable to a person's condition in life and to his actual requirements at the time when the goods or services are supplied.*

If a decision-maker is involved with an act which involves expenditure s 8(1) allows them:

(a) *to pledge P's credit for the purpose of the expenditure, and*

(b) *to apply money in P's possession for meeting the expenditure.*

Similarly, if the expenditure is borne for P by D, it is lawful for D to reimburse himself out of money in P's possession, or to be otherwise indemnified by P.

Key checks for decision-makers

1. What is the act or decision?

2. Why does it need to be performed now?

3. Do you have a reasonable belief that the person lacks capacity in relation to the matter at the particular time of intervention?

4. Can you confirm that it will be in the person's best interests and that you have followed the checklist?

Chapter 8
Lasting Powers of Attorney (sections 9–14 and 22–23)

Introduction

Since the Enduring Powers of Attorney Act 1985 it has been possible to create a Power of Attorney which 'endures' beyond the time when the donor loses mental capacity. However, this has been limited to decisions and acts concerning the donor's property and affairs. It has not been possible to include personal welfare matters (including consenting to medical treatment) within an Enduring Power of Attorney (EPA). This was in line with the general principle of common law that no-one can consent on behalf of another adult to a medical procedure. Hospital consent forms have sometimes been signed by a relative of, for example, an adult with learning difficulties unable to consent for him or herself, without people realising that this does not provide a valid consent in law. Even if the High Court has been approached regarding an issue surrounding the giving or withdrawal of treatment to or from someone who lacks capacity it might grant a declaration that it would be lawful to proceed or not as the case may be, but the court would not consent on behalf of the patient concerned. Thus introducing substituted decision-making in the field of personal welfare, healthcare and consent to medical treatment is one of the more controversial innovations of the Mental Capacity Act, not least because of the additional opportunities for abuse that might be presented. Even if the relationship at the time of creation of the Lasting Power of Attorney was one of unqualified trust, that is no guarantee of the position at some time in the future. The term 'donee' used here equates to the attorney.

What is a Lasting Power of Attorney?

A Lasting Power of Attorney (LPA) is defined in section (s) 9(1) as:

a power of attorney under which the donor ('P') confers on the donee (or donees) authority to make decisions about all or any of the following –

(a) P's personal welfare or specified matters concerning P's personal welfare, and

(b) P's property and affairs or specified matters concerning P's property and affairs, and which includes authority to make such decisions in circumstances where P no longer has capacity.

Section 64(2) states that references in the Act to making decisions in relation to LPAs include, where appropriate, acting on decisions made.

From 1 October 2007 no new EPAs could be made. They are replaced by LPAs, which may be either a property and affairs LPA or a personal welfare LPA. If a person wishes to cover both areas of decision-making, then separate LPAs are required.

What can an LPA cover?

The list of actions and decisions which a property and affairs LPA might cover is not set out in the Act; however, at 7.36 of the Code of Practice numerous examples are given, including:

- buying or selling property;
- operating bank accounts;
- dealing with tax affairs;
- paying outgoings;
- investing savings;
- making gifts;
- applying for entitlement to NHS or social care entitlement;
- claiming, receiving and using benefits.

Similarly, the scope of a personal welfare LPA is not set out in the Act (although s 11(7)(c) provides that it may include giving or refusing consent to medical treatment) but is illustrated in the Code of Practice at 7.21. It could include:

- decisions about where the donor should live;
- who may have contact with him or her;
- day-to-day care;
- rights of access to personal information about the donor;
- whether the donor should take part in social activities, leisure activities, education or training.

Section 11(8) states that where the personal welfare LPA includes refusal of or consent to medical treatment, this will not include life-sustaining treatment (as defined in s 4(10)) unless expressly stated in the LPA.

The formal requirements

Because of the increased opportunities for abuse there has been a corresponding increase in the safeguards which the Government felt it necessary to introduce to give donors additional protections. One such safeguard is the very much more detailed and complex formal requirements needed both to make and register LPAs. These formal requirements are set out in s 10 and in Schedule 1 to the Act, but more particularly in the Lasting Powers of Attorney, Enduring Powers of Attorney and Public Guardian Regulations (2007, No. 1253).

While it is understandable that increased formality might be required in respect of the novel introduction of substituted decision-making for personal welfare and medical matters, it is less obvious why this should be so for a property and affairs LPA covering similar ground to an EPA. So the forms required for each include detailed prescribed information:

- the s 1 principles;
- guidance about choosing an attorney or a replacement;
- when the attorney can act;
- what decisions the attorney can make;
- the restrictions that can be imposed;
- paying the attorney;
- registering the LPA;
- in the case of a personal welfare LPA, the special requirements relating to life-sustaining treatment.

In the LPA the donor can name up to five people who must be notified when an application to register is made. In addition, an independent person has to certify that in his or her opinion the donor is making the LPA of his or her own free will and that he or she understands its purpose and the powers being given to the attorney. Should the donor decide not to name any people who must be first notified, there must then be a second independent person providing an additional certificate.

The LPA cannot be used until it has been registered by the Office of the Public Guardian (which controls and maintains the register of LPAs) and stamped on every page. The degree of formality, complexity and expense consequent upon the enhanced safeguards may prove a longer-term disincentive to the creation of new LPAs. The current fee for registering an LPA is £110 and a separate fee is payable for a property and affairs and a personal welfare LPA. Details of these and other fees are available from the OPG website at **www.gov.uk/government/organisations/office-of-the-public-guardian**.

For the most part the Mental Capacity Act applies to those aged over 16. However, for an LPA both the donor and the attorney must be over 18 and have capacity to execute or operate it respectively. Property and affairs attorneys may not be undischarged bankrupts.

To what controls are attorneys and LPAs subject?

All attorneys are subject to the s 1 principles and the best interests 'checklist' of s 4. In addition s 42(4) requires an attorney to have regard to the Code of Practice. So, for example, an attorney will have to:

- presume capacity on the part of a donor;

- take all practical steps to help him or her to make the decision for him or herself;

- consult as required by s 4;

- so far as is reasonably ascertainable consider the donor's past and present wishes, beliefs and values.

The attorney is also by s 11 subject to similar limitations on the use of restraint imposed generally by s 6 and cannot use restraint or restrictions of movement which amount to a deprivation of liberty within the meaning of Article 5 of the European Convention on Human Rights. Appointing an attorney does not therefore alter the requirements for assessing capacity or determining best interests, nor does it displace the s 1 principles. What the donor is doing is identifying the person who will make the decisions, not changing the requirements of the Act as to how those decisions should be reached.

How might an LPA be limited in scope?

An LPA, whether personal welfare or property and affairs, does not have to cover all possible areas of decision-making. The donor could limit it to financial issues only or to certain types of medical treatment, or to the issue of where the donor is to live. Or the donor could grant a general power but exclude one single area of decision-making such as, for example, who may be allowed to have contact with the donor. Section 9(4)(b) states that the authority conferred by an LPA is subject to any conditions or restrictions specified in it. These could include a requirement that the attorney first consult with a named person before reaching his decision or with different named persons in respect of different areas of decision-making. An attorney could approach the Court of Protection for authority under s 23(2)(b) to make a decision which does not fall within the ambit of the LPA. An example would be where the attorney wishes to make a gift to a relative of the donor other than on a 'customary occasion' permitted by s 12(2).

Several attorneys may be appointed by the donor under an LPA. The donor may wish to appoint different people to deal with his or her property and affairs from those he or she wishes to make personal welfare decisions for him. Where more than one person is appointed, the LPA must specify whether they are to act jointly or jointly and severally. If jointly, then all appointed must agree before the decision can be effective; if jointly and severally, then any of the attorneys will have the authority individually. If the LPA fails to specify whether the attorneys are to act jointly or jointly and severally, it will be assumed that they are to act jointly (s 10(5)). The donor may in the LPA identify a substitute attorney should the original attorney die, become incapacitated, bankrupt or disclaim his appointment, or should the donor's marriage be dissolved. However, the attorney him or herself has no such power to appoint a substitute or successor.

A personal welfare LPA can only be effective once the donor has become, or the attorney believes he or she has become, incapacitated. This contrasts with the situation under an EPA or a property and affairs LPA which may, if the LPA so provides, take effect before the donor loses capacity.

In keeping with the Act's requirement that the question of capacity is decision-specific, in the case of a personal welfare LPA, or a property and affairs LPA which provides that it is only effective once the donor has lost capacity, the attorney will only be able to make those decisions for which the donor lacks capacity at the time. As mentioned above, an attorney must take all practical steps to enable the donor to continue to make decisions in those areas where he or she retains capacity, limiting his or her involvement as decision-maker to those where the donor is incapable of making the decision for him or herself. He or she will have to have regard to the definition of incapacity and the test for the inability to make decisions set out in ss 2 and 3. This could lead to problems in practice where the attorney and health or social care professional have different views as to the person's capacity to make the decision in question or as to what is in that person's best interests. Chapter 15 of the Code of Practice gives guidance on how to resolve such differences (see especially 15.3). Ultimately, the matter may have to be referred to the Court of Protection via the Public Guardian (14.19).

An LPA can be revoked if the donor has capacity to do this (s 13(2)), even if he or she may at the time lack capacity to make the decisions the attorney was empowered to make.

Who may be an attorney?

No-one can be compelled to act as an attorney under an LPA. The attorney's statement in the LPA confirms that he or she has read the prescribed information, and understood his or her duties under the LPA, the Act and the Code of Practice. In signing, he or she accepts this role. After the LPA has been registered, in order to withdraw from his or her appointment he or she must notify the donor, any other attorney and the Office of the Public Guardian, using the prescribed form set out in the Regulations. The Code of Practice gives guidance as to who may be an attorney. An individual has to be named rather than described by reference to a job title. A paid care worker (such as a care home manager) should not agree to act as an attorney, apart from in unusual circumstances (for example, if they are the only close relative of the donor).

The role and duties of an attorney

The duties of an attorney are outlined at 7.58 of the Code of Practice and include a duty of care in decision-making, a duty to act in good faith and not take advantage of his or her position, and a duty to carry out the donor's instructions and to respect his or her confidentiality. The s 44 criminal offence of ill-treatment or neglect is specifically applied to attorneys, including those appointed under an EPA. Even where the decision does not fall clearly within his or her authority under the LPA, an attorney has a right to be consulted when the decision-maker is applying the best interests checklist under s 4.

Advance decisions and Lasting Powers of Attorney

The relationship between advance decisions and LPAs covering personal welfare issues might cause some difficulties in practice. If the advance decision was made after the appointment of an attorney, then the attorney could not consent to treatment specifically refused by the advance decision. If the LPA had been made later then, as discussed above, the issue would be whether the scope of the attorney's authority included consenting to treatments refused in the advance decision. It may be advisable to destroy any earlier advance decisions in case the doctor was unaware of the appointment of an attorney under an LPA. Even where the statement or expression of the person's wishes fell short of constituting a valid and applicable advance decision, the attorney would have to bear those wishes in mind when applying the best interests checklist. Similar principles would apply if the Court of Protection had appointed a deputy with powers to decide personal welfare, including healthcare issues.

Does the law limit the powers of an attorney?

There are a number of limitations on the powers of an attorney imposed either by the Act itself or the general law. So in the same way that a donor, when he or she had capacity, could not directly require a healthcare professional to give specific medical treatment (although he or she could of course refuse such treatment), he or she could not in the LPA authorise his or her attorney to require such treatment. Further, the Act does not apply to treatment for mental disorder regulated under Part 4 of the Mental Health Act (see Chapter 15). Therefore, an attorney could not consent to or refuse such treatment in respect of a formally detained patient. On the other hand, he or she would have authority in relation to treatments for physical conditions or treatment for mental disorder not regulated under Part 4. Where the donor has been made subject to a guardianship order under the Mental Health Act, the Attorney will not be able to make decisions which conflict with those of the Guardian. However, if authorised under the LPA he or she will be able to exercise the donor's rights under the Mental Health Act, such as applying to a Mental Health Review Tribunal (MHRT). It may also be appropriate in some circumstances to involve the attorney in s 117 aftercare planning.

The role and powers of the Court of Protection

As already mentioned among other obligations, an attorney must follow the best interests checklist in deciding how to act where the donor is incapable of deciding for him or herself. The fact that the attorney is effectively the designated decision-maker in areas within the scope of the LPA does not absolve others from challenging his or her decision if they believe that it is not in the donor's best interests. The Court of Protection, through the Office of the Public Guardian, exercises jurisdiction over attorneys.

The court's powers are set out in ss 22–23 and include:

- deciding whether the formal requirements for the creation of an LPA have been met;

- deciding whether an LPA has been revoked;

- deciding whether fraud or undue influence has been exerted over the creation or execution of the LPA, and if so whether to revoke it or not to register it;

- deciding the meaning or effect of an LPA;

- giving authority to the attorney to make decisions, including gifts which fall outside the scope of the LPA;

- giving directions such as to produce records, accounts or information; or directions in respect of the remuneration or expenses of the attorney, or even to relieve the attorney from liability arising from a breach of his duties.

The Code of Practice advises (7.70–72) that, where abuse or exploitation of the donor by the attorney is suspected, this should be reported to the Office of the Public Guardian, which may refer the matter to the Court of Protection. In the case of a personal welfare LPA covering consent to or refusal of medical treatment, if healthcare professionals disagree with the attorney's decision and are unable to persuade him or her to a different view they can apply to the Court of Protection and in the meantime under s 6(7) give life-sustaining treatment or treatment which prevents a deterioration, while the court decides the matter. This almost certainly creates a professional obligation to do so. An attorney will him or herself be protected from liability where an LPA was not effective because, for example, it had been incorrectly created or had been subsequently revoked without his or her knowledge (s 14(2)). In such circumstances, a transaction between the attorney and a third party could be as valid as if the LPA had been effective.

Transitional arrangements for Enduring Powers of Attorney (EPAs)

It has not been possible to make any new EPAs since 1 October 2007. However, existing EPAs will continue until the last donor dies. They will not automatically be extended to include additional areas of decision-making which could have been covered by an LPA. If the donor retains capacity and wishes to cover, for example, personal welfare decisions he or she will have to make an LPA. Existing EPAs will remain valid and will require to be registered with the Office of the Public Guardian when the donor loses capacity. Schedule 4 to the Act essentially reproduces the provisions of the Enduring Powers of Attorney Act 1985. Schedules 7 and 8 to the Lasting Powers of Attorney, Enduring Powers of Attorney and Public Guardian Regulations specify the Notice of Intention to apply for registration of an EPA and the application to register.

Key points and questions relating to Lasting Powers of Attorney

- What area of decision-making does the person wish to cover?

- Does the LPA cover this area of decision-making?

- Have the formal requirements been met?

- If a personal welfare LPA is intended to cover medical treatment decisions, does the donor understand what this includes?

- How old is the donor/attorney? They must both be at least 18.

- The LPA does not bypass best interests checklists and s 1 principles.

- Has the donor of a personal welfare LPA become incapacitated? If so, in relation to which decisions?

- Can the donor make the relevant decision for him or herself?

- Does the LPA cover the same ground as an advance decision?

- Is the attorney failing to act in the best interests of the donor, or abusing him or her?

Chapter 9
Deputies and declarations (sections 15–21)

Introduction

The nature, structure and procedural rules of the Court of Protection are dealt with in Chapter 12. The present chapter will cover the powers of the Court of Protection to make declarations, decisions and to appoint deputies. It will also deal with the approach of the court to the use of its powers. One of the main benefits of the Act is to introduce a single court with the power to deal with all issues concerning people who lack or may lack capacity within the meaning of the Act, whether the issue concerns property and affairs or personal welfare and medical decisions. Not only will there no longer be doubt as to which court should be approached, but also issues concerning the limits to the court's powers and to its willingness to become involved should no longer arise. Gaps in the law requiring appeals to the High Court's inherent jurisdiction have nevertheless emerged. For example, in relation to people unable to make decisions but not because of an impairment of or disturbance in the functioning of the mind or brain (but rather because of, for example, undue influence), see most recently *LB Redbridge v G* (2014); or in relation to a patient detained under the Mental Health Act who cannot be treated under either that Act or the Mental Capacity Act, see *An NHS Trust v Dr A* (2013). Further, there is some evidence of disagreement between judges as to whether, for example, guardianship or an order of the Court of Protection should be used in relation to decisions about residence and accommodation (see *C v Blackburn with Darwen BC* (2011)), which is likely to be exacerbated after the decision in *AM v SLAM* (2013) discussed in Chapter 17. The introduction of the Court of Protection with its greatly increased powers means that a further possible route to action will become available for health and social care professionals, but at least s 21 provides for the ease of transfer of proceedings between courts where appropriate if the wrong choice is made.

The power to make declarations

As a branch of the High Court of Justice the Court of Protection has power to make declarations and this is confirmed by s 15(1) which provides that it may make declarations as to:

(a) whether a person has or lacks capacity to make a decision specified in the declaration;

(b) whether a person has or lacks capacity to make decisions on such matters as are described in the declaration.

It would be appropriate to ask the court for a declaration in circumstances where despite following the procedures set out in the Act and the guidance contained in the Code of Practice, the decision-maker finds it impossible to reach a conclusion as to whether the person has capacity or not. It would not be appropriate to ask for a declaration simply to provide reassurance to the health or social care professional, but only where there is genuine doubt about a person's capacity. Professionals might disagree about the patient's capacity to consent to a medical procedure, or there might be dispute between family members, or the person concerned might wish to challenge a decision that he or she lacked capacity (made perhaps by an attorney under an LPA) (see Code of Practice 8.16).

Section 15(1) also provides that the court may make declarations as to:

(c) the lawfulness or otherwise of any act done, or to be done, in relation to that person.

In this context, an 'act' would include an omission to act and a course of conduct (s 15(2)). Historically, the power of the High Court to make a declaration has been used in relation to controversial areas of medical decision-making. So where there was doubt as to whether a form of treatment should be given or withheld from a person who lacked capacity, a declaration would be sought as to whether to proceed in the way desired by the healthcare professionals would be lawful. Section 15 therefore preserves the right of a healthcare professional to apply to the court in such circumstances. The Code of Practice suggests (8.18) that case law in this field arising before the Act will continue to apply. This would mean, for example, that before withdrawing artificial nutrition and hydration from a persistent vegetative state patient an application would need to be made to the court for a declaration that this would be lawful. Other issues which would need to go to court would be the non-therapeutic sterilisation of an adult with learning disabilities, or the issue as to whether an incapacitated adult could become an organ donor. While this may be so, and declarations may be sought, the power of substituted decision-making by the court introduced by s 16 (see below) may be preferred because of the greater degree of certainty conveyed.

The power to make decisions

While the distinction between the court making a declaration as to the lawfulness of an act in relation to a person lacking capacity on the one hand and making the decision on behalf of that person on the other would appear to be somewhat technical, the reality is that it goes to the heart of one of the more controversial elements of the Act, namely the introduction of substituted decision-making. In the past, while the court might make a declaration that were a doctor to perform a particular procedure in relation to an incapacitated patient that would be lawful, it would not be *consenting* to the procedure on behalf of the patient. Under a personal welfare LPA a person can appoint an attorney to make medical decisions for him or her. Under s 16, the Court of Protection can similarly make a medical decision for an incapacitated person as opposed to simply declaring that a particular procedure would be lawful.

If a person lacks capacity in relation either to a personal welfare or property and affairs matter s 16 (2) provides that the court may:

(a) *by making an order, make the decision or decisions on the person's behalf in relation to the matter or matters, or*

(b) *appoint a person (a 'deputy') to make decisions on the person's behalf in relation to the matter or matters.*

Examples of decisions that the court might make are given in the Code of Practice: terminating a tenancy agreement, making a will, deciding on the validity of an advance decision, deciding upon a medical procedure, or preventing an individual from contacting a person who lacks capacity. As seen in Chapter 8 the Court of Protection has specific powers to determine the validity and operation of LPAs. From these examples alone it can be seen that there is a fine line between applying for a declaration under s 15 and asking the court to make a decision under s 16.

The approach of the court

In making decisions under s 16, subsection (subs) 3 provides that the powers of the court are subject to the provisions of the Act and in particular to s 1 (the principles) and s 4 (best interests). So, for example, the court will start from the presumption that the person has capacity to make the decision for him or herself and in reaching its conclusion will apply both the definition of incapacity and the test for the inability to make a decision under ss 2 and 3. If it reaches the conclusion that the person lacks capacity in relation to the decision in question and that there are no practical steps which might be taken to allow the person to achieve capacity to make the decision for him or herself, it will go through the requirements of the best interests checklist under s 4, consulting where appropriate, seeking to establish what is known of the person's own wishes, and applying the principle of equal consideration.

We have already seen that under s 16 the court may make a decision itself or appoint a deputy (see later) to make the decision or decisions. The default position, however, is that the court should make the decision, requiring the applicant to return to the court should another decision be needed in the future. Section 16(4) provides that a decision by the court is to be preferred to the appointment of a deputy and that where a deputy *is* appointed the powers conferred on him or her should be as limited in scope and duration as is reasonably practicable in the circumstances. This is in keeping with the s 1(6) principle that regard must be had to whether the necessary purpose can be as effectively achieved in a way that is less restrictive of the person's rights and freedom of action. In other words, the court will intervene to the least extent necessary rather than the most that it can.

Personal welfare decisions

The powers of the court to make personal welfare decisions are not exhaustively set out, but s 17 gives examples as follows:

- deciding where the person is to live;

- deciding what contact, if any, the person is to have with any specified persons;

- making an order prohibiting a named person from having contact with the person;

- giving or refusing consent to the carrying out or continuation of a treatment by a person providing healthcare for the person;

- giving a direction that a person responsible for the person's healthcare allow a different person to take over that responsibility.

These are wide powers which would include providing authority for a person to deprive an incapacitated person of liberty within the meaning of Article 5 of the European Convention on Human Rights, where this cannot be authorised as an s 5 act because of the limitations imposed by s 6 (see Chapter 7). This is also spelled out in the amendments to the Act made by the Mental Health Act 2007 (new S4A(3),(4)); but the court's powers will be limited in that it will not be able to make an order depriving a person lacking capacity of liberty where he or she is ineligible under the Deprivation of Liberty Safeguards (DOLS) (see Chapter 16).

Property and affairs decisions

There is similarly no exhaustive list of the s 16 powers of the court in relation to an incapacitated person's property and affairs. However, s 18 provides examples closely modelled on the unamended Mental Health Act s 96 powers of the old Court of Protection, i.e.:

- the control and management of the person's property;

- the sale, exchange, charging, gift or other disposition of the person's property;

- the acquisition of property in the person's name or on the person's behalf;

- the carrying on, on a person's behalf, of any profession, trade or business;

- the taking of a decision which will have the effect of dissolving a partnership of which the person is a member;

- the carrying out of any contract entered into by the person;

- the discharge of the person's debts and of any of the person's obligations, whether legally enforceable or not;

- the settlement of any of the person's property, whether for the person's benefit or for the benefit of others;

- the execution for the person of a will;

- the exercise of any power (including a power to consent) vested in the person whether beneficially or as trustee or otherwise;
- the conduct of legal proceedings in the person's name or on a person's behalf.

The court's powers extend to those under the age of 16 if the court considers it likely that the person will still lack capacity to make such decisions when he or she reaches the age of 18. This is an exception to the general rule that the Act applies only to those aged 16 and above.

The power to appoint a deputy

We have already seen that the court has power under s 16 to appoint a deputy to make decisions on behalf of a person who lacks capacity, but that the starting point for the court will be that it should make the decision for itself and that where it does appoint a deputy it will limit the scope and duration of the appointment. Section 16(8) provides that:

> *The court may, in particular, revoke the appointment of a deputy or vary the powers conferred on him if it is satisfied that the deputy –*
>
> *(a) has behaved, or is behaving, in a way that contravenes the authority conferred on him by the court or is not in the person's best interests, or*
>
> *(b) proposes to behave in a way that would contravene that authority or would not be in the person's best interests.*

The old Court of Protection frequently appointed receivers to manage the property and affairs of a person who lacked capacity. What is new in the Act is that a deputy may be appointed both in respect of property and affairs issues and/or personal welfare issues. The deputy must be over 18 or in the case of property and affairs issues could also be a trust corporation such as a bank or other financial institution. A deputy would naturally have to consent to his or her appointment. Two or more deputies may be appointed to act jointly or jointly and severally. They can even be appointed to act jointly in respect of some matters and jointly and severally in respect of others. When appointing a deputy the court may at the same time appoint a successor to take over in specified circumstances, for example where the deputy appointed dies or him or herself becomes incapable of acting. A deputy can claim reasonable expenses from the estate of the person lacking capacity and may be given power by the court to deal with the control and management of property, including the power to invest. He or she may be required to give security for his or her conduct and to submit reports to the Public Guardian.

The Code of Practice gives guidance at 8.32–33 as to the kind of person who might be appointed a deputy. Clearly, the court will have in mind the nature of the decisions the deputy is empowered to make, whether concerning property and affairs or personal welfare. While a family member may be appropriate in relation to personal welfare issues, the court could appoint a professional deputy in relation to complex financial issues.

When might a deputy be appointed?

For issues concerning property and affairs a deputy is likely to be appointed in similar circumstances to the previous appointment of receivers. So this will be largely unnecessary where the person has no property or assets, but merely social security benefits. It is more difficult to decide when it would be appropriate to apply for a deputy to be appointed in respect of the new area of personal welfare decisions. A deputy would not be needed to make ordinary care and treatment decisions because those would be covered as s 5 acts, needing no specific additional authority. However, it may be appropriate:

- if that person had complex medical needs which would be likely to require repeated difficult treatment decisions to be made over a period of time;

- where family members were repeatedly unable to agree among themselves over what was in that person's best interests;

- where there were regular irreconcilable differences between the health and social care professionals and the family or friends of the person concerned.

What restrictions affect a deputy's powers?

The overriding restriction on a deputy is that at all times he or she must act in accordance with the powers specifically given to him or her by the court and cannot exceed those powers without first going back to the court for extended authority. Section 20 sets out specific limitations on a deputy's powers:

- a deputy cannot act in relation to a matter if he or she knows or has reasonable grounds for believing that a person has capacity in relation to that matter. The fact that a deputy has been appointed does not mean that he or she is free to make decisions even in relation to areas given to him or her by the court if the person has capacity to make the decision him or herself. His or her authority is to be exercised in keeping with the provisions of the Act and in particular the s 1 principles and s 4 best interests checklist. So the deputy would, among other things, have to apply the s 3 functional test (i.e., is *this* person unable to make *this* decision *now*), consider under s 1(3) what practical steps could be taken to assist the person in making the decision for him or herself, and consider whether the decision could safely be put back until a time when the person could make it him or herself. If the person was unable to make the decision and if this was because of s 2 impairment of, or a disturbance in the functioning of, the mind or brain, the deputy, in following the best interests checklist, would have to consult as required and apply the principle of equal consideration.

- The court cannot give a deputy power to prohibit a named person from having contact with the person, nor to require a person responsible for his or her healthcare to allow a different person to take over that responsibility. The court has such powers but they cannot be granted to a deputy.

- In the area of property and affairs a deputy may not be given power to settle any of the person's property, nor to execute a will on his or her behalf nor exercise any power vested in him or her.

- A deputy may not be given power which conflicts with a decision made within the scope of his or her authority by an attorney or attorneys under an LPA.

- A deputy may not be given power to refuse consent to the carrying out of or continuation of life-sustaining treatment in relation to the person.

- A deputy is subject to the limitations on the use of restraint, and the prohibition against deprivation of liberty set out in s 4A. In addition, any use of restraint must fall within the scope of the authority conferred on him or her by the court. On the other hand, where a deputy meets these conditions and is authorised to act in relation to the matter by the court this would prevent anyone else relying on s 5 to make the decision.

- Although a deputy, if given the power by the court, may exercise some of a detained patient's rights under the Mental Health Act on his or her behalf such as the right to apply to a Mental Health Review Tribunal, he or she could not consent or refuse treatment for mental disorder regulated under Part 4 of the Mental Health Act, nor make decisions (for example about where the person should live) which conflict with a Guardianship order (see Chapter 17).

The responsibilities and duties of a deputy

In addition to acting in accordance with the s 1 principles and s 4 best interests checklist dealt with above, a deputy is specifically required to have regard to the guidance contained in the Code of Practice by s 42(4). He or she must also always act within the limits of the authority conferred on him or her by the court. The Code of Practice at 8.56 summarises the duties of a deputy, in keeping with the law of agency which by s 19(6) is specifically applied to deputies, as follows, to:

- *act with due care and skill (duty of care)*;
- *not take advantage of their situation (fiduciary duty)*;
- *indemnify the person against liability to third parties caused by the deputy's negligence*;
- *not delegate their duties unless authorised to do so*;
- *act in good faith*;
- *respect the person's confidentiality; and*
- *comply with the directions of the Court of Protection.*

In relation to property and affairs, they also have a duty to keep accounts and keep the person's money and property separate from their own finances.

The Court of Protection, through the Office of the Public Guardian, exercises control over deputies. Anyone who has concern about the manner in which a deputy is exercising his or her powers should report the matter to the Public Guardian. The Court of Protection can revoke the appointment or amend the powers given to the deputy. The offence under s 44 of ill-treatment or neglect of a person who lacks capacity is specifically applied to court-appointed deputies.

Key points and questions relating to the Court of Protection and deputies

- The Court of Protection deals with all issues concerning a person incapacitated within the meaning of s 2.

- The court can make *declarations* as to incapacity or the lawfulness of actions.

- The court can make *decisions* on behalf of an incapacitated person.

- The court is governed by the best interests checklist and s 1 principles.

- The court will prefer to make the decision itself rather than appoint a deputy.

- The court controls the appointment, actions and powers of a deputy.

- Deputies cannot make decisions where the person retains capacity.

- Deputies must have regard to the Code of Practice and follow the best interests checklist and s 1 principles.

Chapter 10
Advance decisions to refuse treatment (sections 24–26)

Introduction

It is a curious feature of much of the media reporting of the Mental Capacity Act that it focused on one part which in fact introduced very little change to the existing law but which was presented as being one of its more controversial innovations. Advance decisions to refuse treatment, 'living wills', or advance refusals represent a long-established feature of the common law. An adult of sound mind is entitled to refuse medical treatment, whether face to face with the healthcare professional or in advance, anticipating a time when the person may lack capacity to refuse the treatment in question. This is a right protected by Article 8 of the European Convention on Human Rights. The provisions relating to advance decisions to refuse treatment in the Mental Capacity Act are largely a replication and codification of the common law, which is why their description as introducing the concept of preventing a doctor from giving certain treatments, including end-of-life treatments, was misleading.

The statutory provisions

The provisions are contained within sections (ss) 24–26 of the Mental Capacity Act.

Section 24 defines an advance decision (the somewhat misleading shorthand term used in the Act itself) as follows:

(1) 'Advance decision' means a decision made by a person ('P'), after he has reached 18 and when he has capacity to do so, that if –

(a) at a later time and in such circumstances as he may specify, specified treatment is proposed to be carried out or continued by a person providing health care for him, and

(b) at that time he lacks capacity to consent to the carrying out or continuation of the treatment, the specified treatment is not to be carried out or continued.

Note that the provision relates only to the *refusal* of treatment. An advance decision cannot bind a healthcare professional to *give* specified treatment any more than a competent patient can require such treatment face to face. Note also that an advance decision is limited to a refusal of a specified *treatment given by a person providing health care*. It does not cover refusals of other acts. A person could not therefore make a binding advance decision to refuse to be admitted, for example, to a particular care home. A person's wishes in relation to issues outside the field of healthcare could of course be incorporated in a written statement, which the decision-maker would have to bear in mind (but would not be bound by) when deciding best interests under s 4. Even within the field of healthcare it is not possible by an advance decision to refuse consent to the provision of basic care, including nursing care, which may therefore always lawfully be given.

Section 24 further provides that layman's terms may be used, and that if the person retains capacity he or she may withdraw or alter (not necessarily in writing) the advance decision. The Code of Practice (9.21; 9.23; 9.31) emphasises that, particularly where an advance decision or its withdrawal is verbal, this should be documented by the healthcare professional.

An advance decision must be valid

To be effective an advance decision must be *valid* and *applicable*. This is explained in s 25. An advance decision will not be *valid*

- if the person has withdrawn it, although he or she must of course have capacity to do so at the time.

- if the person has subsequently made a Lasting Power of Attorney (LPA) in which the attorney is authorised to give or refuse consent to the treatment covered by the advance decision. It may not be a straightforward matter to decide whether the attorney's authority does indeed relate to the treatment in question as there may be two documents couched in very different language; in fact, the advance decision may not be in writing at all.

- if the person has subsequently acted inconsistently. So, for example, a person may have made an advance decision to refuse blood products. If six months later, while still retaining capacity, he or she accepts blood products, that would be *clearly inconsistent with the advance decision remaining his fixed decision* (s 25(2)(c)). 'Ulysses Pacts' are not effective – i.e. an advance decision purporting to provide that future statements or actions contrary to its provisions are to be ignored; but could that provision be isolated and struck out, leaving the remaining provisions intact and valid?

An advance decision must be applicable

An advance decision will not be *applicable*

- if the treatment is not the treatment specified. This sounds obvious but could give rise to difficulties in practice. A judge would be reluctant to extend the scope of an advance decision on the basis that 'I am sure he or she meant to include that treatment as well'.

- if the person has capacity at the time to give or refuse consent; if that is the case, it is the patient whom the healthcare professional consults and not his or her written advance decision!

- if any specified circumstances are absent or if there are reasonable grounds for believing that circumstances exist which the person did not anticipate at the time and which would have affected his or her decision. This would cover a situation where consent to specific treatment had been refused in an advance decision based on then current medical knowledge and practice, which significantly changed after the person lost capacity. Keyhole surgery might have become possible, or new drug therapies available without the side effects the person particularly wished to avoid.

What are the formal requirements?

In most circumstances no particular formality is required for an advance decision. It may be in writing, verbal, signed, unsigned, dated, undated, witnessed, not witnessed. If it is in writing the Code of Practice (9.19) suggests that it should contain:

- full details of the person making the advance decision, including date of birth, home address and any distinguishing features (in case healthcare professionals need to identify an unconscious person, for example);

- the name and address of the person's GP and whether they have a copy of the document;

- a statement that the document should be used if the person ever lacks capacity to make treatment decisions;

- a clear statement of the decision, the treatment to be refused and the circumstances in which the decision will apply;

- the date the document was written (or reviewed);

- the person's signature (or the signature of someone the person has asked to sign on their behalf and in their presence);

- the signature of the person witnessing the signature, if there is one (or a statement directing somebody to sign on the person's behalf).

Contrast this advice with the complex and very specific formal *requirements* for an LPA.

There is one significant change introduced by the Mental Capacity Act where the advance decision is to apply to life-sustaining treatment. In these circumstances it must be verified by a statement by the person that it is to apply to that treatment even if his or her life is at risk. It must also be in writing, signed by the person or by another person in his or her presence and at his or her direction, and the signature made or acknowledged by the person in the presence of a witness who him or herself signs it or acknowledges his or her signature in the person's presence (s 25(5)(6)). This is an important change in the law because many advance decisions do relate to life-sustaining treatment. Life-sustaining treatment is rather unhelpfully defined in s 4(10) as *treatment which in the view of a person providing health care for the person concerned is necessary to sustain life*. It could include resuscitation, artificial nutrition and hydration, or even antibiotics.

There are transitional arrangements where an advance decision covering life-sustaining treatment was made before 1 October 2007 but does not meet these formal requirements. These arrangements are introduced by Article 5 of the Mental Capacity Act 2005 (Transitional and Consequential Provisions) Order 2007 (SI 2007 No. 1898) and provide that if such an advance decision has been made and the person lacks capacity since 1 October 2007 to comply with the new requirements, then so long as it is in writing and is otherwise valid and applicable it does not need to satisfy the requirements of verification, nor of being signed and witnessed.

The effect of a valid and applicable advance decision

Where an advance decision is both valid and applicable its effect is as if a capacitated adult had decided against a form of treatment in person and at the relevant time. It could not be overturned, even by the Court of Protection. Furthermore, the s 1 principle of presumption of capacity will apply, so that it will be for the person seeking to displace an advance decision to prove that it is either not valid or not applicable.

If it is valid and applicable this will be conclusive as to the best interests of an incapacitated person. This needs to be borne in mind when the decision-maker is considering the best interests checklist under s 4. Further, treatment could not legitimately be given with the protection of an s 5 defence in the face of a valid and applicable advance decision to the contrary.

Protection for healthcare professionals (see also Chapter 7)

In keeping with similar provisions elsewhere in the Act there is protection given depending upon whether a person believes that an advance decision either does or does not exist in relation to the proposed treatment. So a person does not incur liability for treating a patient unless he or she is satisfied that there is a valid and applicable advance decision in existence, which relates to that treatment and nevertheless proceeds to give it. On the other hand, a person does not incur liability if he or she withholds or withdraws treatment from a patient where he or she reasonably believes that a valid and applicable advance decision covering the treatment exists. If the decision-maker suspects that an advance decision exists he or she must make reasonable efforts, time permitting, to find out what it says. The Code of Practice (9.49) suggests this might include discussions with relatives, looking in the clinical records or contacting the person's GP. An emergency might rule out or strictly limit such 'reasonable efforts'.

Problems in practice

Although the law relating to advance decisions is relatively simple, a number of problems can present in practice. There may be a question as to whether the person had capacity at the time of making or withdrawing it; there may be conflicting evidence as to whether the person subsequently changed his or her mind or whether medical developments would have affected his or her decision. Relatives consulted may have differing perceptions of what the person intended. It may be difficult to establish whether the wording used by the person covers the scenario in question; would an advance decision made by a woman continue to apply were she to become pregnant? There may be suspicions that undue influence might have been exerted on the person. The case of *Re T (Adult: Refusal of Medical Treatment)* (1992) 4 All ER 649 rehearses a large number of such issues and was decided on a different basis respectively by the High Court and by the Court of Appeal. The judgment repays careful reading in relation to what might vitiate an apparently effective advance decision. An advance decision may not be what it at first sight appears.

Case law since *Re T* and the Act coming into effect can be confusing (see, for example, *A Local Authority v E* (2012)). Is there in fact a presumption of capacity in relation to the making of the advance decision? Or is it up to the maker to prove capacity at that time? If the matter concerns life-sustaining treatment, is there in practice a higher standard of proof of capacity required? Will advance decisions to refuse life-sustaining treatment be more readily held to be either invalid or not applicable by the court? What does a person need to do in order for his or her advance decision no longer to be valid? Does there need to be a full contemporaneous assessment of capacity to make an advance decision (see Code of Practice 9.8)?

The question will always arise as to how far the decision-maker has to go to establish the existence, validity and applicability of an advance decision. There is no requirement to assume the existence of an advance decision and obsessive efforts to trace an advance decision in circumstances where, even if time permits, there is no suggestion that the patient made one, are not required. However, where the decision-maker suspects that an advance decision exists, then, time permitting, he or she will be obliged to establish the true position. It is part of the best interests checklist that the decision-maker must consider 'so far as is reasonably ascertainable' the person's past and present wishes and feelings (and in particular, any relevant written statement made by him or her when he or she had capacity) (s 4(6)). If, however, there is a valid and applicable advance decision, that will displace consideration of the best interests checklist and will be regarded as conclusive evidence of the person's binding decision.

Even with reasonable efforts, there may be circumstances in which it is far from clear whether an advance decision is valid or applicable or indeed exists at all. Section 26 provides that a declaration may be sought from the Court of Protection on such an issue and that while the court's decision is being sought, life-sustaining treatment or actions reasonably believed to be necessary to prevent a serious deterioration in the patient's condition may be performed without incurring liability.

Advance decisions refusing treatment for mental disorder

What is the situation in respect of a person who makes an advance decision to refuse treatment for mental disorder? There is no reason why under the Mental Capacity Act such an advance decision should not be both valid and applicable. So a patient having made an advance decision to refuse antipsychotic medication could not, if subsequently admitted to hospital informally and at a time when he or she had lost capacity, have such treatment imposed upon him or her. However, s 28 provides that the Act does not apply to people detained under the Mental Health Act whose treatment is being regulated under Part 4 and therefore any advance decision by such a person to refuse such treatment will not be applicable. This is logical because a person detained under the formal provisions of the Mental Health Act who retains capacity can have treatment regulated by Part 4 imposed on him or her under ss 58 and 63 despite his or her competent refusal, provided of course that the necessary formal requirements are met. It would be strange if such treatment could be refused in advance but not at the time. However, such an advance decision would have to be considered as a statement of the person's wishes when decisions as to treatment in that person's best interests were being made, even though it would not be binding.

Two points are worth noting here. First, even if an advance decision is held not to be valid or applicable, and is therefore not binding, it remains a statement of wishes and as such must be taken into account under the best interests checklist of s 4, so the distinction may not necessarily prove decisive. Second, although the Mental Health Act s 63 authorises treatment for mental disorder in the face of an advance decision or capacitated refusal, this is a *power* not an *obligation*, and so a detained patient's responsible clinician may wish to respect the advance decision even where it could be overruled and where the patient's life may be at risk (although an application to court should be made in such circumstances). Is it possible to discern a trend in the courts towards a greater respect for the individual's autonomy as protected by Article 8? See, for example, *Newcastle Foundation Trust v LM* (2014) and *Nottinghamshire Healthcare NHS Trust v RC* (2014).

The introduction of s 58A of the Mental Health Act results in ECT now being subject to different provisions. In particular, a valid and applicable advance decision will prevent ECT being given even to a formally detained patient other than those under the strictly limited exceptions covered by s 62(1A).

The Mental Capacity Act applies to a patient formally detained under the Mental Health Act other than in respect of Part 4 treatment so that, for example, treatments proposed for physical conditions would be governed by Mental Capacity Act principles and a relevant advance decision would be applicable; likewise treatments even for mental disorder where a patient is held under a short-term provision of the Mental Health Act such as s 5 or s 4. What constitutes medical treatment for mental disorder under s 63 is not straightforward and lies outside the ambit of this book. Suffice it to say, the phrase has been broadly interpreted by the courts and includes treatments other than those directly for mental disorder (*B v Croydon Health Authority* (1995)).

Advance decisions and Lasting Powers of Attorney

The relationship between advance decisions and LPAs covering personal welfare issues may cause some difficulties in practice. If the advance decision was made after the appointment of an attorney, then the attorney could not consent to treatment specifically refused by the advance decision. If the LPA had been made later then, as discussed above, the issue would be whether the scope of the attorney's authority included consenting to treatments refused in the advance decision. Even where the statement or expression of the person's wishes fell short of constituting a valid and applicable advance decision, the attorney would have to bear those wishes in mind when applying the best interests checklist. Similar principles would apply if the Court of Protection had appointed a deputy with powers to decide personal welfare including healthcare issues.

Conscientious objections by healthcare professionals

Section 62 confirms for the avoidance of doubt that nothing in the Mental Capacity Act is to be taken to affect the law relating to murder, manslaughter or assisted suicide. An advance decision, which by definition covers only *refusals* of treatment, would be unlikely to raise such issues. But what if the healthcare professional cannot for reasons of conscience comply with an advance decision to refuse life-sustaining treatment? His or her rights in this respect are protected by Article 9 of the European Convention on Human Rights, which covers freedom of thought, conscience and religion. In such circumstances the patient cannot simply be abandoned, nor can the healthcare professional be required to act against his or her conscience. Attempts must be made to transfer the care of the patient to another healthcare professional and in case of difficulty application can be made to the Court of Protection, which has specific power under s 17(1)(e) to direct someone else to take over responsibility for the patient's care.

Key points and questions relating to advance decisions

- If the advance decision is to refuse life-sustaining treatment, does it meet the formal requirements?

- Is there evidence that the person lacked capacity when making the advance decision?

- Is there any evidence of a change of mind or of withdrawal?

- Is there any significant change of circumstances which may have affected the person's decision?

- Does the advance decision clearly cover the treatment in question?

- Did the person mean the advance decision to apply in these circumstances?

- Even if it does not meet the requirements for an advance decision it may still be a statement of wishes to be considered under s 4.

- A valid and applicable advance decision trumps the best interests checklist.

- An advance decision does not cover treatment regulated by Part 4 of the Mental Health Act 1983.

- Is there an LPA covering the same circumstances?

Chapter 11
Independent Mental Capacity Advocates (IMCAs) (sections 35–41)

Introduction

The Independent Mental Capacity Advocacy (IMCA) service was a late addition to the Act. The Joint Parliamentary Committee received considerable volumes of evidence that there was a need for independent advocacy to be available to assist people with capacity problems to make and communicate decisions. The Government accepted the committee's recommendation and so advocacy is included in the Act. The IMCA service has been available since April 2007 in England and since October 2007 in Wales. Practitioners should already be aware of how to contact the service. It should be noted that the service is limited to specific situations and that the amount of time allocated for an IMCA to make a particular decision is also limited.

Most people who lack capacity to make an important decision (for example, about treatment or where to live) will have family or friends who will be consulted by any decision-maker because of the requirements of the Mental Capacity Act. The IMCA service is for people who lack such people to help represent them.

Purpose of the service

Section 35 of the Act sets out the principle and purpose of the IMCA:

> (1) The appropriate authority must make such arrangements as it considers reasonable to enable persons ('independent mental capacity advocates') to be available to represent and support persons to whom acts or decisions proposed under ss 37, 38 and 39 relate.

> (4) In making arrangements under subsection (1), the appropriate authority must have regard to the principle that a person to whom a proposed act or decision relates should, so far as practicable, be represented and supported by a person who is independent of any person who will be responsible for the act or decision.

Money has been allocated to local authorities (in England) or health boards (in Wales) to allow them to commission advocacy services. These have mostly been provided by existing advocacy services which have then organised themselves to be able to take on this function. They have been required to appoint only people who have been trained to provide what is, in effect, non-instructional or 'best interests' advocacy. This is where an advocate represents what he or she considers a person's wishes would be, if they were able to express them. This is a specialist area, as most advocates are used to working with people who can clearly express what they want.

The main circumstances where an IMCA should be appointed have been set out below. The role of the IMCA is to support and represent the person concerned, to ascertain their wishes and feelings and to check that the Act's principles and best interests checklist are followed. The IMCA cannot veto certain decisions, but the relevant authority must take into account any information or submissions provided by the IMCA. If they are very concerned that the person's best interests were not being followed the IMCA could challenge a decision by going to the Court of Protection.

The role of the IMCA is summarised by the Code of Practice at Chapter 10 as:

> *to help particularly vulnerable people who lack the capacity to make important decisions about serious medical treatment and changes of accommodation, and who have no family or friends that it would be appropriate to consult about those decisions. IMCAs will work with and support people who lack capacity, and represent their views to those who are working out their best interests.*

Powers of the advocate

The Act confers certain powers on the IMCA to enable them to carry out their role effectively. Section 35 states that:

> *(6) For the purpose of enabling him to carry out his functions, an independent mental capacity advocate –*
>
> *(a) may interview in private the person whom he has been instructed to represent, and*
>
> *(b) may, at all reasonable times, examine and take copies of –*
>
>   *(i) any health record,*
>
>   *(ii) any record of, or held by, a local authority and compiled in connection with a social services function, and*
>
>   *(iii) any record held by a person registered under Part 2 of the Care Standards Act 2000 (c. 14),*
>
> *which the person holding the record considers may be relevant to the independent mental capacity advocate's investigation.*

This statutory right of access to records is very significant in strengthening the position of the IMCA. Section 36 states that the accompanying Regulations should identify how the IMCA should carry out their primary functions of:

(2) (a) *providing support to the person whom he has been instructed to represent ('P') so that P may participate as fully as possible in any relevant decision;*

   (b) *obtaining and evaluating relevant information;*

   (c) *ascertaining what P's wishes and feelings would be likely to be, and the beliefs and values that would be likely to influence P, if he had capacity;*

   (d) *ascertaining what alternative courses of action are available in relation to P;*

   (e) *obtaining a further medical opinion where treatment is proposed and the advocate thinks that one should be obtained.*

The Regulations also make provision as to circumstances in which the advocate may challenge, or provide assistance for the purpose of challenging, any relevant decision.

England's Regulations are available at:

www.opsi.gov.uk/si/si2006/20061832.htm

The Regulations for Wales are available at:

www.opsi.gov.uk/legislation/wales/wsi2007/20070852e.htm

(Note that these addresses are at slight variance with those given in the Code of Practice as they were giving more direct access as this book went to print. In case of difficulty, enter 'mental capacity act regulations' in your search engine.)

The need for an IMCA

1. Provision of serious medical treatment by an NHS body

Section 37 requires an NHS body to instruct an IMCA to represent a person if:

(i) it is proposing to provide serious medical treatment for that person;

(ii) the person lacks capacity to consent to the treatment; and

(iii) it is satisfied that there is no-one, other than one engaged in providing care or treatment for them in a professional capacity or for remuneration, whom it would be appropriate to consult in determining what would be in the person's best interests.

This would apply to someone who had no suitable family or friends to consult (plus no-one granted LPA, etc.; see list of exceptions below).

This section does not apply if the person's treatment is regulated by Part 4 of the Mental Health Act. This has its own set of rules and requirements for consultation.

If the treatment needs to be provided as a matter of urgency, it may be provided even though the NHS body has not been able to instruct an IMCA.

The IMCA cannot block the provision of treatment but the NHS body must take into account any information given, or submissions made, by them.

'Serious medical treatment' means treatment which involves providing, withholding or withdrawing treatment of a kind prescribed by regulations made by the appropriate authority.

The Mental Capacity Act 2005 (Independent Mental Capacity Advocates) (General) Regulations (2006, No. 1832) at 4(2) describes serious medical treatment as:

> *treatment which involves providing, withdrawing or withholding treatment in circumstances where –*
>
> *(a) in a case where a single treatment is being proposed, there is a fine balance between its benefits to the patient and the burdens and risks it is likely to entail for him,*
>
> *(b) in a case where there is a choice of treatments, a decision as to which one to use is finely balanced, or*
>
> *(c) what is proposed would be likely to involve serious consequences for the patient.*

Point (b) is somewhat surprising and may lead to some debate concerning what are relatively minor procedures but where there is a choice of treatments and where the decision is finely balanced.

Otherwise, the decision-maker will find some general guidance in the Code which gives some examples of treatments (para 10.45) that may be considered serious, including:

- *chemotherapy and surgery for cancer;*
- *electro-convulsive therapy;*
- *therapeutic sterilisation;*
- *major surgery (such as open-heart surgery or brain/neuro-surgery);*
- *major amputations (for example, loss of an arm or leg);*
- *treatments which will result in permanent loss of hearing or sight;*
- *withholding or stopping artificial nutrition and hydration; and*
- *termination of pregnancy.*

The Code goes on to state:

> *These are illustrative examples only, and whether these or other procedures are considered serious medical treatment in any given case, will depend on the circumstances and the consequences for the patient. There are also many more treatments which will be defined as serious medical treatments under the Act's Regulations. Decision-makers who are not sure whether they need to instruct an IMCA should consult their colleagues.*

2. Provision of accommodation by an NHS body

Section 38 requires an NHS body to instruct an IMCA to represent a person, if the NHS body proposes to make arrangements:

(i) for the provision of accommodation in a hospital or care home for a person who lacks capacity to agree to the arrangements; or

(ii) for a change in their accommodation to another hospital or care home; and

(iii) it is satisfied that there is no person, other than one engaged in providing care or treatment for them in a professional capacity or for remuneration, whom it would be appropriate for it to consult in determining what would be in the person's best interests.

As with the provision of serious medical treatment, this excludes anyone dealt with compulsorily under the Mental Health Act. An obligation to reside somewhere may be a condition of s 17 leave, guardianship or supervised aftercare (or a community treatment order when this replaces supervised aftercare).

This applies to any accommodation which is likely to last for more than 28 days in a hospital or eight weeks in a care home, but arrangements can be made in an emergency. As noted above, the IMCA should support and represent the person concerned and the authority must take into account any views expressed by them.

3. Provision of accommodation by a local authority

Section 39 requires a local authority to instruct an IMCA to represent a person if the local authority proposes to make arrangements:

(i) for the provision of residential accommodation for a person who lacks capacity to agree to the arrangements; or

(ii) for a change in the person's residential accommodation; and

(iii) it is satisfied that there is no person, other than one engaged in providing care or treatment for them in a professional capacity or for remuneration, whom it would be appropriate for it to consult in determining what would be in the person's best interests.

Again, this excludes anyone dealt with compulsorily under the Mental Health Act. An obligation to reside somewhere may be a condition of s 17 leave, guardianship or supervised aftercare (or a community treatment order when this replaces supervised aftercare).

This applies to any accommodation which is likely to last for more than eight weeks, but arrangements can be made in an emergency.

The section only applies if the accommodation is to be provided in accordance with s 21 or 29 of the National Assistance Act 1948, or s 117 of the Mental Health Act, as the result of a decision taken by the local authority under s 47 of the National Health Service and Community Care Act 1990.

Exceptions: when an IMCA will not be needed

Section 40 means that if someone has been nominated by the person to be consulted in matters affecting his or her interests, there will be no requirement to instruct an IMCA. This will also be the case if there is:

(i) a donee of a lasting power of attorney created by P,

(ii) a deputy appointed by the court for P, or

(iii) a donee of an enduring power of attorney (within the meaning of Schedule 4) created by P.

Other circumstances when an IMCA could be involved

Section 41 allowed for the expansion of the IMCA role and this has already happened as a result of revised regulations (SI No. 2883).

There is discretion to appoint an IMCA for care reviews and for adult protection procedures (even if family members are involved). The relevant authority must consider in each individual case whether to appoint an IMCA. There needs to be some benefit from having an IMCA for one to be appointed in these circumstances. The Code of Practice (10.61) suggests that there should be a local policy to cover this area and guidance has been issued. This is available on the Department of Health's website at gateway 7557 and is entitled 'Adult protection, care reviews and Independent Mental Capacity Advocates (IMCA): Guidance on interpreting the regulations extending the IMCA role'.

The role of the IMCA

The Code of Practice (10.20) provides a helpful summary of the IMCA's role. It states that the IMCA should decide how best to represent and support the person who lacks capacity and that they:

- *must confirm that the person instructing them has the authority to do so*

- *should interview or meet in private the person who lacks capacity, if possible*

- *must act in accordance with the principles of the Act (as set out in s 1 of the Act and Chapter 2 of the Code) and take account of relevant guidance in the Code*

- *may examine any relevant records that s 35(6) of the Act gives them access to*

- *should get the views of professionals and paid workers providing care or treatment for the person who lacks capacity*

- *should get the views of anybody else who can give information about the wishes and feelings, beliefs or values of the person who lacks capacity*

- *should get hold of any other information they think will be necessary*

- must find out what support a person who lacks capacity has had to help them make the specific decision

- must try to find out what the person's wishes and feelings, beliefs and values would be likely to be if the person had capacity

- should find out what alternative options there are

- should consider whether getting another medical opinion would help the person who lacks capacity, and

- must write a report on their findings for the local authority or NHS body.

Training and procedures for staff on the role of the IMCA

Health and social services authorities should have procedures, training and awareness programmes to ensure that:

- all relevant staff know when they need to instruct an IMCA and are able to do so promptly;

- all relevant staff know how to get in touch with the IMCA service and know the procedure for instructing an IMCA;

- they record an IMCA's involvement in a case and any information the IMCA provides to help decision-making;

- they also record how a decision-maker has taken into account the IMCA's report and information as part of the process of working out the person's best interests (this should include reasons for disagreeing with that advice, if relevant);

- they give access to relevant records when requested by an IMCA under section 35(6)(b) of the Act;

- the IMCA gets information about changes that may affect the support and representation the IMCA provides;

- decision-makers let all relevant people know when an IMCA is working on a person's case; and

- decision-makers inform the IMCA of the final decision taken and the reason for it.

(Department of Health, Code of Practice, 2007, 10.14)

ACTIVITY 11.1

Multiple choice questions

Read each question carefully and tick the appropriate box(es). Where a statement is correct, tick the box next to it; if it is incorrect, leave it blank. You may need to tick more than one box per question.

Appendix 5 (pages 279–83) gives the answers.

11.1 *The IMCA service:*

    (a) *Is based on a statutory requirement*

    (b) *Uses only qualified solicitors*

    (c) *Aims to represent and support people for particular acts*

    (d) *Provides substituted decision-making in relation to healthcare matters*

    (e) *May be involved in vulnerable adult procedures*

    (f) *Has the right to interview certain people in private*

11.2 *IMCAs provide a form of non-instructional advocacy:*

    (a) *True*

    (b) *False*

11.3 *An IMCA has the power to veto any decision made by a local authority or NHS Trust:*

    (a) *True*

    (b) *False*

Chapter 12

The Court of Protection and the Public Guardian (sections 45–61)

Introduction

Section 45(6) of the Act abolished the previous Court of Protection. Section 45(1) establishes a new court bearing the same name. This is unfortunate because the new court is altogether more powerful and wide-ranging in its powers and scope than its predecessor and is not to be confused with it. It has a Central Office, and specialist judges. It will have a regional presence, as the court may sit anywhere in England and Wales on any day at any time (s 45(3)). Any District Registry of the High Court or County Court Office may be designated an additional Registry of the Court of Protection by the Lord Chancellor (s 45(5)).

The Court of Protection deals with all issues concerning people who lack capacity within the meaning of the Act, not merely making orders in respect of their property and affairs but in addition covering issues of personal welfare including the making of medical decisions: from ethical dilemmas posed by novel medical treatments to the investment of assets; from applications to challenge powers being exercised under Lasting Powers of Attorney (LPAs) to authorising deprivation of liberty; from determining where a person lacking capacity should live and who should have contact with him or her to appointing someone to consent to or refuse medical treatment on behalf of the incapacitated person. The Court of Protection is a superior court of record and its judgments are reported and constitute an evolving body of precedents. However, it does not have the inherent jurisdiction of the High Court, which will therefore have to be applied to in circumstances where a remedy cannot be provided by the Court of Protection under the Act. An example would be *An NHS Trust v Dr A* (2013) in which necessary treatment could not be provided under either the Act or the Mental Health Act and the High Court had recourse to its inherent jurisdiction.

The powers of the Court of Protection, and the principles which guide the use of those powers (such as the requirement to follow the best interests checklist of s 4) are set out in ss 15–23 (see Chapters 8 and 9). This chapter deals with the court process and functions, together with the role of the Public Guardian, who is in many ways its gatekeeper, executive arm and public face.

The court structure

The judges of the Court of Protection are nominated by or on behalf of the Lord Chancellor from a long list set out in s 46(2). Section 47 provides that the court has the same powers, rights, privileges and authority as the High Court. These include High Court powers in relation to witnesses, contempt of court, and enforcement of its orders. Section 48 provides that the court will have power to make interim orders or directions if there is reason to believe that the person lacks capacity in relation to the matter in question, that the matter is one to which the court powers under this Act extend, and that it is in the person's best interests to make the order or give the directions without delay. See *Re F* (2009) for the approach to be taken by the court. In order to discharge its functions, the court can by s 49 call for reports covering whatever it directs, from the Public Guardian or from Court of Protection Visitors, or if necessary requiring a local authority or NHS body to arrange for such reports to be made. The report may be in writing or oral. If the Public Guardian or a Visitor is providing a report required by the Court of Protection, then they may examine and take copies of Health and Social Services records. They may also interview the person in private. A Court of Protection Special Visitor may, if the court so directs, carry out in private a medical, psychiatric or psychological examination of the person's capacity and condition (s 49(9)).

When might an application be made?

Most acts in connection with the care or treatment of a person lacking capacity can lawfully be performed under s 5, subject to the restrictions and limitations imposed by s 6 (see Chapter 7) and there will be no need to make an application to the Court of Protection. In particular, it would be inappropriate to apply to the court where the situation was clear but the health or social care professional simply wanted the security of the court's sanction. The following are some examples of where an application might be appropriate:

- where the cumulative restrictions or restraints imposed upon a person who lacked capacity amounted to a deprivation of liberty and therefore could not lawfully be imposed as an s 5 act (Deprivation of Liberty Safeguards (DOLS) might be available if this was in a care home or hospital);

- where the court has determined that certain categories of decisions in respect of people who lacked capacity required an application (for example, withdrawing artificial nutrition and hydration from a patient in a persistent vegetative state);

- where there were genuine concerns about the manner in which an attorney or a deputy was acting (for example, apparently ignoring the best interests checklist);

- where there was doubt over the meaning or construction of an LPA or whether an advance decision was valid or applicable;

- where it was felt that there might be the need for a deputy to be appointed;

- where an existing receiver under an EPA wished to have clarification or an extension of his powers;

- where despite following the statutory provisions and the guidance contained in the Code of Practice a decision-maker found it impossible to decide either whether the person lacked capacity in relation to a matter or, if he lacked capacity, whether what was proposed was in his or her best interests;

- where a provision in the Act was unclear and needed interpretation (for example, whether a particular form of treatment constituted life-sustaining treatment);

- where a person wished to challenge a determination that he or she lacked capacity in relation to a matter;

- where a person wished to challenge a DOLS authorisation;

- where an IMCA believed that a decision-maker was failing to take into account his or her submissions as to what was in the best interests of a person lacking capacity.

This is not intended to be an exhaustive list but rather one designed to illustrate the broad range of decisions and declarations that the Court of Protection has power to make if requested. If in doubt about whether a court decision is needed, the Office of the Public Guardian should be approached for advice (see below, page 80).

Who can apply to the Court of Protection?

From the above list of circumstances in which an application to the Court of Protection might be considered, it can be seen that the application itself could come from an NHS Trust, a local authority, an allegedly incapacitated person, or from somebody wanting to be able to deal with the money and property of a person lacking capacity.

Comprehensive rules have been issued (Court of Protection Rules 2007, No. 1744) which govern the practice and procedure of the Court of Protection. Section 50(1) sets out a list of those people who do not need to have prior permission before applying to the Court of Protection, and these have been extended by rule 51 as follows:

- a person who lacks or allegedly lacks capacity (and if under 18 anyone with parental responsibility for him or her);

- the donor or donee (attorney) of an LPA to which the application relates;

- a deputy appointed by the court for a person to whom the application relates;

- a person named in an existing order of the court if the application relates to that order;

- the Official Solicitor or the Public Guardian;

- anyone, if the application concerns an LPA purportedly created under the Act;

- anyone, if the application concerns an Enduring Power of Attorney (EPA) within the meaning of Schedule 4 to the Act;

- anyone, if (with certain exceptions set out in rule 52) the application relates solely to the exercise of the court's powers in relation to a person's property and affairs;

- the relevant person's representative where a DOLS authorisation has been given.

In any other circumstances (apart from declarations as to private international law), permission is required to make an application to the Court of Protection. In deciding whether to grant permission the court must in particular have regard to:

- the applicant's connection with the person to whom the application relates;

- the reasons for the application;

- the benefit to a person to whom the application relates of a proposed order or directions; and

- whether the benefit can be achieved in any other way.

The Procedural Rules also include: when hearings can be dispensed with (rule 84), when the hearing may be held in private, the form in which evidence is to be given (Part 14) and orders for costs (rules 156–7). The general rule in respect of costs is that the court will not order one party to pay the costs of another and can order in appropriate circumstances that costs are paid out of the estate of the person lacking capacity. Permission to appeal will normally be required (except from an order for committal) and if the original order was made by a district judge appeal will be to a circuit judge; if from a circuit judge then to a High Court judge and thence to the Court of Appeal with permission.

The Code of Practice deals with the availability of public funding at 15.38–44. The fees for application to the Court of Protection and for the services provided by the Public Guardian are set out respectively in the Court of Protection Fees Order 2007, No. 1745, and the Public Guardian (Fees, etc.) Regulations 2007, No. 2051.

Court of Protection Visitors

Court of Protection Visitors are appointed by the Lord Chancellor. There are two panels: a panel of Special Visitors and a panel of General Visitors. Special Visitors must be either registered medical practitioners or appear to the Lord Chancellor to have other suitable qualifications or training and to have special knowledge of and experience in cases of impairment of or disturbance in the functioning of the mind or brain. They may be requested either by the court or by the Public Guardian to visit and make reports on people who lack capacity. They may interview the person in private and have a right to see and take copies of relevant health and social care records. Special Visitors may, if directed by the court, carry out in private a medical, psychiatric or psychological examination of the person's capacity and condition. The Code of Practice at 14.10–11 highlights the Visitors' role in also interviewing attorneys or deputies and supporting them in carrying out their duties. General Visitors could come from a range of backgrounds and report to the court on issues such as whether attorneys are acting within their legal remit as well as in a person's best interests.

The Public Guardian

Section 57 creates a new public official known as the Public Guardian, appointed by the Lord Chancellor. The functions of the Public Guardian are set out in s 58 and include the following:

- establishing and maintaining registers of LPAs and court-appointed deputies;

- supervising deputies;

- directing Court of Protection Visitors to visit and report to him or her on LPA attorneys, deputies or the person lacking capacity;

- receiving reports from deputies or attorneys;

- providing reports to the Court of Protection as directed under s 49(2);

- dealing with representations and complaints about the way in which attorneys or deputies are exercising their powers.

In carrying out his or her functions under the second and last of the above, the Public Guardian is empowered to work co-operatively with other people who have responsibilities for the care or treatment of persons lacking capacity.

The Public Guardian's functions are expanded upon in the Lasting Powers of Attorney, Enduring Powers of Attorney and Public Guardian Regulations (SI 2007, No. 1253), in particular in relation to requiring security or the manner in which information is sought from attorneys under LPAs and EPAs.

How will the Public Guardian operate in practice?

From comments made on behalf of the Government and by the Public Guardian, it was clearly anticipated that the role of the Public Guardian should not be confined to the formal exercise of his or her powers and functions. So in the Department of Constitutional Affairs' overview of the original Mental Incapacity Bill it was stated that the Public Guardian:

> will also offer advice to the public on matters to do with adults who lack capacity . . . we envisage that the Public Guardian will work with other organisations involved in the care and well-being of adults who lack capacity in order to provide a complete approach to problems and possible abuse. The Public Guardian will also work with attorneys and deputies who may need help and support in carrying out their duties.

No doubt mindful of the restriction on the availability of public funding for applications to the Court of Protection and in relation to the Act generally (there is specialist limited publicly funded legal advice available where necessary for cases of particular seriousness and complexity), the Government envisaged that the Public Guardian would offer a telephone information line. In an early statement the Public Guardian stated:

Working in effective partnership with the judiciary it will be our role to ensure that appropriate supervision regimes are in place which balance the autonomy of the individual with the most appropriate protection against abuse. We are currently considering how this regime can be effective yet as unobtrusive as possible. We will also have a role in providing the public with information about mental capacity issues and signposting people to the most appropriate form of help and assistance.

This emphasis on the broader constructive role that the Public Guardian will play is highlighted in the Code of Practice. So along with the responsibility for maintaining the registers, checking documentation before registration, and investigating allegations of abuse by attorneys and deputies, the focus is on:

- providing information to help potential donors understand the impact of making an LPA, what they can give an attorney authority to do, and what to consider when choosing an attorney (14.12);

- supporting deputies in carrying out their duties (14.15);

- working co-operatively with local authorities and NHS Trusts (14.14; 14.20);

- running checks on potential deputies, including risk assessments *to determine what supervision a deputy will need once they are appointed* (14.17);

- being available to *anybody who is caring for a person who lacks capacity, whether in a paid or unpaid role, who is worried about how attorneys or deputies carry out their duties* (14.19);

- being approached for guidance and advice in relation to disagreements about the finances of a person lacking capacity (15.34);

- referring concerns about personal welfare LPAs or personal welfare deputies to the relevant agency including, in certain circumstances, the police (14.21).

ACTIVITY **12.1**

Multiple choice questions

Read each question carefully and tick the appropriate box(es). Where a statement is correct, tick the box next to it; if it is incorrect, leave it blank. You may need to tick more than one box per question.

Appendix 5 (pages 279–83) gives the answers.

12.1 The following would be typical situations where the Court of Protection would be involved.

    (a) It was felt that there might be the need for a deputy to be appointed ☐

    (b) A person was appealing against detention under the Mental Health Act ☐

(Continued)

(Continued)

(c) *A person wished to challenge a decision that he or she lacked capacity in relation to a matter*

(d) *A nearest relative wanted to make an application for guardianship*

(e) *Someone alleged that an attorney was not applying the best interests checklist*

(f) *An IMCA believed a decision-maker was failing to take into account his or her submissions as to what was in the best interests of a person lacking capacity*

12.2 *The Court of Protection can only intervene if the person in question has a mental disorder as defined by the Mental Health Act 1983:*

(a) *True*

(b) *False*

12.3 *The Public Guardian is responsible for:*

(a) *Establishing and maintaining registers of LPAs*

(b) *Establishing and maintaining registers of guardianships under the Mental Health Act*

(c) *Supervising court-appointed deputies*

(d) *Supervising nearest relatives appointed by the County Court*

(e) *Directing Court of Protection Visitors to visit and report on persons lacking capacity*

(f) *Receiving reports from deputies or attorneys*

Chapter 13
Other issues

Ill-treatment and neglect (section 44)

A new criminal offence of ill-treatment or neglect is created by section (s) 44. While not a central part of the scheme of the Act, it is one of a number of protective mechanisms and safeguards reinforcing other measures such as Adult Protection Committees. The section does not create a single offence but rather separate offences of ill-treatment or neglect, carrying a maximum sentence of five years' imprisonment. Based on earlier court decisions ill-treatment must be either deliberately or recklessly undertaken, whether or not actual harm was caused. 'Wilful neglect' is not defined, but the Code of Practice states that it usually means that a person has deliberately failed to carry out an act they knew they had a duty to do.

The offence can be committed by:

- a person having care of someone who lacks or whom he or she reasonably believes to lack capacity;
- a person appointed under a Lasting Power of Attorney or an Enduring Power of Attorney created by the victim;
- a deputy appointed by the Court of Protection for the victim.

The victim may be under the age of 16. This is one of the rare occasions when the Act does not apply just to those over the age of 16 (see Chapter 15).

No further definition is given of a person who lacks capacity. For the prosecution this has created difficulties in practice given the scheme of the Act, which emphasises the time- and decision-specific nature of capacity; in other words the Act and Code of Practice strongly discourage unqualified assertions of lack of capacity, requiring the functional test to be applied to the specific circumstances in which the person finds him or herself. The question is not 'does this person lack capacity?' but rather 'in relation to *what* does he or she lack capacity?' What is the act in respect of which the person must lack capacity in order for him or her to constitute a potential victim of this offence? Is it whether he or she has capacity to make a decision to protect him or herself, or to make other kinds of decisions, and if so which? It is both curious and unfortunate that the concept of lack of capacity is neither defined nor qualified in this context. However, in a series of cases (see in particular *R v Dunn* (2010)) the courts have held that the lack of capacity referred to the person's ability to make decisions concerning their care.

Exclusions

Chapter 17 examines the interface between the Mental Capacity Act and the Mental Health Act, in particular the provisions of s 28 relating to someone detained under the Mental Health Act whose treatment is regulated under Part 4. The non-applicability of the Mental Capacity Act in relation to such patients is strictly limited and so does not cover, for example, the issue of consenting to *admission* to hospital but only to treatment covered by Part 4. In many circumstances the Mental Capacity Act will apply in relation to a patient formally detained under the Mental Health Act, for example when treatment for a physical condition rather than for mental disorder is in issue. It will also apply of course to informal patients. The definition of incapacity in s 2(1) is qualified by the words *for the purposes of this Act*, and the standard of proof set out in s 2(4) by the words *in proceedings under this Act or any other enactment*; Schedule 6 makes a number of amendments to other Acts to make their interpretation of incapacity consistent with the Act but does not affect the test for insanity or fitness to plead to a criminal charge; the Code of Practice refers (4.32) to the continued applicability of other tests of capacity in different contexts such as capacity to make a will. While this may be strictly true, if the functional test is applied, and the specific decision placed in context, the use of the Act's test of the inability to make a decision in such other contexts is unlikely to result in a different outcome. What is more likely to differ is the identity of the decision-maker, the person who will make the assessment of capacity. Thus, in practice the definition and test for incapacity set out in the Act are likely to be used ever more widely in future.

Specific exclusions

Section 27 sets out certain specifically excluded decisions, which cannot be made on behalf of a person lacking capacity. Section 27 precludes:

- consenting to marriage or a civil partnership;

- consenting to sexual relations;

- consenting to a decree of divorce or the dissolution of a civil partnership on the basis of two years' separation;

- consenting to a child being placed for adoption or to the making of an adoption order;

- discharging parental responsibilities in matters not relating to a child's property;

- giving consent under the Human Fertilisation and Embryology Acts 1990 and 2008.

Section 29 precludes voting at an election or at a referendum on behalf of a person lacking capacity.

Section 62 provides that for the avoidance of doubt nothing in the Act is to be taken to affect the law relating to murder, manslaughter or assisting suicide. This declaratory provision is strictly speaking unnecessary and was inserted to give reassurance to those who argued or who were concerned that the provisions in particular relating to personal welfare Lasting Powers of Attorney (LPAs) and advance decisions constituted a slippery slope leading towards euthanasia.

Finally, it needs to be remembered that s 2(5) provides that the powers exercisable under the Act in relation to a person lacking or reasonably thought to lack capacity are not exercisable in relation to a person under 16; this is subject to the power of the Court of Protection under s 18(3) to make an order in respect of a person's property and affairs even though he is under the age of 16 if it considers it likely that he or she will still lack capacity to make decisions in respect of that matter when he or she reaches 18; this does not include the making of a statutory will. Remember also that a person under the age of 18 may not make an advance decision, or execute an LPA or be appointed an attorney.

Chapter 14
Research

Introduction

Sections 30–34 of the Mental Capacity Act, together with associated Regulations, provide a comprehensive set of safeguards in relation to research projects involving a person who lacks capacity. Research is not defined in the Act but includes direct medical interventions and also covers asking patients' views about health and social care services, observing them in a social care setting and research on medical notes (where not anonymised).

What research is affected by the Act?

Section (s) 30 provides that 'intrusive research' carried out on or in relation to a person who lacks capacity is unlawful unless it is part of an approved research project and complies with the provisions relating to consultation and other safeguards contained in ss 32 and 33. 'Intrusive research' means research which would be unlawful unless, where consent was required, the research subject had capacity to consent to his or her involvement and did consent. A research project must be approved by an appropriate body which Regulations define as a recognised Research Ethics Committee.

The Act does not apply to clinical trials which are subject to the provisions of the Medicines for Human Use (Clinical Trials) Regulations 2004 as amended, because these regulations already provide for participants who lack capacity. Because of the way intrusive research is defined the Act will not cover research not requiring the consent of a participant. So research on anonymised medical data or (provided Research Ethics Committee approval has been obtained) on anonymised human tissue is not included.

It is also possible to obtain approval under s 251 of the NHS Act 2006 to use confidential patient information without the patient's consent. Although the Act does not repeat the requirements of the Human Tissue Act 2004 in relation to the storage or use of tissue, for example for transplants and research, the relevant provisions so far as they concern adults lacking capacity are covered in the Code of Practice at chapter 11.37–40.

The requirements for approval

Before approval can be given for a research project s 31 sets out a number of pre-qualifying conditions.

- The research must be connected with an 'impairing condition' or its treatment. 'Impairing condition' means one that is or may be attributable to or causes or contributes to the impairment of or disturbance in the functioning of the person's mind or brain. As the Explanatory Notes to the Act set out, this limits the sort of research projects that the person may be involved in but will include research into the effects of the impairment on his or her health and day-to-day life as well as into the causes or possible causes of the impairment and its treatment.

- There must be reasonable grounds for believing that research of comparable effectiveness cannot be carried out if it has to be confined to people who have capacity to consent.

- The research must *either* (1) have the potential to benefit the person lacking capacity without imposing on him or her a burden disproportionate to the potential benefit to him or her *or* (2) be intended to provide knowledge of the causes or treatment of or of the care of persons affected by the same or a similar condition. If relying on (2) above, there must be reasonable grounds for believing that the risk to the person lacking capacity is negligible and does not constitute a significant interference with his or her privacy or freedom or be unduly invasive or restrictive. There is, at least in theory, a conflict between this provision and the 'best interests' principle of s 1(5). In addition, he or she must be withdrawn from the project if the researcher believes at any time that these conditions no longer apply, unless to do so would pose a significant risk to his or her health (s 33(5)). At chapter 11.14 the Code of Practice gives examples of potential benefits of research for a person who lacks capacity. These could be: developing more effective ways of treating a person or managing his or her condition; improving the quality of healthcare, social care or other services to which he or she has access; discovering the cause of his or her condition; or reducing the risk of his or her being harmed, excluded or disadvantaged.

The requirement of consultation

The consultation requirements of the Act are set out in s 32. Before enrolling a person into an approved research project the researcher must take reasonable steps to identify someone with whom he or she can consult; this must not be somebody professionally involved with the care of that person nor a paid carer but someone interested in his or her welfare and who is prepared to be consulted. An attorney appointed under a Lasting Power of Attorney (LPA) or a deputy appointed by the court could fulfil this role.

If the researcher is unable to identify such a person he or she must nominate somebody unconnected with the research project but willing to be consulted. Guidance to be followed in respect of this process was issued in February 2008.

Once the consultee has been identified he or she must be provided with relevant information about the project and asked whether the person lacking capacity should take part and what he or she thinks that person would have said if he or she had capacity. If the consultee advises that the person would not have wished to take part in the research project the researcher must ensure that he or she does not participate;

if he or she is already participating he or she must be withdrawn from it unless the researcher believes on reasonable grounds that to do so would pose a significant risk to the person's health.

If the person lacking capacity is having or is about to have urgent treatment and the researcher believes that it is necessary for him or her to take urgent action for the purposes of the research and that it is impracticable to follow the consultation requirements, he or she can proceed (for so long as it remains urgent) if he or she obtains the agreement of a doctor (unconnected with the research project) or, where there is no time, he or she follows a procedure covering such an eventuality which will have been approved in advance by the Research Ethics Committee. As the Code of Practice points out (11.36), this exception to the duty to consult is likely to be limited to research into procedures or treatments used in emergencies. The Explanatory Notes give as an example a paramedic or doctor making measurements in the first few minutes following a serious head injury or stroke. The exception does not apply where the researcher simply wants to act quickly.

Other safeguards

Section 33 imposes further limits on what can be done to a person lacking capacity who has been enrolled in an approved research project. The researcher cannot do anything to which the person appears to object unless it is necessary to do so to protect him or her from harm or reduce pain or discomfort suffered by him or her. In addition, the researcher must withdraw the person without delay from the project if he or she indicates in any way that he or she wishes to be withdrawn. If the person has made a valid and applicable advance decision or any other form of statement refusing consent to anything being done or proposed to be done to him or her during the research project the researcher may not proceed. There is a presumption in favour of the interests of the person lacking capacity outweighing those of science and society.

Section 34 deals with the situation where a person loses capacity during a research project begun before s 30 was in force and provides that Regulations may be made permitting the person's continued involvement in accordance with the requirements of the Regulations, which may include provisions similar to those contained in ss 31–33. The Regulations have been issued as the Mental Capacity Act 2005 Loss of Capacity during Research Project (England) Regulations 2007, No. 679 and do indeed contain such provisions.

Chapter 15
Links with other areas of law

Links with the Human Rights Act 1998

The relationship between the Mental Capacity Act and the Human Rights Act is a crucial one for practitioners. The Human Rights Act 1998 became operational in October 2000. It does not incorporate the whole of the European Convention on Human Rights but it does include the following Articles, which are relevant in varying degrees in the field of mental capacity:

Article 2   **Right to life.** Everyone's right to life shall be protected by law.

Article 3   **Prohibition of torture.** No-one to be subject to torture or inhuman or degrading treatment or punishment. *This has a fairly high threshold but might be breached by excessive use of control and restraint.*

Article 4   **Prohibition of slavery and forced labour**

Article 5   **Right to liberty and security of person.** 5.1 No-one shall be deprived of their liberty except for specific cases and in accordance with procedure prescribed by law . . . , e.g. after conviction, lawful arrest on suspicion of having committed an offence, lawful detention of person of unsound mind, to prevent spread of infectious diseases. 5.4 Everyone deprived of liberty by arrest or detention shall be entitled to take proceedings by which the lawfulness of the detention shall be decided speedily by a Court and release ordered if the detention is not lawful.

Article 6   **Right to a fair trial.** Everyone is entitled to a fair and public hearing within a reasonable time by an independent and impartial Tribunal.

Article 7   **No punishment without law**

Article 8   **Right to respect for private and family life.** Everyone has the right to respect for his private and family life, his home and his correspondence.

Article 9   **Freedom of thought, conscience and religion**

Article 10   **Freedom of expression**

Article 11   **Freedom of assembly and association**

Article 12   Right to marry. Men and women of marriageable age have the right to marry and to found a family. *This is largely outside the remit of the Mental Capacity Act because of the exclusions in s 27.*

Article 14   Prohibition of discrimination. Enjoyment of the rights and freedoms set forth in this Convention shall be secured without discrimination on any ground such as sex, race, colour, language, religion, political or other opinion, national or social origin, association with a national minority, property, birth or other status.

Relevance of the Human Rights Act 1998 in the passage of the Bill

It is not surprising that the Parliamentary Joint Committee on Human Rights concentrated so heavily in its deliberations, reports and questioning of Government about the Mental Incapacity Bill on the question of potential breaches of Article 5 of the European Convention (Council of Europe, 1950). These largely took place in the aftermath of the European Court decision in *HL v UK*, when in the context of the Bill concerns surrounding deprivation of liberty, its extent and process were very much to the fore. The concern that the Bill permitted involuntary placement of incapacitated people on the authority of section (s) 5, and the absence of any proposals to fill the 'Bournewood Gap' preoccupied the committee.

The Government's eventual response was, in relation to the first issue, to prohibit the use of s 5 to deprive an incapacitated person of liberty, and, in relation to the second issue, to produce in the Mental Health Bill (now Mental Health Act 2007) its proposals for a new procedure prescribed by law to authorise deprivations of liberty. Both these responses create problems of their own. If an incapacitated person could not lawfully be deprived of his or her liberty under s 5, this raised the difficulty of what lawful avenues were open to care for people in such circumstances, certainly until the advent of the new Court of Protection in October 2007. The 'Bournewood Gap' (Deprivation of Liberty Safeguards (DOLS)) provisions did not take effect until April 2009, leaving health and social care professionals with a period of uncertainty as to whether they are providing care in circumstances amounting to an unauthorised deprivation of liberty. These issues are covered in detail in Chapter 16.

Elsewhere within the Act there is potential for breaches of Articles 2, 3, 6, 8 and 14. The role, powers of and access to the new Court of Protection are likely to ensure that the Act is compliant with the Article 6 right to a fair trial, which covers not merely criminal proceedings but all proceedings where an individual's civil rights are in issue. Whether the DOLS procedures proposals are sufficiently compliant with Article 6 remains to be seen. The principle of equal consideration, namely that a determination as to a person's best interests must not be made merely on the basis of the person's age or appearance, or a condition of his or her, or an aspect of his or her behaviour, which might lead others to make unjustified assumptions about what might be in his or her best interests, coupled with the presumption of capacity goes a long way towards ensuring that the Act complies with the Article 14 prohibition against discrimination of an individual's enjoyment of rights and freedoms guaranteed by the Convention.

This leaves for more detailed consideration Article 2 (the right to life), Article 3 (the prohibition against torture or inhuman and degrading treatment or punishment) and Article 8 (the right to respect for private and family life).

Articles 2, 3 and 8 of the European Convention on Human Rights

It might be thought that an Act which has, as one of its principal objectives, the active promotion of the rights of people lacking capacity (both in the process of assessing their capacity to make decisions, and in the way that decisions are made in their best interests when they lack capacity) would be unlikely to come into conflict with provisions of the European Convention. Indeed, the scheme for personal welfare Lasting Powers of Attorneys (LPAs) is compatible with the Convention because the attorney is chosen by a person who must have capacity to make the appointment and understand its implications. In addition, the attorney is governed by the best interests checklist and by guidance contained within the Code of Practice and is ultimately accountable for his or her actions to the Court of Protection.

Even around the question of withholding or withdrawing consent to life-sustaining treatment, the human rights issues arise from consideration of the adequacy of the safeguards rather than from the principle itself. Advance decisions to refuse treatment have been an accepted part of the common law for many years. It is generally accepted that the requirement to give life-sustaining treatment in the face of a valid and applicable advance refusal (which might be argued as implicit in Article 2 as a result of the positive nature of the obligation of the state to secure Convention rights for its citizens) gives way to the Article 8 right of a competent person to medical autonomy and indeed in appropriate cases to the Article 3 prohibition against inhuman and degrading treatment.

On the other hand, the possibility of abuse or misunderstanding has to be considered. So, in codifying and clarifying the common law principle on which advance decisions are based, a number of safeguards are provided – the requirement that an advance decision be valid and applicable, and spelling out circumstances in which it is not. The formal requirements where an advance decision is made to refuse life-sustaining treatment go beyond the previous requirements of the common law. The fact that a doctor is free to treat unless he or she is satisfied that there is a valid and applicable advance decision in existence (s 26(2)), dealt with in Chapter 10, is a considerable safeguard, resolving doubts in favour of the presumption of preserving life.

Is there a requirement to go further? The Joint Committee urged the Government to introduce a requirement that *all* advance decisions be in writing to reduce possible misunderstanding, but there seems no logical reason why a person who has capacity should not be able simply in conversation with, for example, a healthcare professional to declare his or her refusal of specific treatment without being required to put it in writing. The healthcare professional may well decide to make a careful note as a sensible safeguard, but given the presumption referred to above and the requirement to be satisfied as to the validity and applicability of an advance decision, to go further appears unnecessary, particularly when set against the declared aim of empowering people to make more decisions for themselves when they have the capacity to do so. It may add to the difficulties for a healthcare professional in deciding whether a verbal advance decision is valid or applicable, but that is insufficient reason to add such a formal requirement. Overall, the additional safeguards and clarifications provided in the Act compared to the vagueness of the common law position make it very unlikely that the framework for advance decisions will lead to breaches of Article 2 or 3.

The Joint Committee had a particular concern in respect of decisions to withdraw artificial nutrition and hydration (ANH). This was because they feared that the decision in *Airedale NHS Trust v Bland* that giving artificial nutrition and hydration constituted medical treatment which could therefore in appropriate circumstances lawfully be withdrawn by healthcare professionals was not widely understood by the general public. The committee was concerned that in making advance decisions covering refusal of life-sustaining treatment, or in appointing a personal welfare attorney with power to consent to or refuse life-sustaining treatment, it would not be appreciated that this would cover ANH. The Government declined to amend the definition of life-sustaining treatment in the Act to include specific reference to ANH, but did agree that the Code of Practice should make the position clear, which it does at chapter 9.26. This seems sufficient in the circumstances.

Where there is no valid and applicable advance decision in existence it must be remembered that in appointing a personal welfare deputy the Court of Protection cannot give him or her power to refuse consent to the carrying out or continuation of life-sustaining treatment (s 20(5)). Further, for a personal welfare LPA covering consent to medical treatment, if this is intended to include consent to or refusal of life-sustaining treatment that must be explicitly stated. In addition, the prescribed information contained in the form for creating a personal welfare LPA contains an explanation of life-sustaining treatment. These provisions, together with s 62 which declares for the avoidance of doubt that nothing in the Act is to be taken to affect the law relating to murder or manslaughter or assisted suicide, almost certainly provide sufficient safeguards to satisfy the positive obligation of the state to protect life.

A similar issue regarding the adequacy of safeguards concerned the Joint Committee in relation to research involving people lacking capacity, drawing unfavourable comparisons with the stringent requirements of the Convention on Human Rights and Biomedicine as to the nature of the benefit of the research to the person lacking capacity or others with the same or similar conditions, the nature of the risk of harm, and the meaning and effect of the 'no alternative' criterion (i.e. that the research could not equally well be carried out on individuals able to consent). This seems a little harsh, given the welter of safeguards relating to the initial approval of the project, the requirement of consultation, the provision for participants losing capacity part way through the project (see Chapter 14), and it is unlikely that if the requirements of the Act and Regulations are followed there will be any breach of the participant's Article 2 or 3 rights, and any breach of his or her Article 8 rights is likely to be justified under Article 8(2).

Links with the Mental Health Act 1983

There are several areas where working within the remit of the Mental Capacity Act is likely to bring people into contact with the Mental Health Act. These are:

(i) informal admissions to psychiatric hospitals of those who lack capacity to make a decision about admission;

(ii) treatment within psychiatric hospital of those who lack capacity to give valid consent to the treatment in question;

(iii) decisions on matters that fall outside the remit of the Mental Health Act for those who are subject to compulsion within its provisions;

(iv) decisions on matters that fall within the remit of the Mental Health Act but where someone has been appointed as a deputy or where an LPA exists.

A key issue will be whenever a person's circumstances amount to a deprivation of liberty rather than restriction of movement, as there are serious limitations on what can be dealt with under the Mental Capacity Act in these circumstances. This is discussed and developed in Chapters 16–18. It is not just a question which occurs when a person is detained, as the definition of mental disorder also applies to informal patients, whether they are in effect 'voluntary' or lacking capacity to make a decision on admission and are in hospital in their best interests.

Mental incapacity compared with mental disorder

It is important to avoid assumptions that people who have a mental disorder will lack the capacity to make decisions about health and social matters. It is also important not to assume that a lack of capacity to make a particular decision must be caused by a mental disorder. This, however, is a little more difficult to assert when the definition of mental disorder is so broad, and becoming broader. At one point in the Government's moves to reform mental health law, the definition of mental disorder was almost identical to that of mental incapacity, as it was then described in the Mental Incapacity Bill. If this had remained the case, there would potentially have been even more problems with people muddling up the two concepts.

Starting with the first assertion, that people who have a mental disorder will not automatically lack the capacity to make decisions about health and social matters, this should be clear as soon as an individual situation is looked at. Even if a mental disorder, say severe depression, affects capacity in some areas of a person's decision-making it is unlikely to rob the individual of all decision-making powers. Even in cases of severe depression, dementia or severe learning difficulties there will be some decisions that the individual will be able to make. The definition of mental incapacity in the Mental Capacity Act starts with the phrase *unable to make a decision for himself in relation to the matter*, which should help clarify the issue. No-one should have the general label 'mentally incapacitated' attached to them; 'mental incapacity' only has meaning in relation to a specific issue.

The second assertion, that there are causes of incapacity which are other than mental disorder, is usually accepted. Note that the new definition of 'mental disorder' in the amended Mental Health Act 1983 is simply 'any disorder or disability of the mind'. It is not clear as to which *impairments or disturbances in the functioning of the mind or brain* (the phrase used in the Mental Capacity Act but which does not appear in the Mental Health Act) will *not* amount to mental disorder.

Now that the Bournewood safeguards (DOLS) have been implemented, this will become an issue in many cases, as there will be a 'mental disorder' test before the new provisions can be used. Areas of controversy will probably include: strokes, physical illnesses which can affect thinking (e.g. diabetes), and the long-term effects of drugs or alcohol. For other areas of the Mental Capacity Act where there may be requests for immediate interventions, there would, again, be issues associated with the effects of drugs or alcohol as well as situations such as concussion following a head injury. These impairments are not usually seen as 'mental disorders' for the purposes of the Mental Health Act, although they are *impairments or disturbances in the functioning of the mind or brain*. It will be interesting to see how custom and practice, and/or case, law develop in this area. It is not an area of idle speculation, as important matters such as funding can hang on such decisions.

Consent to treatment under the Mental Health Act 1983

Section 28 of the Mental Capacity Act states:

(1) *Nothing in this Act authorises anyone –*

(a) *to give a patient medical treatment for mental disorder, or*

(b) *to consent to a patient's being given medical treatment for mental disorder, if, at the time when it is proposed to treat the patient, his treatment is regulated by Part 4 of the Mental Health Act.*

(1a) *Subsection (1) does not apply in relation to any form of treatment to which section 58A of that Act (electro-convulsive therapy, etc.) applies if the patient comes within subsection (7) of that section (informal patient under 18 who cannot give consent).*

(1b) *Section 5 does not apply to an act to which section 64B of the Mental Health Act applies (treatment of community patients not recalled to hospital).*

(2) *'Medical treatment', 'mental disorder' and 'patient' have the same meaning as in that Act.*

Patients not covered by Part 4 of the Act are in the same position as any other patients in any hospital and cannot be treated without their consent except where the Mental Capacity Act will allow it. In addition, not all detained patients are included. Generally, those patients liable to detention under the Mental Health Act 1983 for periods of more than 72 hours are covered (e.g. ss 2 and 3), with the exception of people remanded for reports by the courts under s 35.

Part 4 of the Mental Health Act outlines the circumstances in which treatment for mental disorder may be given without the consent of a detained patient. The main principle adopted by the Act is that there are some patients who are liable to be detained who may need to be given treatment without their consent. Further, this may be seen as reasonable given the fact of their detention. However, certain safeguards were seen as necessary and were introduced by the 1983 Act.

Some more serious forms of treatment are subject to procedures which should be followed to offer these safeguards. These essentially involve a second medical opinion from outside the hospital in those cases where valid consent cannot be obtained from the patient. This absence of consent could either be the result of the patient objecting to the treatment, or of their being unable to give valid consent (e.g. because of mental incapacity). For the most serious treatments (such as psychosurgery), a second opinion *and* the consent of the patient are required. Because of the invasive nature of these treatments, the safeguards are also extended to informal patients.

The Care Quality Commission has a general duty to oversee the operation of this part of the Act.

Other links with the Mental Health Act 1983

The nearest relative under the Mental Health Act 1983 has certain specific powers such as being able to apply for detention, or to exercise discharge powers, and they also have rights to information and to be consulted. It is possible that a nearest relative might also have an LPA for an individual or there may a conflict of opinion between a nearest relative and someone with an LPA or who is acting as a deputy. For a fuller description of this and how other Mental Health Act provisions operate in practice readers are referred to two books in the same series as this text: *The Approved Mental Health Professional's Guide to Psychiatry and Medication* (Brown, Adshead and Pollard, 2012) and *The Approved Mental Health Professional's Guide to Mental Health Law* (Brown, 2013).

The interface between the Act and the Mental Health Act 1983 are extensively discussed in Chapter 17.

Links with the children's law

In general, the Mental Capacity Act does not apply to children under the age of 16. However, the criminal offence of ill-treatment or wilful neglect under s 44 will apply if the child's incapacity meets the Act's definition (particularly in relation to its cause). Further, the Court of Protection could make an order in relation to the property and affairs of a child if it was persuaded that this was necessary because the child would continue to lack capacity beyond the age of 18 (s 18(3)).

The Act broadly applies to 16- and 17-year-olds, but with a few exceptions:

- No-one may make or be appointed under an LPA if under the age of 18;

- the court cannot make a statutory will for an under 18-year-old;

- an under 18-year-old cannot make an advance decision;

- the DOLS provisions only apply to those over the age of 18.

So health and social care professionals will still be faced with a number of possible routes to take in relation to an under 18-year-old:

- the Children Act 1989;

- the Mental Health Act 1983;

- the Mental Capacity Act 2005; and indeed

- the common law and the inherent jurisdiction of the High Court.

The need for relief to extend beyond the child's 18th birthday will no doubt encourage application to the Court of Protection under the Mental Capacity Act rather than using the Children Act, but transfer between jurisdictions will be straightforward (under the Mental Capacity Act 2005 (Transfer of Proceedings) Order 2007, No. 1899), should this subsequently become appropriate. The considerations to be borne in mind in determining the route will remain largely unaltered, particularly in relation to the choice between the Mental Health Act and the Children Act.

More detailed consideration of this area of potential overlap is outside the scope of this book and practitioners are referred to Chapter 12 of the Code of Practice to the Mental Capacity Act and to 'Mentally Disordered Children and the Law' by Anthony Harbour (2008).

Links with the common law

Some practitioners struggle with the concept of common law. Although many professionals' tasks are rooted firmly in statute, there are frequent overlaps with the common law. It is therefore necessary for professionals to have a working grasp of what is meant by common law and how it might relate to their practice. The *Oxford Dictionary of Law* (Martin and Law, 2006, page 104) gives three basic definitions of common law:

1. *The part of English law based on rules developed by the royal courts during the first three centuries after the Norman Conquest (1066) as a system applicable to the whole country, as opposed to local customs . . .*

2. *Rules of law developed by the courts as opposed to those created by statute.*

3. *A general system of law deriving exclusively from court decisions.*

Montgomery (2002, page 7) has described common law as:

> *The rules which are extrapolated from the practice of the judges in deciding cases.*

Some practitioners have referred to this as 'common sense under a wig'.

The Mental Capacity Act takes, adapts and clothes in statutory form a number of areas of common (judge-made) law, in particular:

- the test for incapacity;

- the means of establishing 'best interests';

- the authority to intervene in relation to a person lacking capacity and the limits to that authority;

- the law relating to advance decisions.

So for many areas of practice what used to be common law is now covered by the statute. Just when the common law will continue to apply in relation to dealing with those lacking capacity is an interesting issue and outside the scope of this book. What is left of the common law will depend to some extent upon how the courts construe the Mental Capacity Act, whether broadly or narrowly. Perhaps the safest advice would be to confine the use of common law powers in relation to a person lacking capacity to emergencies and short-term interventions.

ACTIVITY **15.1**

Multiple choice questions
Read each question carefully and tick the appropriate box(es). Where a statement is correct, tick the box next to it; if it is incorrect, leave it blank. You may need to tick more than one box per question.

Appendix 5 (pages 279–83) gives the answers.

15.1 *'An impairment of, or a disturbance in the functioning of, the mind or brain' is a key phrase to be found in* **BOTH** *the Mental Health Act 2007 and the Mental Capacity Act 2005:*

    (a) True ☐

    (b) False ☐

15.2 *In HL v UK the European Court ruled that there had been breaches of:*

    (a) Article 3 – prohibition of torture ☐

    (b) Article 5.1 – right to liberty and security of person ☐

(Continued)

(Continued)

    (c) Article 5.4 – right to a speedy review of detention   ☐

    (d) Article 8.1 – right to respect for private and family life   ☐

    (e) Article 12 – right to marry and found a family   ☐

    (f) Article 14 – prohibition of discrimination   ☐

15.3 The Mental Capacity Act limits the following areas to people of 18 or over:

    (a) Making an advance decision   ☐

    (b) Any intervention under s 5 on the basis of mental incapacity   ☐

    (c) Making a Lasting Power of Attorney   ☐

    (d) Being a named person for consultation as part of the best interests checklist   ☐

    (e) Becoming an attorney under a Lasting Power of Attorney   ☐

    (f) Use of the new Bournewood safeguards when implemented   ☐

Chapter 16
Deprivation of Liberty Safeguards

Introduction

The Mental Health Act 2007 (MHA) amended the Mental Capacity Act 2005 (MCA) by introducing the Deprivation of Liberty Safeguards (DOLS). The new section (s) 4A and Schedule A1 created a procedure for authorising a deprivation of liberty. The procedure is intended to provide a lawful means of depriving a person of their liberty within hospital or care home settings. This procedure only applies to adults in England and Wales who have a mental disorder, and who lack the capacity to consent to being accommodated for the purpose of being given care or treatment in circumstances that amount to a deprivation of liberty. The deprivation of liberty must be necessary to protect the person from harm and be in their best interests. The procedures, which came into force on 1 April 2009, were envisaged by the government to be most likely to apply to people with significant learning disabilities, people who have dementia or those with neurological conditions. The procedures allow for standard and urgent authorisations of deprivation of liberty. Initially, uptake of DOLS was slow; however, developments in case law resulting in a broad definition of deprivation of liberty have led to a surge in requests for standard authorisations.

This chapter will outline the DOLS procedures. Chapter 17 looks at the interface between the MCA and the MHA, and considers the factors that might be influential in deciding which Act provides the more appropriate means of depriving someone of their liberty. Chapter 18 then considers the distinction between restriction of movement and deprivation of liberty. These chapters should be read in conjunction with the DOLS procedures described in this chapter.

Lawful ways to deprive someone of their liberty

The Mental Capacity Act provides three ways of lawfully depriving a person of their liberty.

- Deprivation of Liberty Safeguards (s 4A and Schedules A1 and 1A).
- A personal welfare order (s 4A and s 16(2)(a)) The court is able to make decisions in relation to a person's welfare which may include matters such as: deciding where the person should live; what contact the person should have with other specified people

(this includes enforced and prohibited contact); giving or refusing consent to treatment; and determining who is responsible for healthcare.

- Deprivation of liberty for the purpose of life-sustaining treatment (s 4B). The new section 4B allows a decision-maker to deprive a person of his or her liberty where this is necessary (wholly or partly) for the purpose of giving life-sustaining treatment, or to prevent a serious deterioration in the person's condition, while a decision is sought from the Court of Protection.

The Deprivation of Liberty Safeguards (DOLS) procedure

Schedule A1, 'Hospital and Care Home Residents: Deprivation of Liberty', sets out the procedure for depriving a person of their liberty in either a care home or hospital setting. Where a care home or hospital, termed the 'managing authority', identifies that a person is being, or is likely to be, deprived of their liberty within the next 28 days, they must apply for an authorisation (Schedule A1 para 24). The request for such an authorisation is made to the 'supervisory body'. The DOLS Code (Ministry of Justice, 2008) sets out the following guidance regarding identification of the managing authority.

Managing authority

Para 3.1 states:

- *In the case of an NHS hospital, the managing authority is the NHS body responsible for the running of the hospital in which the relevant person is, or is to be, a resident.*

- *In the case of a care home or a private hospital, the managing authority will be the person registered, or required to be registered, under part 2 of the Care Standards Act 2000 in respect of the hospital or care home.*

Supervisory body

From 1 April 2013, when primary care trusts ceased to exist, their supervisory body responsibilities relating to hospitals were transferred to local authorities in England. This means that local authorities are the only supervisory bodies in England authorising deprivations of liberty (in hospital and care home settings). The supervisory body responsibilities of the National Assembly for Wales were unchanged. Therefore, supervisory body responsibilities following amendments to Schedule A1 of the MCA by Schedule 5 of the Health and Social Care Act 2012 are as follows.

Hospitals situated in England:

- *Where the deprivation of liberty safeguards are applied to a person in a hospital situated in England, the supervisory body will be the local authority for the area in which the person is ordinarily resident.*

- *Where the deprivation of liberty safeguards are applied to a person not ordinarily resident in England and the National Assembly for Wales or the Local Health Board commission the relevant care or treatment, the National Assembly are the supervisory body.*

- *In any other case, the supervisory body is the local authority for the area in which the relevant hospital is situated.*

Hospitals situated in Wales:

- *Where the deprivation of liberty safeguards are applied to a person in a hospital situated in Wales, the supervisory body will be the National Assembly for Wales.*

- *Where the deprivation of liberty safeguards are applied to a person ordinarily resident in the area of a local authority in England, the supervisory body is that local authority.*

Care homes:

- *Where the deprivation of liberty safeguards are applied to a person in a care home, whether situated in England or Wales, the supervisory body will be the local authority for the area in which the person is ordinarily resident. However, if the person is not ordinarily resident in the area of any local authority (for example a person of no fixed abode), the supervisory body will be the local authority for the area in which the care home is situated.*

(Ministry of Justice, 2008, para 3.3)

Request for a standard authorisation

Managing authorities are required to request a standard authorisation in the following circumstances:

- where it appears that a current or future resident is being, or is likely within the next 28 days to be, accommodated in circumstances that amount to a deprivation of liberty;

- the relevant person is already subject to an authorisation of deprivation of liberty and moves. In these circumstances the responsibility to apply rests with the managing authority of the new place of residence;

- where a personal welfare order granting deprivation of liberty is about to expire and the person will continue to be deprived of their liberty.

Managing authorities must keep written records of any requests made and the reasons for the request. The DOLS Code (3.6) provides guidance to managing authorities about the decision to apply for an authorisation, stating:

Managing authorities should have a procedure in place that identifies:

- *whether deprivation of liberty is or may be necessary in a particular case*

- *what steps they should take to assess whether to seek authorisation*

- *whether they have taken all practical and reasonable steps to avoid a deprivation of liberty*

- *what action they should take if they do need to request an authorisation*

- *how they should review cases where authorisation is or may be necessary, and*

- *who should take the necessary action.*

The Act allows a third party (someone other than the managing authority) to require the supervisory body to decide whether there is an unauthorised deprivation of liberty. See 'Assessment to establish if an unauthorised deprivation of liberty is occurring' below. In addition to managing authorities' responsibilities to identify deprivation of liberty, the case of *AJ v A Local Authority* (2015) EWCOP5 has given guidance to local authorities in relation to the need to obtain a DOLS authorisation in advance where it is anticipated that a person will become deprived of their liberty. This might include cases where residential care is arranged ostensibly for respite, where the underlying plan is for a permanent residential placement.

Standard authorisation application information

An application for an authorisation of deprivation of liberty must be in writing. Prescribed forms are available for this purpose, but they are not statutory forms and therefore do not have to be used. The Mental Capacity Act (Deprivation of Liberty: Standard Authorisations, Assessment and Ordinary Residence) Regulations 2008 ('The Regulations') set out the information to be provided by the managing authority to the supervisory body when requesting a standard authorisation. These regulations apply in England. For those operating this legislation in Wales, separate regulations must be observed. The information required in England is:

- *the name and gender of the relevant person;*

- *the age of the relevant person or, where this is not known, whether the managing authority believes that the relevant person is aged 18 years or older;*

- *the address and telephone number where the relevant person is currently located;*

- *the name, address and telephone number of the managing authority and the name of the person within the managing authority who is dealing with the request;*

- *the purpose for which the authorisation is requested;*

- *the date from which the standard authorisation is sought; and*

- *whether the managing authority has given an urgent authorisation under paragraph 76 of Schedule A1 to the Act and, if so, the date on which it expires.*

The following information must also be included where it is available and could be obtained by the managing authority. However, where there is an existing authorisation in force and a further authorisation is sought, the following information is not required provided that it has not changed.

- *any medical information relating to the relevant person's health that the managing authority considers to be relevant to the proposed restrictions to the relevant person's liberty;*

- *the diagnosis of the mental disorder (within the meaning of the Mental Health Act 1983 but disregarding any exclusion for persons with learning disability) that the relevant person is suffering from;*

- *any relevant care plans and relevant needs assessments;*

- *the racial, ethnic or national origins of the relevant person;*

- *the person's religion or belief, sexual orientation and disability;*

- *whether the relevant person has any special communication needs;*

- *details of the proposed restrictions on the relevant person's liberty;*

- *whether it is necessary for an IMCA to be instructed;*

- *whether section 39A of the Act (person becomes subject to Schedule A1) applies;*

- *where the purpose of the proposed restrictions to the relevant person's liberty is to give treatment, whether the relevant person has made an advance decision that may be valid and applicable to some or all of that treatment;*

- *whether the relevant person is subject to –*

  - *the hospital treatment regime,*

  - *the community treatment regime, or*

  - *the guardianship regime;*

- *the name, address and telephone number of –*

  - *anyone named by the relevant person as someone to be consulted about his welfare,*

  - *anyone engaged in caring for the person or interested in his welfare,*

  - *any donee of a lasting power of attorney granted by the person,*

  - *any deputy appointed for the person by the Court of Protection, and*

  - *any independent mental capacity advocate appointed in accordance with sections 37 to 39D of the Act; and*

- *whether there is an existing authorisation in relation to the detention of the relevant person and, if so, the date of the expiry of that authorisation.*

Once an application is complete it must be sent to the supervisory body, which will keep a record of its receipt and acknowledge its receipt from the managing authority. The supervisory body then commissions six assessments: age, mental health, mental capacity, eligibility, best interests and no refusals. These assessments must involve at least two assessors as the mental health and the best interests assessments must be carried out by different people. The regulations set out who are eligible persons to carry out assessments (see Appendix 1B, pages 265–72). Once in receipt of the assessments, the supervisory body must scrutinise the assessments to ensure the authorisation is legally valid (*Hillingdon v Neary* (2011)). If these conditions are not met, the supervisory body is prevented from giving a standard authorisation. In this case, those providing care and treatment should consider alternative means of authorising a lawful deprivation of liberty, for example detention under the MHA or a personal welfare order authorised under s 16 of the MCA. Alternatively, they might stop depriving the person of their liberty.

Assessment to establish if an unauthorised deprivation of liberty is occurring

Paragraph 69 of Schedule A1 allows an eligible person (someone other than the managing authority of the relevant hospital or care home) to request the supervisory body to decide whether or not an unauthorised deprivation of liberty is occurring. The supervisory body must select and appoint a person to carry out an assessment of whether or not the relevant person is a detained resident unless one of the following applies:

- they consider the request to be frivolous or vexatious; or
- it has already been established whether or not an unauthorised deprivation of liberty is occurring; and
- since that decision, there has not been a change that would merit a reassessment.

This assessment may take place in isolation to the other assessments. However, where an unauthorised deprivation of liberty is identified, further assessments are likely to take place to establish if the person should be made subject to DOLS.

The six assessments

The assessments are detailed within Part 3 of Schedule A1 to the MCA and are referred to as 'the qualifying requirements'. The requirements relate to: age, mental health, mental capacity, best interests, eligibility and no refusals. The relevant person must meet all of the above requirements for an authorisation to be given. Failure to meet one or more of these requirements would halt the assessment process and prevent the use of DOLS. Assessors may examine and take copies of any health, local authority or care home records which are considered relevant to their assessment. A list of the examined records should be detailed within the assessment report(s). Assessors must keep a written record of any assessments they have completed and give copies to the supervisory body. The supervisory body will then distribute copies of these reports to the managing authority, the relevant person's representative and any Independent Mental Capacity Advocate (IMCA) who has been instructed. Assessments must be completed within a specified time frame.

In England, all assessments for a standard authorisation must be completed within 21 days beginning with the date the supervisory body received the request for an authorisation. Where an urgent authorisation has been given, the assessments must be completed within the time period that the urgent authorisation is in force.

In Wales, where a standard authorisation is sought the assessments must be completed within 21 days from the date the assessors are instructed by the supervisory body. Where an urgent authorisation has been given and a standard authorisation is being sought assessments must be completed within five days of the date of instruction.

The following table sets out: the assessments, who is eligible to carry out the assessments (in England), and which forms should be completed.

Table 16.1 DOLS assessors

Assessments	Persons eligible to assess	Original form(s)	Revised form(s)
Age	Anyone eligible to carry out a best interests assessment	5 or 10	3
Mental health	A doctor approved under s 12 of the MHA, or a doctor with a minimum of 3 years post-registration experience in the diagnosis or treatment of mental disorder. Both need to complete a DOLS course provided by the Royal College of Psychiatrists	6	4
Mental capacity	A doctor approved as a mental health assessor or a best interests assessor (BIA)	7	3 or 4
Best interests	Approved Mental Health Professional (AMHP), social worker, nurse, occupational therapist or psychologist. All need to be two years post qualification and have completed approved BIA training	10	3 or 3A
Eligibility	A doctor approved as a mental health assessor or a BIA who is also an AMHP	9	4
No refusals	Anyone eligible to carry out a best interests assessment	8	3

Age

The person must be, or believed to be, 18 years of age or older. The age assessment can be completed as a separate assessment or as part of the best interests assessment when using the original forms 5 or 10, or it may be assessed alongside mental capacity, no refusals and best interests when using the revised form 3. The assessments are intended to be completed with information which will be accurate at the time the authorisation comes into force. Therefore, there is nothing to prevent a 17-year-old being assessed, provided that they will have attained the age of 18 by the time the authorisation takes effect. If the assessor is unable to ascertain a date of birth, they must state that to the best of their knowledge and belief the person will be aged 18 or over when the authorisation comes into force. Where a person does not meet the age requirement consideration should be given to alternative provisions within the MHA or the Children Act 1989.

Mental health

A doctor must establish whether the relevant person has a mental disorder, i.e. 'any disorder or disability of the mind', as defined by s 1 of the amended MHA. This will exclude those solely with dependence upon alcohol or drugs, but will include those with a learning disability. The requirement that the learning disability should be associated with 'abnormally aggressive or seriously irresponsible conduct' does not apply when considering the DOLS procedure. Therefore, the MCA may well be used for people with a learning disability who fall outside the scope of the MHA in the case of a deprivation of liberty lasting for more than 28 days. The mental health assessor must also consider how (if at all) the relevant person's mental health is likely to be affected by being a detained resident. They must notify the best interests assessor (BIA) of their conclusions. The mental health assessment can be completed as a separate assessment when using the original form 6, or it may be assessed alongside mental capacity and eligibility when using the revised form 4.

If a person was assessed as meeting the requirements of the mental capacity assessment but not the mental disorder test, then DOLS could not be authorised and an application to the Court of Protection would need to be considered. With the mental health test being so broad, this seems likely to be a rare occurrence.

Mental capacity

The relevant person's capacity must be assessed in relation to the decision about accommodation in a care home or hospital for the purpose of providing care or treatment. The test for incapacity must be in accordance with ss 1–3 of the MCA. This test is contained within Chapter 5 above. The mental capacity assessment can be completed as a separate assessment when using the original form 7, or it may be assessed alongside age, no refusals and best interests, or mental health and eligibility when using the revised forms 3 and 4, respectively.

Best interests

Schedule A1, para 16 states that the BIA must satisfy themselves that:

- the person is, or is going to be, a detained resident in a care home or hospital. This requires the BIA to establish if the person's care and treatment is, or will amount to, a deprivation of liberty;
- it would be in the person's best interests to be a detained resident;

- it is necessary for the person to be a detained resident to prevent harm to him or herself (note that this does not include the prevention of harm to others); and

- deprivation of liberty is a proportionate response to the likelihood of the person suffering harm, and the seriousness of that harm.

Schedule A1, para 3 states that the BIA must also consult the managing authority (which will be either the care home or hospital where the relevant person is, or is likely to become, resident), have regard to the conclusion of the mental health assessor (in relation to the likely impact of deprivation of liberty on the relevant person's mental health), and have regard to any relevant needs plan and care plan.

Schedule A1 of the Act defines a relevant needs assessment at para 39(4) as

an assessment of the relevant person's needs which was carried out in connection with the relevant person being accommodated in the relevant hospital or care home, and was carried out by or on behalf of the managing authority of the relevant hospital or care home, or the supervisory body.

A relevant care plan is defined at para 39(5) as

a care plan which sets out how the relevant person's needs are to be met whilst he is accommodated in the relevant hospital or care home, and was drawn up by or on behalf of the managing authority of the relevant hospital or care home, or the supervisory body.

The managing authority or supervisory body must give the BIA a copy of the needs assessment.

The BIA:

- must state the name and address of every interested person they have consulted as part of the assessment process,

and where they conclude that the relevant person meets the best interests requirement they:

- must state the maximum length of time of the authorisation;

- may include recommendations about conditions that may, or may not be imposed;

- will identify a representative for the person (see 'Relevant person's representative' below).

The best interests assessment can be completed as a separate assessment when using the original form 10, or it may be assessed alongside age, mental capacity and no refusals when using the revised form 3. Where they conclude that the best interests requirement is not met because there is no unauthorised deprivation of liberty occurring, they must make a statement to this effect within their report. This can be recorded on the original form 10 or the revised form 3A, which is specifically for the purpose of recording the absence of deprivation of liberty.

In order to carry out this assessment, the BIA must comply with s 4 of the MCA (see Chapter 6 for more information). In addition to the best interests checklist, the BIA must consider the factors outlined at para 4.61 of the Code:

- *whether any harm to the person could arise if the deprivation of liberty does not take place*

- *what that harm would be*

- *how likely that harm is to arise (i.e. is the level of risk sufficient to justify a step as serious as depriving a person of liberty?)*

- *what other care options there are which could avoid deprivation of liberty, and*

- *if deprivation of liberty is currently unavoidable, what action could be taken to avoid it in future.*

Relevant person's representative

The relevant regulations are set out at Appendix 1A, see pages 260–4. The supervisory body must appoint someone to be the relevant person's representative as soon as practicable after a standard authorisation is given. A representative must not be appointed unless the person making the selection is satisfied that the prospective representative would maintain contact with, represent and support the relevant person. The importance of this role in securing the relevant person's Article 5(4) right to a legal challenge has been highlighted in the case of *AJ v A Local Authority* (2015) EWCOP5. The supervisory body must, therefore, scrutinise the selection of the representative, and where the representative does not meet the criteria above, for example a potential conflict of interest arises as a result of them being involved in the placement of the relevant person, the supervisory body must refer the matter back to the BIA. Where the representative has already been appointed, and a conflict is identified, the supervisory body must consider terminating the representative's appointment on the grounds that they are no longer eligible. Where the representative or IMCA appointed under s 39D of the MCA fail to challenge the authorisation, the supervisory body should consider applying to the court itself.

The BIA must establish if the relevant person has the capacity to select his or her own representative; if this is the case he or she may select a representative.

Where the relevant person has capacity but does not wish to make a choice, the BIA may select a representative, provided that any donee or deputy does not wish to make a selection. However, the BIA is unable to make the proposed selection in the face of an objection by a donee or deputy. Where the relevant person lacks capacity to make a selection, the BIA may make the selection provided that there is no donee or deputy, or where there is a donee or deputy but selecting a representative is outside the scope of their authority. Where the BIA is unable to select an eligible representative, they must inform the supervisory body which is able to appoint a representative in a professional capacity. A representative appointed by the supervisory body may receive payment.

Where the BIA has established that the relevant person lacks capacity to select a representative and the relevant person has a donee or deputy with the authority to select a representative, then that person may select a representative. The donee may select him or herself to be the representative. Where the donee or deputy does not wish to select a representative the BIA may select a representative.

The above selections (other than the donee or deputy selecting themselves) may be of a family member, a friend or a carer. Where anyone other than the BIA selects the representative, the eligibility of the selected family member, friend or carer must be confirmed by the BIA, and be recommended by them to the supervisory body. Where the BIA is unable to confirm the eligibility of the proposed representative they must advise the person who made the selection, give reasons and invite them to make a further selection. The offer of appointment of a representative must be in writing and must outline the duties of the representative. The proposed representative must reply to the offer in writing, stating that they have understood the duties imposed upon them.

Eligibility

Schedule 1A sets out the circumstances in which a relevant person would be ineligible for DOLS. This is a very complex schedule, but in essence a relevant person would be ineligible if:

- he or she is a patient who is subject to a 'hospital treatment regime' section of the Mental Health Act 1983 (i.e. ss 2, 3, 4, 35, 36, 37, 38, 44, 45A, 47, 48 or 51); or

- he or she is a patient subject to either s 17 leave of absence, s 7 guardianship, 17A community treatment order (CTO) or conditional discharge and is subject to a condition which would conflict with the proposed authorisation, an example being a requirement of residence elsewhere (if, however, there are no conflicting requirements a person could be subject to DOLS and the above provisions); or

- he or she is a patient subject to recall provisions of either s 17, CTO or conditional discharge; or

- if the purpose of detention is treatment (partly or wholly) for mental disorder in a hospital (not in a care home), it would be possible for the patient to be detained under the MHA, and the patient objects to the treatment. The objection may be a current objection or be based upon historical information established as part of the best interests assessment, for example an understanding of the person's past wishes, feelings, values or beliefs.

This last paragraph is key to avoiding the creation of a new gap in the legislation. There are some learning disabled patients (who may even have been detained on s 2 of the MHA) where it will not be possible for them to be detained under s 3 of the

MHA, as they are not 'abnormally aggressive or seriously irresponsible'. Even if such a patient objects to treatment, they may be made subject to the DOLS procedures because of the way Schedule 1A has been worded. In contrast, a patient who was 'abnormally aggressive or seriously irresponsible' could be detained under s 3 of the MHA and would be ineligible for DOLS.

If the eligibility assessor is a doctor, they may require the BIA to provide them with any information which will assist them in determining whether or not the relevant person will be ineligible. Where a person is ineligible for DOLS s 16A of the MCA prevents the Court of Protection from making a personal welfare order that amounts to a deprivation of liberty.

The eligibility assessment can be completed as a separate assessment when using the original form 9, or it may be assessed alongside mental capacity and mental health when using the revised form 4.

No refusals

This assessment is to establish if a deprivation of liberty would conflict with any advance or substituted decision-making. Examples would be: a valid and applicable advance decision made by the relevant person refusing all or part of the proposed treatment; a refusal by a donee under a Lasting Power of Attorney (LPA); or, a refusal by a deputy appointed by the Court of Protection. It is important to note that treatment cannot be authorised under DOLS. The assessor would need to establish whether any refusal is within the scope of the person's authority. Faced with a refusal, an assessor might wish to consider whether the provisions of the MHA would be appropriate. The purpose of the no refusals assessment is to place the relevant person in the same position as someone who had capacity to refuse consent to the proposed course of action.

The no refusals assessment can be completed as a separate assessment when using the original form 8, or it may be assessed alongside age, mental capacity and best interests when using the revised form 3.

Authorisation of deprivation of liberty

Only a supervisory body may give a standard authorisation. Schedule A1 para 50 sets out that it must give an authorisation when the managing authority has requested an authorisation, all the assessments are positive, and it has written copies of all those assessments. Schedule A1 para 55 states that the supervisory body must give the authorisation in writing and state the following:

- the name of the relevant person;
- the name of the relevant hospital or care home;
- the period during which the authorisation is to be in force (this must be for no longer than the time period stated in the best interests assessment);

- the purpose for which the authorisation is given;

- any conditions subject to which the authorisation is given (having regard to any recommendations in the best interests assessment);*

- the reason why each of the qualifying requirements is met. In the case of the eligibility requirement, the reason why the patient is eligible must be recorded by stating the applicable case as listed in para 2 of Schedule 1A (see Appendix 1).

> *Note: The managing authority has the responsibility to ensure that any conditions are complied with.

Once the authorisation is given the supervisory body must, as soon as practicable, give a copy of the authorisation to the relevant person, their representative, the relevant managing authority, any IMCA appointed and anyone consulted by the BIA. If, however, the supervisory body is prevented from giving an authorisation they must give notice to those listed above.

Authorisation of deprivation of liberty is situation specific. Therefore, a change in residence of a person subject to DOLS would require fresh assessment.

Giving information

Schedule A1 para 59(2) states that where a standard authorisation is given, the managing authority must as soon as practicable take reasonable steps to ensure that the relevant person understands:

- the effect of the authorisation;

- the right to apply to the Court of Protection to appeal the authorisation;

- the right to request a review;

- the right to, and how to, appoint an IMCA.

This information must be given orally and in writing to the relevant person and their representative. Where an IMCA has been appointed the above information must also be given to them in writing.

Selection of assessors

It is the responsibility of the supervisory body to select assessors to complete the six assessments required for a standard authorisation or for a review of a standard authorisation. The supervisory body must not select an assessor unless it appears to it that the assessor is suitable to carry out the assessment (suitability may include the type of assessment and the person being assessed) and that they are eligible to carry out the assessment(s). Supervisory bodies must also ensure that no conflicts arise as a result of the selection of assessors.

Selection of assessors: relative and financial interests

Conflicts will arise in the following circumstances:

- where the assessor is a relative of the relevant person;
- where the assessor is a relative of a person who has a financial interest in the care of the relevant person;
- where the assessor has a financial interest in the case.

Selection of best interests assessor

Conflicts will arise in the following circumstances:

- where the assessor is involved in the care, or making decisions about the care, of the relevant person;
- where the supervisory body and managing authority are a single organisation the BIA must not be an employee of that organisation or be providing services to it.

The Mental Capacity (Deprivation of Liberty: Standard Authorisations, Assessments and Ordinary Residence) Regulations 2008 contain further information about potential conflicts of interest (see Appendix 1B, pages 265–72).

Equivalent assessments

The Act allows equivalent assessments, which have already been carried out, to be used to meet any of the six requirements listed above. However, there are certain conditions that must be met if equivalent assessments are to be used. First, the supervisory body must have a written copy of the assessment already carried out. Second, the assessment must comply with the requirements of Schedule A1. Third, any equivalent assessment, other than the age assessment, must have been carried out within the previous 12 months. The fourth condition is that the supervisory body is satisfied that the assessment remains accurate. This is particularly important where the equivalent assessment is to be used as the best interests assessment, as the Act places a requirement on the supervisory body to take into account any information from the relevant person's representative and any IMCA appointed for the relevant person. The DOLS Code suggests that equivalent assessments should not be used as a matter of routine. Further guidance regarding the use of equivalent assessments can be found in chapter 4 of the DOLS Code.

Expiry of an authorisation

A deprivation of liberty may be authorised for a maximum period of one year. The duration of a deprivation of liberty will be stipulated by the BIA. Where deprivation of liberty needs to continue beyond the prescribed time, a further authorisation must be sought. All requirements must be met using new assessments or equivalent assessments carried out within the previous 12 months, other than the age assessment. See 'Equivalent assessments' above for more information. Also see 'Suspension of an authorisation' below for the circumstances in which an authorisation may be terminated. While the statute does not determine a time frame within which a subsequent deprivation of liberty must be sought, the DOLS Code states at para 3.19:

> an authorisation should not be applied for too far in advance as this may prevent an assessor from making an accurate assessment of what the person's circumstances will be at the time the authorisation will come into force.

Urgent authorisation

A managing authority may self-authorise a deprivation of liberty for a period not exceeding seven days. The authorisation must be in writing and state the name of the relevant person, the name of the relevant hospital or care home, the time period the authorisation is to be in force, and the purpose for which the authorisation is given.

The managing authority must give an urgent authorisation if either of the following apply:

- they are required under paras 24 or 25 of Schedule A1 (see Appendix 1) to make a request for a standard authorisation, and they believe that the need for the relevant person to be detained is so urgent that it needs to begin before the request is made, or

- an authorisation has been requested, but the need for the relevant person to be detained is so urgent that it needs to begin before the request is dealt with. This means that no urgent authorisation can be given unless the managing authority reasonably believes it is likely that a standard authorisation will be obtained. (See DOLS Code para 6.1.)

Information in relation to record keeping and the giving of information is contained within paras 82 and 83 of Schedule A1.

Extension of an urgent authorisation

Where an urgent authorisation has been given the supervisory body may, in exceptional circumstances, extend that authorisation for a maximum of a further seven days at the request of the managing authority. Upon making a request the managing authority must keep a written record of why they have made the request and must give the relevant person notice of the request. The supervisory body may extend the duration of the original authorisation if the following criteria are met:

- the managing authority have made a request for a standard authorisation;

- there are exceptional reasons why it has not yet been possible for all of the assessments required for a standard authorisation to have been completed; and

- it is essential that the detention of the relevant person continues until the end of the assessment process required for a standard authorisation.

The Act does not define 'exceptional circumstances'. Paragraphs 84–90 of Schedule A1 give additional information about urgent authorisations. It follows that the six assessments have to be completed within a maximum of 14 days where there has been an urgent authorisation.

The Government introduced transitional provisions to allow managing authorities to give an urgent authorisation for up to 21 days, rather than seven days where the authorisation was made on or before 30 April 2009. However, no alteration to the duration of urgent authorisations has been made following the judgment in the case of *P v Cheshire West and Chester Council and Another* and *P and Q v Surrey County Council* (2014), which has resulted in a significant increase in requests for standard authorisations. An inability to meet legislative timeframes, for example putting in place a standard authorisation during the period of an urgent authorisation, is likely to amount to an unlawful deprivation of liberty.

Independent Mental Capacity Advocates (IMCA)

The role of the IMCA is set out in Chapter 11 of this text, but the IMCA instructed at the initial stage of the deprivation of liberty has additional rights and responsibilities. The DOLS Code sets out these rights at para 3.23. IMCAs have the right to:

- *as they consider appropriate, give information or make submissions to assessors, which assessors must take into account in carrying out their assessments*

- *receive copies of any assessments from the supervisory body*

- *receive a copy of any standard authorisation given by the supervisory body*

- *be notified by the supervisory body if they are unable to give a standard authorisation because one or more of the deprivation of liberty assessments did not meet the qualifying requirements*

- *receive a copy of any urgent authorisation from the managing authority*

- *receive from the managing authority a copy of any notice declining to extend the duration of an urgent authorisation*

- *receive from the supervisory body a copy of any notice that an urgent authorisation has ceased to be in force, and*

- *apply to the Court of Protection for permission to take the relevant person's case to the Court in connection with a matter relating to the giving or refusal of a standard or urgent authorisation (in the same way as any other third party can).*

IMCAs should familiarise themselves with the relevant person's circumstances. They will need to share relevant information with the assessors and highlight their concerns about the giving of an urgent or standard authorisation. The DOLS Code, para 3.25 gives advice about the resolution of disagreements an IMCA may have with assessors. In essence, the Code advocates informal resolution where possible, but also highlights the potential need to inform the supervisory body and ultimately involve the Court of Protection where informal resolution cannot be reached. The role of the IMCA ceases once the relevant person's representative is appointed. However, if there is a delay in, or gap between, the appointment of the relevant person's representative, an IMCA must remain involved. IMCAs may be instructed when the relevant person does not have a paid professional representative, when the relevant person or their representative requests the involvement of an IMCA to help them, or a supervisory body believes that an IMCA will assist in making sure the person's rights are protected.

Reviews

The supervisory body may at any time carry out a review of a standard authorisation. It must carry out a review if the relevant person, the relevant person's representative or the managing authority request a review. There is no statutory provision limiting the frequency of requests for reviews.

Managing authorities should at all times keep under review the necessity for continued deprivation of liberty. Managing authorities must request a review if they consider that one or more of the qualifying requirements are no longer met. An example would be where it is no longer necessary for the relevant person to be managed in circumstances amounting to a deprivation of liberty.

The eligibility requirement would cease to be met where the relevant person objected to receiving mental health treatment in hospital and they met the criteria for an application for admission under s 2 or 3 of the MHA. Where a person with a learning disability was objecting, they would not meet the criteria for detention under s 3 of the MHA if their learning disability was not associated with abnormally aggressive or seriously irresponsible conduct. Thus, they would not be ineligible and would continue to meet the requirements for DOLS.

There must also be a review of the deprivation of liberty when there has been a change in the relevant person's circumstances resulting in a change, removal of or addition to one of the conditions, or where the reasons that the person meets the qualifying requirements have changed since the authorisation was given.

The supervisory body must tell the relevant person, their representative and the managing authority if it is going to carry out a review. They must also decide which of the qualifying requirements needs reviewing. The supervisory body must establish if a full reassessment is necessary, because where this is the case assessors should be selected to review the qualifying requirements in the same way as for the initial deprivation of liberty. However, minor changes such as a change to a condition may be made by the supervisory body without full reassessment (DOLS Code 8.14). If any of the requirements are no longer met, the authorisation must be terminated and that outcome given in writing to the managing authority, the relevant person, their representative and any IMCA who has been instructed.

Suspension of an authorisation

Short-term suspension of DOLS can occur under Schedule A1 Part 6 for up to 28 days where a person is detained as a hospital in-patient under the MHA. Managing authorities must inform the supervisory body of any such detention to allow the suspension to take place. Should a period of detention under the MHA last for more than 28 days or where the managing authority fails to inform the supervisory body (within 28 days) that detention under the MHA has ended the DOLS authorisation will be terminated.

Protection from liability

Those operating this provision will be protected from liability provided that they comply with the legal framework. Decisions made and actions taken will be as though the relevant person had had capacity to consent and had consented to it. However, there will be no protection for those that act negligently.

Key points

- The MHA 2007 amended the MCA introducing the Deprivation of Liberty Safeguards.

- The DOLS procedure allows for a lawful deprivation of a person's liberty within a hospital or care home.

- The DOLS procedure does not authorise treatment.

- DOLS cannot be used in group-home settings. Where an unauthorised deprivation of liberty is occurring in such a setting use of s 16 of the MCA should be considered.

- Managing authorities are responsible for requesting an authorisation where a deprivation of liberty exists, or is likely to occur.

- Managing authorities are able to self-authorise a deprivation of liberty for up to seven days, while simultaneously requesting a standard authorisation.

- Supervisory bodies are responsible for accepting requests, appointing assessors, providing information to relevant people and authorising deprivation of liberty (when the requirements are met).

- There are six qualifying requirements (assessments), to be completed by at least two assessors.

- A DOLS authorisation can last for up to one year.

- DOLS authorisations can be reviewed and must be terminated if any of the qualifying requirements are no longer met.

- Appeals against DOLS authorisations are to the Court of Protection.

- The relevant person and their representative are entitled to an IMCA in certain circumstances.

Multiple choice questions

Read each question carefully and tick the appropriate box(es). Where a statement is correct, tick the box next to it; if it is incorrect, leave it blank. You may need to tick more than one box per question.

Appendix 5 (pages 279–83) gives the answers.

16.1 The Government has introduced measures to close the 'Bournewood Gap'. For relevant cases supervisory bodies will commission which of the following assessments:

(a) Best interests ☐

(b) No refusals (e.g. from LPA) ☐

(c) Age ☐

(d) Financial ☐

(e) Eligibility ☐

(f) Whether receiving MHA s 117 after-care ☐

(g) Mental capacity ☐

(h) Abnormally aggressive or seriously irresponsible conduct ☐

(i) Mental health ☐

16.2 Under the new DOLS measures one professional could carry out all of the required assessments:

(a) True ☐

(b) False ☐

16.3 Under the new DOLS measures a representative will be appointed for the individual after deprivation of liberty has been authorised:

(a) True ☐

(b) False ☐

Chapter 17

The interface between the Mental Capacity Act and the Mental Health Act

Introduction

The Mental Capacity Act introduced a statutory framework for the care or treatment of individuals lacking capacity: section (s) 5 acts; the giving of treatment that is life-sustaining or to prevent a serious deterioration of the person's condition; the Court of Protection personal welfare powers; Lasting Powers of Attorney; and, more recently, the Deprivation of Liberty Safeguards (DOLS). The provisions of the MCA, the MHA and the remaining elements of common law have led to the potential for confusion of those charged with the responsibility for deciding which provision will best meet an individual's need. The situation is further complicated by the different approaches of the two statutes: the MCA which, in the majority of cases, must be utilised for those who fall within its scope, and the MHA, which allows for professionals' discretion whether or not to apply the Act, even where statutory criteria are met. However, developments in case law and the introduction of a new chapter concerning mental capacity and deprivation of liberty within the Mental Health Act 1983 Code of Practice help guide professionals when deciding which Act is applicable.

This chapter sets out the statutory criteria for each of the main provisions of the MCA and MHA. It then outlines which provisions allow treatment to be given, or the requirement of residence to be imposed, in circumstances that amount to a restriction of movement or a deprivation of liberty. It then goes on to detail which provisions may, and may not, be used together, and sets out guidance and arguments for the preferred means of providing care or treatment.

A person cannot become subject to any of the above provisions unless they meet the statutory criteria. However, establishing whether the legal criteria are met will not by itself be sufficient to establish if the provision will meet an individual's needs. Those providing care or treatment will need to establish: first, if the statutory criteria are met; second, what care or treatment the person needs; and third, whether the care or treatment amounts to, or is likely to amount to, a restriction of the person's movement or a deprivation of their liberty. The distinction between restriction of movement and deprivation of liberty is discussed within Chapter 18. Once these three elements have been established, those making decisions will be able to establish which Act(s) and provision(s) will meet individual needs. The different provisions are detailed below, setting out what the provisions allow (treatment or accommodation) and whether they allow a restriction of movement or a lawful means of deprivation of liberty.

Table 17.1 The Mental Capacity Act: legal criteria

Provision	Criteria
Section 5	• aged 16 and over • specific decision to be made at a specific time • mental incapacity: the person has an inability to make the specific decision because of an impairment of, or disturbance in, the functioning of the mind or brain • the decision is in the person's best interests, as defined in s 4 of the MCA • See Chapter 7 for more information
Section 4A and Schedule A1 – Deprivation of Liberty Safeguards (DOLS)	• aged 18 and over • mental disorder, i.e. 'any disorder or disability of the mind' • mental incapacity (as above) in relation to the decision whether to be accommodated • best interests, as defined in s 4 of the MCA • eligibility (see Schedule 1A of MCA) • no refusals
Sections 4A and 16 – personal welfare order or appointment of a deputy	• aged 16 and over (18 and over for deputy) • the person lacks capacity in relation to a personal welfare or property and affairs matter • the decision(s) or appointment of a deputy is in the best interests of the person
Section 4B – life-sustaining treatment, etc.	• aged 16 and over • a decision is being sought from the court • the deprivation of liberty is wholly or partly for the purpose of giving life-sustaining treatment or to prevent a serious deterioration in a person's condition • a deprivation of liberty is necessary to give life-sustaining treatment or to prevent a serious deterioration in the person's condition

Table 17.2 The Mental Health Act: legal criteria

Provision	Criteria
Informal/voluntary admission (s 131)	• no lower age restriction • mental disorder, i.e. 'any disorder or disability of the mind' • the person has capacity and is consenting to admission and treatment (voluntary), or the person lacks capacity to consent to admission and treatment (informal), is not objecting to admission and admission will not amount to a deprivation of liberty

(Continued)

119

Table 17.2 (Continued)

Provision	Criteria
	• note: where the admission of an incapable person amounts to deprivation of liberty a lawful means of deprivation of liberty must be used, i.e. MHA detention or MCA DOLS
Civil admission (e.g. ss 2 and 3)	• no lower age restriction • mental disorder, i.e. 'any disorder or disability of the mind', of a nature or degree warranting detention in hospital • risk to the health or safety of patient or for the protection of others • informal admission is not appropriate (for s 2 and s 3) • treatment cannot be provided unless detained under this section (for s 3) • it is the most appropriate way of providing care and medical treatment • appropriate medical treatment is available (for s 3)
Guardianship (s 7)	• aged 16 and over • mental disorder of a nature or degree warranting reception into guardianship • necessary in the interests of the patient's welfare or for the protection of others
Leave of absence (s 17 leave)	• may be granted by the responsible clinician for many patients who are liable to be detained under the Act
Community treatment order (s 17A)	• patient is subject to s 3 or is an unrestricted Part 3 patient • the patient is suffering from a mental disorder of a nature or degree which makes it appropriate for him or her to receive medical treatment • it is necessary for his or her health or safety or for the protection of other persons that he or she should receive such treatment • subject to his or her being liable to be recalled as mentioned below, such treatment can be provided without his or her continuing to be detained in a hospital • it is necessary that the responsible clinician should be able to exercise the power to recall the patient to hospital, and • appropriate medical treatment is available

Note: Part 3 provisions are not included in detail here as they can only be imposed by a court when an offence has been committed and so they are not a realistic option for professionals in most situations. See Barber, Brown *et al.* (2012).

Treatment (amounting to a restriction of movement)

Section 5, Mental Capacity Act 2005

Section 5 allows care or treatment to be provided to an incapacitated person using proportionate restraint, provided that they are 16 years of age or older, that the care or treatment is in their best interests and that the care or treatment does not amount to a deprivation of their liberty. Treatment for physical and mental ill health can be provided under this section, without time limit. Chapter 7 gives details regarding s 5 of the MCA.

Common law doctrine of necessity

The common law doctrine of necessity provides for the care or treatment of incapacitated adults in their best interests. The common law has largely been replaced in practice in this field by the MCA, and in particular s 5 acts (detailed above and in Chapter 7). However, there are arguably two areas of common law remaining: the first being the ability to intervene in emergency situations where there is not time to operate legislative provisions; the second being the necessity to intervene to prevent a person causing harm to others, as s 6 of the MCA does not allow for restraint to be used to prevent harm to others. Chapter 7 details the limitations to the use of restraint contained within the MCA.

Treatment (amounting to a deprivation of liberty)

Detention, Mental Health Act 1983

The MHA allows for the detention of a person of any age, provided that they have a mental disorder and meet the relevant criteria of the section of the Act to be used. Detention under the MHA complies with Article 5 of the European Convention on Human Rights (ECHR) as the detention is in accordance with a procedure prescribed by law and those detained are entitled to a Mental Health Tribunal, which provides a legal challenge to detention. Those detained under the Act (other than those detained under ss 4, 5, 35, 135 or 136) are covered by Part 4 of the Act. Part 4 allows for the compulsory treatment of patients regardless of capacity (with one exception regarding electro-convulsive therapy (ECT) – see s 58A of the MHA). The treatment provisions are limited to treatment for mental disorder. Therefore, if a patient needs treatment for physical ill health (unrelated to their mental disorder) their capacity should be assessed in relation to that treatment, and where they are assessed as lacking capacity s 5 of the MCA will apply.

Section 4A and section 16(2)(a) personal welfare order: Mental Capacity Act 2005

The Court of Protection is able to make a personal welfare order which is, in effect, a form of substituted decision-making for a person who lacks capacity. The court is able to make decisions about where the person is to live, what contact, if any, the person is to have with specified persons, can prevent contact with specified persons, give or refuse consent to carry out or continue treatment, and determine who is responsible for healthcare. The court is able to make decisions that amount to a deprivation of liberty.

Section 4B, life-sustaining treatment, etc.: Mental Capacity Act 2005

A patient may be treated in circumstances that amount to a deprivation of their liberty provided that the deprivation is wholly or partly for the purpose of giving life-sustaining treatment, or treatment to prevent a serious deterioration in the person's condition, and that it is necessary to deprive the person of their liberty to give such treatment. Such treatment can only be given in these circumstances while a decision is sought from the Court of Protection.

Common law doctrine of necessity

The common law and the circumstances in which it may be used are detailed above. Arguably, the common law may also be used in circumstances that amount to a deprivation of a person's liberty for a short period, in cases of urgency where there is not enough time to operate specific legislative provision. The length of time that common law may be relied upon is not clear. The case of *HL v UK* (2005) stated that the use of common law to detain HL for a period of approximately three months was too long, but did not state what would have been an acceptable period. Since then, in the case of *Sessay v South London & Maudsley NHS Foundation Trust, Commissioner of Police for the Metropolis* (2011), the undue delay in assessing Sessay, having been taken to a place of safety by police (who purported to have acted under the MCA), amounted to an unlawful deprivation of liberty. Sessay was unlawfully detained for 13 hours before being lawfully detained under s 2 of the MHA. Each case of deprivation of liberty will be assessed on its facts; in any event it should be for the minimum time, and accompanied by the minimum restrictions necessary to achieve the legitimate objective.

Accommodation (amounting to a restriction of movement)

Section 7, guardianship: Mental Health Act 1983

Guardianship may be used for patients who have a mental disorder, who have attained the age of 16 and who meet the criteria set out in s 7(2), detailed above. Section 8 of the Act allows the guardian only three specific powers in relation to the patient: the power to require the patient to reside in a specified place; the power to require the patient to attend at places and times for the purpose of medical treatment, occupation, education or training; and the power to require access to the patient to be given, at any place where he or she is residing to any doctor, Approved Mental Health Professional (AMHP) or other specified person.

The requirement of residence is not seen by the Government as permitting the lawful deprivation of a person's liberty. However, the Act itself does not state this, but the case of *NL v Hampshire County Council* (2014) helped clarify the relationship between guardianship and deprivation of liberty. Deprivation of liberty is defined as 'continuous supervision *and* control, *and* not free to leave'. Where the power to require the patient to reside in a specified place is imposed, the second element of deprivation of liberty is met, as the patient is not free to leave the place of residence. However, this alone is not sufficient to amount to a deprivation of liberty; the person must also be under continuous supervision and control. Decision-makers must therefore establish: first, is there a requirement of residence and (if so), second, does the care plan amount to continuous supervision and control. Where these two elements are answered in the positive and the patient lacks capacity to consent to the arrangements, guardianship alone cannot be relied upon and a lawful means of deprivation of liberty must be sought.

Guardianship does have some limitations. While a person can be conveyed to the place of residence in the first instance, and be returned if they leave with the intention of not returning, it cannot be used as a means of stopping vulnerable people from leaving the place of residence on a day-to-day basis. (Although it is worth noting that DOLS is also limited as it lacks specific powers of conveyance, only allowing a deprivation of liberty in a specific establishment.) The ability to require a guardianship patient to attend places does not give the authority to convey them, or to enforce engagement in an activity when they do attend. For example, while a person may be required to attend for the purpose of medical treatment, there is no authority to treat them once there. Any treatment would be administered on the basis of a capacitated consent, or under s 5 of the MCA where the person lacked capacity. Similarly, the power to gain access does not permit forced access. Forced entry in the face of a refusal would be a trespass unless authorised by a warrant under s 135 of the MHA (obtained from a Magistrates' Court) or under the provisions of the Police and Criminal Evidence Act 1984.

Community treatment order (CTO), non-mandatory condition: Mental Health Act 1983

A responsible clinician is able, with the initial agreement of an AMHP, to set non-mandatory conditions as part of a patient's CTO. Any conditions may be set provided that they are necessary or appropriate to ensure that the patient receives medical treatment, to prevent risk of harm to the patient's health or safety, or to protect others. This may include the requirement of residence in a specified place. However, there are limited enforcement powers. The patient's responsible clinician is only able to recall a patient to hospital if they break a mandatory condition (the requirement of residence is not a mandatory condition) or where the patient requires medical treatment in hospital for his or her mental disorder and there would be a risk of harm to the health or safety of the patient or to other persons if the patient were not recalled for treatment. Given the limited powers to impose non-mandatory conditions and limited ability of the responsible clinician to recall patients, CTOs may not provide a robust requirement of residence to those who do not wish to comply. In this case, guardianship could provide a more effective means of imposing a condition of residence.

Section 17: leave requirements under Mental Health Act 1983

The responsible clinician, when granting a patient leave of absence from hospital, may impose conditions of residence. This is not necessarily granted in a way that places the person in the custody of another and therefore, although the patient remains 'liable to be detained', may be seen as a restriction of movement rather than a deprivation of liberty. It is of some interest to note that such a patient could then either be made subject to DOLS (as long as this did not conflict with the residence requirement) or the responsible clinician could place the patient in someone's custody.

Section 16: Mental Capacity Act 2005

Section 16 of the MCA allows the Court of Protection to make a personal welfare order, detailed above. A personal welfare order may stipulate that a person must live in a specified place.

Accommodation (amounting to a deprivation of liberty)

Deprivation of Liberty Safeguards (DOLS): Mental Capacity Act 2005 (as amended by the MHA 2007)

The Deprivation of Liberty Safeguards allow for the lawful deprivation of liberty of a person within a hospital or care home setting for the purpose of being given care or treatment, provided that they meet the criteria detailed above. However, DOLS do not give authority to provide the actual care or treatment to a detained resident. The capacitated consent of the resident, or s 5 of the MCA (where the person lacks capacity to consent) could be relied upon to provide any necessary care or treatment. Chapter 7 above discusses s 5 acts.

Section 17: leave requirements under Mental Health Act 1983

The responsible clinician, when granting a patient leave of absence from hospital, may place them in the custody of someone else. This could be in another hospital, care home or other establishment and could amount to deprivation of liberty.

Section 16: Mental Capacity Act 2005

The Court of Protection has the ability to make a personal welfare order, detailed above. Any order made under this section compelling a person to reside in a specified place would comply with Article 5 of the ECHR.

Sometimes one Act or provision alone will not meet the needs of an individual. For example, a patient may be detained and treated under the MHA for mental disorder, but that Act does not allow for the treatment of physical ill health unrelated to mental disorder. In this case, any treatment for physical ill health must have a separate authority. The separate authority could be the consent of the patient, where they have capacity to consent (and have consented), or s 5 of the MCA where they are assessed as lacking the capacity to consent and the treatment is considered to be in their best interests. There are some provisions, such as these, that may operate together, and others that are prevented from operating together; some examples of this interface are detailed below.

Examples of provisions that can be used together

Detention under the MHA and section 5 of the MCA

As identified above, the MHA does not allow for the treatment of physical health problems unrelated to mental disorder. Therefore, a patient detained under the MHA requiring treatment for physical ill health may be treated under the provision of s 5 of the MCA provided that they lacked capacity in relation to that treatment decision.

DOLS and section 5 of the MCA

DOLS merely provides for the lawful detention of a person within a hospital or care home setting. It does not authorise the giving of care or treatment. Therefore, s 5 of the MCA could be used to authorise care or treatment where the person is assessed as lacking the capacity to consent. Where a person has capacity in relation to a treatment decision, s 5 of the MCA will not apply and they are entitled to make their own decision; sometimes this might require consideration of the compulsory powers of the MHA.

DOLS and CTO

In theory, these provisions can operate together. An example would be where a patient has a number of non-mandatory CTO conditions imposed upon them, including a condition to reside in a residential establishment. The limited enforcement powers of non-mandatory conditions, for example the inability to return a CTO patient to the place of residence specified as a condition, may lead to a decision to impose residence under the DOLS provisions. This would allow the legal enforcement of residence (provided the place of residence is a registered care home), and the imposition of other non-mandatory conditions under the CTO regime. These conditions could include *where and when the patient is to receive treatment in the community . . . and avoidance of known risk factors or high-risk situations relevant to the patient's mental disorder* (Department of Health, 2015, para 29.32). However, there are some potential problems with this approach. First, the MHA Code of Practice (para 29.33) suggests that patients agree to keep to the conditions; agreement would suggest capacity, in which case the patient may be ineligible for DOLS. Second, the principles of both the MHA and MCA require consideration of less restrictive principles, and CTO conditions must not amount to a deprivation of liberty, and so clear justification for both provisions would be necessary.

DOLS and guardianship

On the basis that guardianship is not recognised (by the Government or courts) as a lawful means of deprivation of liberty, a person subject to guardianship (in circumstances that amount to a deprivation of liberty) may also be made subject to DOLS, which would then provide a lawful means of depriving someone of their liberty. This may only happen where the place of residence determined under DOLS does not conflict with the place of residence determined by the guardian. While in some circumstances DOLS alone may be sufficient to meet a person's need of residence, it may be appropriate to maintain guardianship in addition to DOLS to enforce the other powers of guardianship, the powers of attendance and access, which DOLS does not provide for. However, in these circumstances the MHA Code of Practice (para 30.32) requires local authorities to consider whether the need for guardianship remains, in light of the least restrictive option and maximising independence principle.

DOLS and section 17 leave of absence (MHA)

This combination may be used where a person is to be deprived of their liberty (under the DOLS procedure) within a residential care establishment following a period of detention under the MHA. Section 17 leave of absence may be a good means of ensuring that the person gets to the place where they will be required to reside (under the DOLS procedure). This would resolve any issue of conveyance, as DOLS does not have an explicit power to convey a person to the place in which they are required to reside. This may seem a strange use of DOLS given that s 17 could authorise a deprivation of liberty.

Examples of provisions that cannot be used together

Detention under the MHA and section 7, guardianship

Section 8(5) of the MHA prevents a patient being liable to detention and guardianship at the same time.

DOLS and actual detention under the MHA

Schedule 1A prevents a person being made subject to DOLS while detained in a hospital under the MHA. That said, once a person is subject to DOLS, but requires compulsory treatment for mental disorder under the MHA, they may be detained for up to 28 days, with DOLS suspended in the meantime. If a person ceases to be detained within the 28 days they remain subject to DOLS; if, however, their detention exceeds 28 days the DOLS authorisation expires and fresh assessments would be required if DOLS were needed after the period of detention under the MHA.

DOLS and guardianship

Schedule 1A prevents DOLS and guardianship operating together where there is a conflict between the DOLS procedure and the guardian regarding the place of residence. However, in the absence of such a conflict these provisions can operate together (see above).

Choice of Act

The Code of Practice to the MCA offers some guidance about the relationship between the MCA and the MHA. It aims to help those making a choice between the legal frameworks, albeit with strong encouragement to use the less restrictive framework of the MCA. For example, para 13.20 states:

> decision-makers must never consider guardianship as a way to avoid applying the MCA

and para 13.11 suggests that it might be unlawful to use the MHA if the MCA could safely be used. Chapter 13 of the Code goes on to state at pages 225 and 226:

> Professionals may need to think about using the MHA to detain and treat somebody who lacks capacity to consent to treatment (rather than use the MCA), if:
>
> - it is not possible to give the person the care or treatment they need without doing something that might deprive them of their liberty
>
> - the person needs treatment that cannot be given under the MCA (for example, because the person had made a valid and applicable advance decision to refuse an essential part of treatment)
>
> - the person may need to be restrained in a way that is not allowed under the MCA
>
> - it is not possible to assess or treat the person safely or effectively without treatment being compulsory (perhaps because the person is expected to regain capacity to consent, but might then refuse to give consent)
>
> - the person lacks capacity to decide on some elements of the treatment but has capacity to refuse a vital part of it – and they have done so, or
>
> - there is some other reason why the person might not get treatment, and they or somebody else might suffer harm as a result.
>
> Before making an application under the MHA, decision-makers should consider whether they could achieve their aims safely and effectively by using the MCA instead.
>
> Compulsory treatment under the MHA is not an option if:
>
> - the patient's mental disorder does not justify detention in hospital, or
>
> - the patient needs treatment only for a physical illness or disability.
>
> The MCA applies to people subject to the MHA in the same way as it applies to anyone else, with four exceptions:
>
> - if someone is detained under the MHA, decision-makers cannot normally rely on the MCA to give treatment for mental disorder or make decisions about that treatment on that person's behalf
>
> - if somebody can be treated for their mental disorder without their consent because they are detained under the MHA, healthcare staff can treat them even if it goes against an advance decision to refuse that treatment

- *if a person is subject to guardianship, the guardian has the exclusive right to take certain decisions, including where the person is to live, and*

- *Independent Mental Capacity Advocates do not have to be involved in decisions about serious medical treatment or accommodation, if those decisions are made under the MHA.*

Chapter 14 of the Code of Practice to the MHA equally encourages the use of the MCA wherever possible, stating at paras 14.11 to 14.13:

In deciding whether it is necessary to detain patients, doctors and AMHPs must always consider the alternative ways of providing the treatment or care they need. Decision-makers should always consider whether there are less restrictive alternatives to detention under the Act, which may include: . . . treatment under the Mental Capacity Act (MCA) if the person lacks capacity to consent to admission and treatment. If a deprivation of liberty occurs, or is likely to occur, either the Act, a DOLS authorisation or a deprivation of liberty order by the Court of Protection must be in place.

In considering whether it is necessary for the person to be detained under the Act, decision-makers must consider whether the person has capacity to consent to or refuse admission and treatment. This should be assessed in accordance with the MCA, which makes clear that a person must be assumed to have capacity unless it is established that they do not.

Professionals must consider available alternatives, having regard to all the relevant circumstances, to identify the least restrictive way of best achieving the proposed assessment or treatment. This will include considering what is the person's best interests (if the person lacks capacity, this will be determined in accordance with the MCA).

In essence, Government guidance promotes the use of the MCA rather than the MHA wherever possible. However, the following facts may lead to a decision to rely upon the MHA in preference to the MCA.

Examples of when the MCA may not be relied upon

- Where a person has made a valid and applicable advance decision refusing treatment for mental disorder. Detention under the MHA (to which Part 4 of that Act applies) will enable the advance decision to be overridden if necessary, having considered competing human rights. However, an advance decision refusing ECT may not be overridden unless the treatment is immediately necessary to save the patient's life or (not being irreversible) is immediately necessary to prevent a serious deterioration of his or her condition. The same applies where a patient has appointed an attorney: the attorney may not consent to or refuse treatment that is governed by Part 4 of the Mental Health Act.

- Restraint is necessary which goes beyond that provided for in s 6 of the MCA. For example, a patient needs restraining to prevent harm to others when unwell.

- The patient is expected to regain capacity (perhaps once treatment starts) and might then refuse treatment. Once capacity is regained the MCA can no longer be relied upon, therefore detention under the MHA will allow continued treatment regardless of capacity. This may also apply where a person has fluctuating capacity, but not to the extent that a decision can be reached that they lack capacity.

- The person has a mental disorder, but retains capacity to refuse some or all of the necessary treatment. In which case the MCA does not apply.

- Where a person is already detained under the MHA, s 28 of the MCA prevents treatment for mental disorder from being given under the MCA.

- The applicant, when faced with the responsibility under s 13 of the MHA to satisfy him or herself that detention in a hospital is in all the circumstances of the case the most appropriate way of providing the care and treatment the patient needs, considers that the protections contained within the MHA provide better human rights safeguards to the patient, and therefore is the most appropriate way of providing care and treatment.

- Note that s 3(2) of the MHA requires that treatment *cannot be provided unless he is detained under this section*. Therefore, if treatment could be provided under the MCA, it would be difficult to justify the treatment under s 3 of the MHA.

Table 17.3 might help decision-makers identify which Act is applicable.

Table 17.3 Acts applicable in particular circumstances

Issue	Mental Capacity Act	Mental Health Act
Age	The person is aged 16 or over (18 or over for DOLS).	There are no age limits to detention (although a person must have attained the age of 16 for guardianship).
Capacity	The person lacks capacity to consent to care or treatment.	The person has capacity in relation to the decision (or lacks capacity but is likely to regain capacity during treatment).
Restraint	The person requires restraint to prevent harm to self (the MCA does not allow for restraint to prevent harm to others).	The person requires restraint to prevent harm to self or others.
Treatment	Treatment can be provided for physical or mental ill health, (however, s 28 MCA prevents treatment for mental disorder from being given to patients detained under a section of the MHA to which Part 4 of that Act applies).	Treatment may only be given for mental disorder or physical ill health related to the mental disorder. Where treatment for physical ill health (unrelated to mental disorder) is required, this can be given on the basis of a capacitous consent, or under the MCA where the person lacks capacity and treatment is in their best interests.

(Continued)

129

Table 17.3 (Continued)

Issue	Mental Capacity Act	Mental Health Act
Establishment	Care or treatment may be provided to an incapable person in their own home, a supported living environment, a registered care home or a hospital under s 5 of the MCA, provided the care and treatment does not amount to a deprivation of liberty. Care or treatment amounting to deprivation of liberty in a registered care home or a hospital may be authorised by DOLS, or in a home or supported living arrangement by the Court of Protection.	Care and treatment may be provided to a mentally disordered person in the community or in a hospital. Care and treatment in the community should not generally amount to a deprivation of liberty, for example under guardianship or a community treatment order. Care and treatment in a hospital may be provided to a capacitous consenting patient irrespective of whether the care and treatment amounts to a restriction of movement or a deprivation of liberty. However, where the person lacks capacity to consent to care or treatment it may be provided under a combination of s 131 of the MHA and s 5 of the MCA where it does not amount to a deprivation of liberty. Where care and treatment in a hospital amounts to a deprivation of liberty, either detention under the MHA or a DOLS authorisation will be required. See below.

Care or treatment in a hospital amounting to deprivation of liberty

As set out above, a DOLS authorisation or MHA detention may be used in certain circumstances to provide a lawful means of deprivation of liberty in a hospital. This situation leaves a choice between Acts; the following information sets out the potential problem areas, and the guidance offered to decision-makers when making this choice.

The two sets of circumstances that present potential confusion concern: first, the incapable person with mental and physical ill health that requires treatment in hospital (amounting to deprivation of liberty) and, second, the passive, incapable person requiring treatment in a hospital for mental disorder (amounting to deprivation of liberty). Both sets of circumstances have been before the court and, as a result, the judgments help direct professional decision-making. In both sets of circumstances, the eligibility requirement of DOLS must be considered. In short, the decision-makers must answer the following three questions:

- Does the person have a mental disorder requiring treatment in a hospital?

- Does the person meet the detention criteria for s 2 or 3 of the MHA?

- Is the person objecting (past or present) to all or part of their treatment?

Where these three questions are answered in the positive, the MHA must be used, as the person becomes ineligible for DOLS. However, where one or more of the questions are answered in the negative, the person is not ineligible for DOLS and therefore a choice between Acts emerges. In the first of the potential areas for confusion identified above, the case of *GJ* (2009) helped clarify which Act should be used in the case of a person with both physical and mental ill health. GJ lacked capacity to make decisions about his care and treatment, and was deprived of his liberty under a DOLS authorisation in a psychiatric hospital. He suffers with vascular dementia and Korsakoff's syndrome (both mental disorders) and poorly controlled diabetes (a physical illness unconnected with, and not caused by, his mental disorders). His mental and physical ill health were therefore separate, and so the reason for GJ's detention had to be established. The 'but for' test was adopted; in short, the question posed was, but for his physical ill health did his mental disorder require treatment in hospital? In this case, the need for detention arose as a result of GJ's physical ill health, and therefore the first of the three questions above was answered in the negative, which meant that GJ was not ineligible for DOLS, and therefore the standard authorisation was not unlawful. Where mental and physical ill health are viewed as separate, it follows that the MHA is used to authorise deprivation of liberty for the purpose of providing treatment for mental disorder, and the MCA DOLS regime is used where care and treatment for physical ill health amounts to deprivation of liberty.

In the second of the potential areas for confusion, the case of *AM v SLAM* (2013) helped clarify which Act should be used in the case of a passive, incapable person deprived of their liberty in a hospital for treatment of mental disorder. AM was detained under s 2 of the MHA (which was continuing under s 29 of the MHA), and the Tribunal was to decide whether s 2 of the MHA should be discharged and her assessment continued under the MCA.

It was agreed that AM required ongoing assessment and treatment in hospital for mental disorder; however, she was not objecting, and therefore the third of the three questions above was answered in the negative, and as a result she was not ineligible for DOLS. As AM's care and treatment was for mental disorder the MHA could be used, as could the MCA DOLS regime. To determine which Act should be used, the 'necessary', 'warranted' and 'less restrictive' test was applied. The first of these two words mirror the language of s 2 and s 72 of the MHA, and 'less restrictive' is integral to the principles of both Acts. The balancing of the relevant factors was therefore necessary to promote the best interests of AM in the less restrictive way. In this case, use of the MCA was viewed as less restrictive as the MHA was seen as carrying a stigma, and more restrictive, for example, *in respect of family visits or to the community* (para 65). However, it is not to be assumed that the MCA DOLS regime will always be the correct choice. The case of *AM v SLAM* highlighted that *there may be cases in which a compliant incapacitated person may properly and lawfully be admitted, assessed or treated and detained under Part II MHA when he or she could be assessed or treated pursuant to s 131 MHA and ss 5 and 6 MCA and be the subject of the DOLS* (para 68). Therefore, decision-makers faced with a passive, incapable person requiring assessment or treatment in a hospital for mental disorder in circumstances that amount to deprivation of liberty must consider whether the MHA is necessary, warranted and less restrictive.

The Code of Practice to the MHA offers guidance when faced with a choice between Acts, stating at paras 13.58 and 13.59:

- *The choice of legal regime should never be based on a general preference for one regime or the other, or because one regime is more familiar to the decision-maker than the other. Such considerations are not legally relevant and lead to arbitrary decision-making. In addition, decision-makers should not proceed on the basis that one regime is generally less restrictive than the other. Both regimes are based on the need to impose as few restrictions on the liberty and autonomy of patients as possible. In the particular circumstances of an individual case, it may be apparent that one regime is likely to prove less restrictive. If so, this should be balanced against any potential benefits associated with the other regime.*

- *Both regimes provide appropriate procedural safeguards to ensure the rights of the person concerned are protected during their detention. Decision-makers should not therefore proceed on the basis that one regime generally provides greater safeguards than the other. However, the nature of the safeguards provided under the two regimes are different and decision-makers will wish to exercise their professional judgement in determining which safeguards are more likely to best protect the interests of the patient in the particular circumstances of each individual case.*

This guidance is, however, potentially open to question. The first of the points deters the decision-maker from proceeding on the basis that one regime is generally less restrictive than another (which seems at odds with *AM v SLAM* (2013), above), and the second argues that both regimes provide appropriate procedural safeguards. Both statements might be refuted on the basis of the greater safeguards afforded to a patient detained under the MHA; for example, the nearest relative and the treatment safeguards, the entitlement to s 117 aftercare for those detained under ss 3, 37, 45A, 47 and 48 MHA (not available to those detained under DOLS), and the availability of an appeal to hospital managers and the Mental Health Tribunal (with automatic reference to the Mental Health Tribunal in certain circumstances), again not available to those subject to DOLS). Decision-makers must, however, clearly state their rationale for choosing one regime over the other.

Key points

- The MCA allows for the care or treatment (for physical illness or mental disorder) of incapacitated people in their best interests.

- The MHA allows for informal and compulsory treatment of mental disorder.

- Different criteria apply to the different sections of the MCA and MHA.

- Making the distinction between restriction of movement and deprivation of liberty is essential in determining which Act or provision may lawfully be used.

- The mental capacity of individuals must be assessed, as the outcome of the assessment will determine which Act or provision may lawfully be used.

- The MCA and MHA are not mutually exclusive. Some provisions of the Acts may be used together. However, some provisions are prevented from operating together.

- When detained under the MCA or MHA the patient has the right to a legal challenge to the detention.

- Government guidance tends to advocate the use of the MCA rather than the MHA where possible.

Chapter 18

The distinction between restriction of movement and deprivation of liberty

Introduction

The European Convention on Human Rights (ECHR) is partly incorporated into English law by the Human Rights Act 1998. One of the Articles so incorporated is Article 5, and as a result it is necessary to draw a distinction between restriction of movement and deprivation of liberty. Restricting a person's movement may be lawful in many circumstances, whereas depriving a person of their liberty is unlawful unless it complies with the requirements of Article 5, the Right to Liberty and Security. This distinction becomes relevant whenever care or treatment is to be provided under the Mental Capacity Act 2005 (MCA) or the Mental Health Act 1983 (MHA) because both statutes contain specific provisions which authorise deprivation of liberty. This chapter will explain Article 5 of the ECHR and will consider some of the relevant case law. It will give further detail on why it is necessary to make the distinction between restriction of movement and deprivation of liberty, and set out the guidance available to professionals when making this distinction in practice.

Article 5 of the ECHR and related case law

Article 5 of the ECHR, the Right to Liberty and Security, has two essential elements concerned with deprivation of liberty. Article 5 of the ECHR states:

> *Everyone has the right to liberty and security of person. No one shall be deprived of his liberty save in the following cases and in accordance with a procedure prescribed by law: . . . (e) the lawful detention of persons . . . of unsound mind.* (Article 5(1))

> *Everyone who is deprived of his liberty by arrest or detention shall be entitled to take proceedings by which the lawfulness of his detention shall be decided speedily by a court and his release ordered if the detention is not lawful.* (Article 5(4)).

The Winterwerp judgment (*Winterwerp v Netherlands*, 1979) established that any deprivation of liberty must satisfy the following criteria if it is to comply with Article 5(1) (e):

- there is objective medical expertise establishing a true mental disorder (except in emergencies);

- the mental disorder must be of a kind or degree warranting compulsory confinement;

- the validity of continued confinement depends upon the persistence of mental disorder.

It is clear that detention must comply with Article 5 of the ECHR to be lawful. However, drawing the distinction between restriction of movement and deprivation of liberty is difficult, and the law in relation to this distinction has changed over time. Those providing care or treatment to incapacitated adults must consider the question: is a deprivation of liberty occurring, or likely to occur? If they answer yes, they must ensure that the deprivation of liberty meets the above Article 5 requirements. If, however, they consider that the care and treatment falls short of a deprivation of liberty (constituting a mere restriction of movement) Article 5 becomes largely irrelevant.

For a deprivation of liberty to be occurring the following must be met:

- the objective component of the confinement in a particular restricted place for a not negligible length of time (deprivation of liberty);

- the subjective component of lack of valid consent; and

- the attribution of responsibility to the state (*Storck v Germany* (2005), paras 74 and 89).

The following case assists in determining whether the first of these three elements is met, in that a test for deprivation of liberty is given.

P v Cheshire West and Chester; P & Q v Surrey County Council (2014)

This case concerns the criteria for judging whether the living arrangements for mentally incapable people amount to a deprivation of liberty. P is an adult male born with cerebral palsy and Down's syndrome, and a history of cerebral vascular accidents. P lives in a bungalow with 24-hour care arranged by the local authority as he lacks the mental capacity to make decisions about his care and residence. The circumstances in which P lives are detailed below:

- P's room and nearby bathrooms are personalised to his needs;

- P receives one-to-one supervision during the day;

- P attends a day centre four days a week, and a hydrotherapy pool one day a week (with one-to-one staffing);

- P goes to a club, the pub, and sees his mother regularly;

- P can walk short distances but needs a wheelchair to go further;

- P requires prompting and assistance for activities of daily living (e.g. eating, personal hygiene and continence);

- intervention is needed to manage challenging behaviours;

- P wears a body suit to stop him accessing and ingesting his continence pads; and

- finger sweeping is used to remove matter from his mouth when he ingests pieces of his continence pads.

By 2014, this case had been before the courts twice; first the Court of Protection in 2011 before Baker J who concluded (paras 118–20):

> *his life is completely under the control of members of staff . . . He cannot go anywhere or do anything without their support and assistance. More specifically, his occasionally aggressive behaviour, and his worrying habit of touching and eating continence pads, require a range of measures, including at times physical restraint and when necessary, the intrusive procedure of inserting fingers into his mouth whilst being restrained . . . the steps required to deal with his challenging behaviour lead to a clear conclusion, looked at overall, P is being deprived of his liberty.*

This decision was in keeping with the approach adopted in the case of *HL v UK* (2005), in which the exercise of 'complete and effective control' over HL's care and movements was regarded as a deprivation of liberty. However, the second occasion on which the case of P came before the court, Munby LJ in the Court of Appeal concluded that P was not deprived of his liberty. Munby LJ introduced the 'relevant comparator' test; essentially a comparison was to be made with an *adult of similar age, with the same capabilities and affected by the same condition or suffering the same inherent mental and physical disabilities* (para 86). If, having made that comparison, the care and treatment being provided was considered 'normal' for people who are inherently restricted by their condition, a deprivation was unlikely to occur. But in 2014 this judgment was overruled by the Supreme Court in the case of *Cheshire West* and *P & Q*. The tests of 'relevant comparator' and 'relative normality' were viewed as discriminatory, affording differing levels of liberty dependent upon the differing characteristics of individuals. A new 'acid test' of deprivation of liberty was established, to be applied to all regardless of mental or physical disability.

Deprivation of liberty

When assessing whether a deprivation of liberty is occurring, decision-makers should establish whether the care and treatment regime the individual is subject to amounts to continuous/complete supervision *and* control, *and* that the person would not be free to leave. If all elements of this test are met, the person lacks capacity to consent to the arrangements, and the state is involved, a deprivation of liberty is occurring.

Establishing the presence of deprivation of liberty, a practice guide

Are the following present?	Guidance
Deprivation of liberty (continuous/ complete supervision *and* control, *and* not free to leave) . . .	Ask whether the person(s) or body responsible for the individual has a plan which means that they need always broadly to know: • where the individual is; and • what they are doing at any one time. If 'yes' to both, this is a strong pointer to continuous/complete supervision, and control (Law Society, 2015, page 26). See below in relation to those aged under 18. In relation to 'not free to leave', focus on the actions or potential actions of those providing care, not the individual. For example, what would those providing care do should the person or the person supported by a member of their family leave the place of residence? If attempts would be made to return the person, this is a strong indicator that the person is not free to leave.
for a not negligible length of time	This is difficult to define. In the case of *HL v UK* three months was considered too long in the absence of an authority; in the case of *Sessay* (2011), 12 hours of detention in a psychiatric hospital amounted to a deprivation of liberty; and in the case of *ZH* (2013) 40 minutes of police intervention and restraint amounted to deprivation of liberty.
a lack of valid consent	Is the person unable to make a decision because of an impairment of, or disturbance in, the functioning of the mind or brain? See Chapter 5 and Appendix 7 for more information in relation to the test for incapacity.
responsibility to the state	This is not clearly defined, but will include involvement of a public authority, and may include those self-funding, and utilising direct payments for residential accommodation in an establishment inspected by the state. See the Law Society's *Identifying a Deprivation of Liberty: A Practical Guide* (2015) for more information.

Where all the above elements are met, and there is no way of reducing the restrictions to avoid a deprivation of liberty, a lawful means of deprivation of liberty must be found. Where there is uncertainty about the existence of deprivation of liberty, Lady Hale urged that professionals should 'err on the side of caution' in deciding what constitutes deprivation of liberty.

Deprivation of liberty: aged under 18

A DOLS authorisation is not available to those aged under 18. Therefore, authority for deprivation of liberty for those aged 16 and 17 must be sought from the Court of Protection or via the Mental Health Act 1983. Under the MCA, the courts will therefore determine whether a 16- or 17-year-old is deprived of their liberty and, if so, whether it is in their best interests. Guidance from the Law Society suggested *the test for deprivation of liberty is more nuanced when it comes to this age group because children and young persons are compared with those of the same age and maturity* (2015, page 95). Therefore, the concepts of 'relevant comparator' and 'relative normality' may be helpful in determining whether the care and treatment of a 16- or 17-year-old amounts to deprivation of liberty. The following guidance is offered by the Law Society when making this decision:

> *These questions may help establish whether an individual is deprived of their liberty in this context:*
>
> - *Compared to another person of the same age and relative maturity who is not disabled, how much greater is the intensity of the supervision, support, and restrictions?*
>
> - *Can the person go out of the establishment without the carer's permission? Can they spend nights away? How do the arrangements differ to the norm for someone of their age who is not disabled?*
>
> - *To what extent is the person able to control his or her own finances? How does this differ to the norm for someone of the same age who is not disabled?*
>
> - *Can the person choose what to wear outside school hours and buy his or her own clothes?*
>
> - *To what extent do the rules and sanctions differ from non-disabled age appropriate settings?*
>
> - *Are there regular private times, where the person has no direct carer supervision?*
>
> - *What is the carer to person ratio and how different is this to what would usually be expected of someone of that age who is not disabled?*
>
> - *Is physical intervention used? If so, what type? How long for? And what effect does it have on the person?*
>
> - *Is medication with a sedative effect used? If so, what type? How often? And what effect does it have on the person?*
>
> - *How structured is the person's routine compared with someone of the same age and relative maturity who is not disabled?*
>
> - *To what extent is contact with the outside world restricted?*

This guidance is however limited to those aged 16 and 17 who fall within the jurisdiction of the Court of Protection. Where a deprivation is, or may occur in relation to a child below the age of 16, or those aged 16 and over who lack capacity resulting from immaturity (outside the scope of ss 2 and 3 of the MCA) an application to the High Court should be considered. Decision-makers concerned with those under the age of 16 should also consider the case of *Trust A and X, A local authority, Y and Z* (2015), in which the accommodation of a 15-year-old male with mental disorder within a psychiatric hospital would have amounted to deprivation of liberty, had it not been for the consent of his parents. The decision suggests that the placing of a child in an environment where they will be subject to restrictions upon their life falls within the scope of parental responsibility. This consent negates a deprivation of liberty. What falls within the scope of parental responsibility was held to by the court to differ according to the disabilities and therefore needs of the child; i.e. the comparator is a child with, rather than free from, disabilities, and therefore the decision is arguably inconsistent with *Chester v West*.

Why is the distinction relevant to practice?

The distinction between restriction of movement and deprivation of liberty will, in many cases, need to be made by those wishing to provide care or treatment under the provisions of the MCA, MHA or in cases of urgency, the common law doctrine of necessity. The following table gives examples of circumstances in which those providing care or treatment will need to draw this distinction.

Table 18.1 The need to make a distinction between restriction of movement and deprivation of liberty

Mental Capacity Act 2005	Mental Health Act 1983
• Section 5 Acts are only lawful where the care or treatment being provided amounts to a mere restriction of movement.	• Detention under the Act provides a lawful means of deprivation of liberty.
• DOLS can only be authorised when an individual's care or treatment amounts to a deprivation of liberty.	• Where a person lacks capacity to consent to admission to hospital for treatment, and that treatment would amount to a deprivation of liberty, they must be detained, rather than being admitted informally.
• Treatment authorised under s 4B can only be given where deprivation of liberty is considered necessary to give life-sustaining treatment or prevent a serious deterioration in the person's condition.	• Section 7 (guardianship) is viewed by the Government as allowing a restriction of movement, not a deprivation of liberty.
• The Court of Protection may make a personal welfare order under s 16 which may amount to deprivation of liberty.	

Note that there will be no breach of Article 5(1) where deprivation of liberty is not occurring.

The Mental Capacity Act 2005

The MCA is largely concerned with those aged 16 and over who lack, or may lack, capacity to make their own decisions. The MCA provisions detailed above, other than the Court of Protection, require those making decisions about care or treatment to draw the distinction between restriction of movement and deprivation of liberty. Section 5 of the Act allows decision-makers to provide care or treatment in the best interests of a person, provided that the care or treatment amounts to a mere restriction of a person's movement. Care or treatment that amounts to a deprivation of liberty cannot be authorised under this section, and if challenged would be unlawful. In contrast, an authorisation of deprivation of liberty under the Deprivation of Liberty Safeguards (DOLS) may only be granted where a best interests assessor establishes that deprivation of liberty exists, or is going to occur. (See Chapter 16 for more information.) Similarly, decision-makers are only authorised to administer life-sustaining treatment, or treatment to prevent a serious deterioration in the person's condition under s 4B, where they are satisfied that deprivation of liberty is considered necessary to give that treatment. The Court of Protection is able to make personal welfare decisions which may, or may not, amount to deprivation of liberty. (See Chapter 12 for more information.)

The Mental Health Act 1983

Detention under the MHA authorises a deprivation of liberty which complies with Article 5 of the ECHR, as the process of detention is set out in statute. Those detained are entitled to appeal to a Tribunal (which is able to discharge detention) which complies with the requirements of Article 5(4). While the MHA allows for detention, the spirit of the Act is to use compulsory powers as a last resort (see s 131, s 13 and the principles). Consideration of informal admission forms part of the assessment process, and should be facilitated wherever appropriate. However, the outcome of *HL v UK* (2005) established that the admission of an incapacitated person, whose care or treatment amounts to deprivation of liberty, must now be formalised to ensure compliance with Article 5 of the ECHR.

Guardianship may be used for those aged 16 and over, and allows the guardian to impose requirements upon a person, including the requirement of residence. The Government takes the view that guardianship allows for a restriction of movement but not a deprivation of liberty. This view was subsequently supported in *NL v Hampshire CC* (2014). While the requirement of residence meets one element of the 'acid test' for deprivation of liberty (not free to leave), a deprivation of liberty will not be occurring unless the requirements of the care plan result in complete and effective control. Where both elements are met, a lawful means of deprivation of liberty must be sought and this could sit alongside guardianship.

Common law doctrine of necessity

Common law may be relied upon (for a short period) to provide care or treatment to an incapacitated person where relying upon legislative provisions would cause an undesirable delay, provided that any restrictions are proportionate to the risks posed to the individual or others, constitute the minimum intervention necessary to sustain life or prevent a deterioration in his or her condition, and are for the minimum period necessary. It may also be relevant in some circumstances to intervene in the case of a vulnerable adult who falls outside the statutory provisions. (See *Re SA* (2006).)

Decision-making

Before setting out to establish whether or not a person is deprived of their liberty, professionals must first ask themselves whether the person lacks capacity to make their own decision about the circumstances in which care or treatment is to be provided. A person is presumed to have capacity, and this presumption can only be displaced if the decision-maker has applied the correct test for incapacity, and established that the person meets that test. The legal test for incapacity is set out within ss 2 and 3 of the MCA and is discussed in Chapter 5. Where a person has capacity, they are permitted to make their own decisions about the way in which care or treatment is, or is not to be provided. However, where a person is assessed as lacking capacity, the distinction between restriction of movement and deprivation of liberty must be made, as this distinction will determine which Act(s) or provision(s) are available to meet their needs. The ECHR and UK courts have determined a number of cases about deprivation of liberty, and the Government has issued guidance to assist those making this distinction in practice (see below).

- *The DoLS are part of the MCA and as such are rooted in the MCA's five statutory principles. The DoLS only apply to individuals who lack the capacity to consent to accommodation in a care home or hospital where care and/or treatment provided in that accommodation amounts (or is likely to amount) to a deprivation of liberty.*

- *A DoLS authorisation does not in itself authorise care or treatment, only the deprivation of liberty that results from the implementation of the proposed care plan. Any necessary care or treatment should be provided in accordance with the MCA.*

- *When considering whether to apply for a DoLS authorisation, decision-makers should first assess the capacity of the person to consent to the arrangements for their care or treatment, in accordance with the MCA.*

- *Next, decision-makers should consider whether the circumstances of the proposed accommodation and treatment amount (or are likely to amount) to a deprivation of liberty. Consideration must also be given at this stage to whether the patient's care plan can be amended to avoid any potential deprivation of liberty.*

- *The precise scope of the term 'deprivation of liberty' is not fixed. In its 19 March judgment P v Cheshire West and Chester Council and another and P and Q v Surrey County Council ('Cheshire West'), the Supreme Court clarified that there is a deprivation of liberty in circumstances where a person is under continuous control and supervision, is not free to leave and lacks capacity to consent to these arrangements.*

- *The Supreme Court also noted that factors which are not relevant in determining whether there is a deprivation of liberty include the person's compliance or lack of objection and the reason or purpose behind a particular placement. The relative normality of the placement (whatever the comparison made) is also not relevant.*

- *A deprivation of liberty can occur in domestic settings where the state is responsible for such arrangements. In such cases, an order should be sought from the Court of Protection.*

- *The definition of a deprivation of liberty develops over time in accordance with the case law of the European Court of Human Rights and UK courts on article 5 of the ECHR. In order for decision-makers to be able to assess whether the situation they are faced with constitutes (or is likely to constitute) a deprivation of liberty, they should keep abreast of the latest case law developments.*

(Department of Health, 2015)

Conclusion

Those making the distinction will need to apply the 'acid test' and determine whether a deprivation of liberty is, or is likely, to occur. This process is likely to differ dependent on whether an adult, young person or child is being assessed. Where deprivation of liberty is occurring, or likely to occur, an authority is needed; again this will differ dependent on the age of the person, and the environment in which they reside.

It is important to remember that, however well intentioned, any restrictions placed upon an individual are, nevertheless, restrictions which could amount to deprivation of liberty. The fact that restrictions are imposed in the individual's best interests does not preclude a deprivation of liberty.

Key points

- There is a legal test for deprivation of liberty.
- Case law and guidance assists us in making the distinction between restriction of movement and deprivation of liberty.
- The requirements of Article 5 of the ECHR must be met for a deprivation of liberty to be lawful.
- Where a person lacks capacity to make care or treatment decisions, the distinction between restriction of movement and deprivation of liberty must be made, as this will determine which provision(s) and Act(s) may lawfully be used.
- The common law has largely been replaced by the MCA. It may only be relied upon in cases of urgency for a short period or possibly for vulnerable adults who are not covered by the MCA.

Appendix 1
The Mental Capacity Act 2005

Contents

Part 1   Persons who lack capacity

Part 2   The Court of Protection and the Public Guardian

Part 3   Miscellaneous and general

145

Schedules

The Mental Capacity Act 2005

Part 1 Persons who lack capacity

The principles

1 The principles

(1) The following principles apply for the purposes of this Act.

(2) A person must be assumed to have capacity unless it is established that he lacks capacity.

(3) A person is not to be treated as unable to make a decision unless all practicable steps to help him to do so have been taken without success.

(4) A person is not to be treated as unable to make a decision merely because he makes an unwise decision.

(5) An act done, or decision made, under this Act for or on behalf of a person who lacks capacity must be done, or made, in his best interests.

(6) Before the act is done, or the decision is made, regard must be had to whether the purpose for which it is needed can be as effectively achieved in a way that is less restrictive of the person's rights and freedom of action.

Preliminary

2 People who lack capacity

(1) For the purposes of this Act, a person lacks capacity in relation to a matter if at the material time he is unable to make a decision for himself in relation to the matter because of an impairment of, or a disturbance in the functioning of, the mind or brain.

(2) It does not matter whether the impairment or disturbance is permanent or temporary.

(3) A lack of capacity cannot be established merely by reference to –

    (a) a person's age or appearance, or

    (b) a condition of his, or an aspect of his behaviour, which might lead others to make unjustified assumptions about his capacity.

(4) In proceedings under this Act or any other enactment, any question whether a person lacks capacity within the meaning of this Act must be decided on the balance of probabilities.

(5) No power which a person ('D') may exercise under this Act –

    (a) in relation to a person who lacks capacity, or

    (b) where D reasonably thinks that a person lacks capacity, is exercisable in relation to a person under 16.

(6) Subsection (5) is subject to section 18(3).

3   Inability to make decisions

(1) For the purposes of section 2, a person is unable to make a decision for himself if he is unable –

- (a) to understand the information relevant to the decision,
- (b) to retain that information,
- (c) to use or weigh that information as part of the process of making the decision, or
- (d) to communicate his decision (whether by talking, using sign language or any other means).

(2) A person is not to be regarded as unable to understand the information relevant to a decision if he is able to understand an explanation of it given to him in a way that is appropriate to his circumstances (using simple language, visual aids or any other means).

(3) The fact that a person is able to retain the information relevant to a decision for a short period only does not prevent him from being regarded as able to make the decision.

(4) The information relevant to a decision includes information about the reasonably foreseeable consequences of –

- (a) deciding one way or another, or
- (b) failing to make the decision.

4   Best interests

(1) In determining for the purposes of this Act what is in a person's best interests, the person making the determination must not make it merely on the basis of –

- (a) the person's age or appearance, or
- (b) a condition of his, or an aspect of his behaviour, which might lead others to make unjustified assumptions about what might be in his best interests.

(2) The person making the determination must consider all the relevant circumstances and, in particular, take the following steps.

(3) He must consider –

- (a) whether it is likely that the person will at some time have capacity in relation to the matter in question, and
- (b) if it appears likely that he will, when that is likely to be.

(4) He must, so far as reasonably practicable, permit and encourage the person to participate, or to improve his ability to participate, as fully as possible in any act done for him and any decision affecting him.

(5) Where the determination relates to life-sustaining treatment he must not, in considering whether the treatment is in the best interests of the person concerned, be motivated by a desire to bring about his death.

(6) He must consider, so far as is reasonably ascertainable –

- (a) the person's past and present wishes and feelings (and, in particular, any relevant written statement made by him when he had capacity),
- (b) the beliefs and values that would be likely to influence his decision if he had capacity, and
- (c) the other factors that he would be likely to consider if he were able to do so.

(7) He must take into account, if it is practicable and appropriate to consult them, the views of –

- (a) anyone named by the person as someone to be consulted on the matter in question or on matters of that kind,
- (b) anyone engaged in caring for the person or interested in his welfare,

(c) any donee of a lasting power of attorney granted by the person, and

(d) any deputy appointed for the person by the court, as to what would be in the person's best interests and, in particular, as to the matters mentioned in subsection (6).

(8) The duties imposed by subsections (1) to (7) also apply in relation to the exercise of any powers which –

(a) are exercisable under a lasting power of attorney, or

(b) are exercisable by a person under this Act where he reasonably believes that another person lacks capacity.

(9) In the case of an act done, or a decision made, by a person other than the court, there is sufficient compliance with this section if (having complied with the requirements of subsections (1) to (7)) he reasonably believes that what he does or decides is in the best interests of the person concerned.

(10) 'Life-sustaining treatment' means treatment which in the view of a person providing health care for the person concerned is necessary to sustain life.

(11) 'Relevant circumstances' are those –

(a) of which the person making the determination is aware, and

(b) which it would be reasonable to regard as relevant.

4A Restrictions on deprivation of liberty

(1) This Act does not authorise any person ('D') to deprive any other person ('P') of his liberty.

(2) But that is subject to –

(a) the following provisions of this section, and

(b) section 4B.

(3) D may deprive P of his liberty if, by doing so, D is giving effect to a relevant decision of the court.

(4) A relevant decision of the court is a decision made by an order under section 16(2)(a) in relation to a matter concerning P's personal welfare.

(5) D may deprive P of his liberty if the deprivation is authorised by Schedule A1 (hospital and care home residents: deprivation of liberty).

4B Deprivation of liberty necessary for life-sustaining treatment etc.

(1) If the following conditions are met, D is authorised to deprive P of his liberty while a decision as respects any relevant issue is sought from the court.

(2) The first condition is that there is a question about whether D is authorised to deprive P of his liberty under section 4A.

(3) The second condition is that the deprivation of liberty –

(a) is wholly or partly for the purpose of –

(i) giving P life-sustaining treatment, or

(ii) doing any vital act, or

(b) consists wholly or partly of –

(i) giving P life-sustaining treatment, or

(ii) doing any vital act.

(4) The third condition is that the deprivation of liberty is necessary in order to –

(a) give the life-sustaining treatment, or

(b) do the vital act.

(5) A vital act is any act which the person doing it reasonably believes to be necessary to prevent a serious deterioration in P's condition.

5 Acts in connection with care or treatment

(1) If a person ('D') does an act in connection with the care or treatment of another person ('P'), the act is one to which this section applies if –

    (a) before doing the act, D takes reasonable steps to establish whether P lacks capacity in relation to the matter in question, and

    (b) when doing the act, D reasonably believes –

      (i) that P lacks capacity in relation to the matter, and

      (ii) that it will be in P's best interests for the act to be done.

(2) D does not incur any liability in relation to the act that he would not have incurred if P –

    (a) had had capacity to consent in relation to the matter, and

    (b) had consented to D's doing the act.

(3) Nothing in this section excludes a person's civil liability for loss or damage, or his criminal liability, resulting from his negligence in doing the act.

(4) Nothing in this section affects the operation of sections 24 to 26 (advance decisions to refuse treatment).

6 Section 5 acts: limitations

(1) If D does an act that is intended to restrain P, it is not an act to which section 5 applies unless two further conditions are satisfied.

(2) The first condition is that D reasonably believes that it is necessary to do the act in order to prevent harm to P.

(3) The second is that the act is a proportionate response to –

    (a) the likelihood of P's suffering harm, and

    (b) the seriousness of that harm.

(4) For the purposes of this section D restrains P if he –

    (a) uses, or threatens to use, force to secure the doing of an act which P resists, or

    (b) restricts P's liberty of movement, whether or not P resists.

(5) . . .

(6) Section 5 does not authorise a person to do an act which conflicts with a decision made, within the scope of his authority and in accordance with this Part, by –

    (a) a donee of a lasting power of attorney granted by P, or

    (b) a deputy appointed for P by the court.

(7) But nothing in subsection (6) stops a person –

    (a) providing life-sustaining treatment, or

    (b) doing any act which he reasonably believes to be necessary to prevent a serious deterioration in P's condition, while a decision as respects any relevant issue is sought from the court.

7 Payment for necessary goods and services

(1) If necessary goods or services are supplied to a person who lacks capacity to contract for the supply, he must pay a reasonable price for them.

(2) 'Necessary' means suitable to a person's condition in life and to his actual requirements at the time when the goods or services are supplied.

8 Expenditure

(1) If an act to which section 5 applies involves expenditure, it is lawful for D –

    (a) to pledge P's credit for the purpose of the expenditure, and

    (b) to apply money in P's possession for meeting the expenditure.

(2) If the expenditure is borne for P by D, it is lawful for D –

    (a) to reimburse himself out of money in P's possession, or

    (b) to be otherwise indemnified by P.

(3) Subsections (1) and (2) do not affect any power under which (apart from those subsections) a person –

    (a) has lawful control of P's money or other property, and

    (b) has power to spend money for P's benefit.

Lasting powers of attorney

9   Lasting powers of attorney

(1) A lasting power of attorney is a power of attorney under which the donor ('P') confers on the donee (or donees) authority to make decisions about all or any of the following –

    (a) P's personal welfare or specified matters concerning P's personal welfare, and

    (b) P's property and affairs or specified matters concerning P's property and affairs, and which includes authority to make such decisions in circumstances where P no longer has capacity.

(2) A lasting power of attorney is not created unless –

    (a) section 10 is complied with,

    (b) an instrument conferring authority of the kind mentioned in subsection (1) is made and registered in accordance with Schedule 1, and

    (c) at the time when P executes the instrument, P has reached 18 and has capacity to execute it.

(3) An instrument which –

    (a) purports to create a lasting power of attorney, but

    (b) does not comply with this section, section 10 or Schedule 1, confers no authority.

(4) The authority conferred by a lasting power of attorney is subject to –

    (a) the provisions of this Act and, in particular, sections 1 (the principles) and 4 (best interests), and

    (b) any conditions or restrictions specified in the instrument.

10   Appointment of donees

(1) A donee of a lasting power of attorney must be –

    (a) an individual who has reached 18, or

    (b) if the power relates only to P's property and affairs, either such an individual or a trust corporation.

(2) An individual who is bankrupt may not be appointed as donee of a lasting power of attorney in relation to P's property and affairs.

(3) Subsections (4) to (7) apply in relation to an instrument under which two or more persons are to act as donees of a lasting power of attorney.

(4) The instrument may appoint them to act –

    (a) jointly,

    (b) jointly and severally, or

    (c) jointly in respect of some matters and jointly and severally in respect of others.

(5) To the extent to which it does not specify whether they are to act jointly or jointly and severally, the instrument is to be assumed to appoint them to act jointly.

(6) If they are to act jointly, a failure, as respects one of them, to comply with the requirements of subsection (1) or (2) or Part 1 or 2 of Schedule 1 prevents a lasting power of attorney from being created.

(7) If they are to act jointly and severally, a failure, as respects one of them, to comply with the requirements of subsection (1) or (2) or Part 1 or 2 of Schedule 1 –

    (a) prevents the appointment taking effect in his case, but

    (b) does not prevent a lasting power of attorney from being created in the case of the other or others.

(8) An instrument used to create a lasting power of attorney –

    (a) cannot give the donee (or, if more than one, any of them) power to appoint a substitute or successor, but

    (b) may itself appoint a person to replace the donee (or, if more than one, any of them) on the occurrence of an event mentioned in section 13(6)(a) to (d) which has the effect of terminating the donee's appointment.

11   Lasting powers of attorney: restrictions

(1) A lasting power of attorney does not authorise the donee (or, if more than one, any of them) to do an act that is intended to restrain P, unless three conditions are satisfied.

(2) The first condition is that P lacks, or the donee reasonably believes that P lacks, capacity in relation to the matter in question.

(3) The second is that the donee reasonably believes that it is necessary to do the act in order to prevent harm to P.

(4) The third is that the act is a proportionate response to –

    (a) the likelihood of P's suffering harm, and

    (b) the seriousness of that harm.

(5) For the purposes of this section, the donee restrains P if he –

    (a) uses, or threatens to use, force to secure the doing of an act which P resists, or

    (b) restricts P's liberty of movement, whether or not P resists, or if he authorises another person to do any of those things.

(6) . . .

(7) Where a lasting power of attorney authorises the donee (or, if more than one, any of them) to make decisions about P's personal welfare, the authority –

    (a) does not extend to making such decisions in circumstances other than those where P lacks, or the donee reasonably believes that P lacks, capacity,

    (b) is subject to sections 24 to 26 (advance decisions to refuse treatment), and

    (c) extends to giving or refusing consent to the carrying out or continuation of a treatment by a person providing health care for P.

(8) But subsection (7)(c) –

    (a) does not authorise the giving or refusing of consent to the carrying out or continuation of life-sustaining treatment, unless the instrument contains express provision to that effect, and

    (b) is subject to any conditions or restrictions in the instrument.

12   Scope of lasting powers of attorney: gifts

(1) Where a lasting power of attorney confers authority to make decisions about P's property and affairs, it does not authorise a donee (or, if more than one, any of them)

to dispose of the donor's property by making gifts except to the extent permitted by subsection (2).

    (2) The donee may make gifts –

        (a) on customary occasions to persons (including himself) who are related to or connected with the donor, or

        (b) to any charity to whom the donor made or might have been expected to make gifts, if the value of each such gift is not unreasonable having regard to all the circumstances and, in particular, the size of the donor's estate.

    (3) 'Customary occasion' means –

        (a) the occasion or anniversary of a birth, a marriage or the formation of a civil partnership, or

        (b) any other occasion on which presents are customarily given within families or among friends or associates.

    (4) Subsection (2) is subject to any conditions or restrictions in the instrument.

13   Revocation of lasting powers of attorney etc.

    (1) This section applies if –

        (a) P has executed an instrument with a view to creating a lasting power of attorney, or

        (b) a lasting power of attorney is registered as having been conferred by P, and in this section references to revoking the power include revoking the instrument.

    (2) P may, at any time when he has capacity to do so, revoke the power.

    (3) P's bankruptcy revokes the power so far as it relates to P's property and affairs.

    (4) But where P is bankrupt merely because an interim bankruptcy restrictions order has effect in respect of him, the power is suspended, so far as it relates to P's property and affairs, for so long as the order has effect.

    (5) The occurrence in relation to a donee of an event mentioned in subsection (6) –

        (a) terminates his appointment, and

        (b) except in the cases given in subsection (7), revokes the power.

    (6) The events are –

        (a) the disclaimer of the appointment by the donee in accordance with such requirements as may be prescribed for the purposes of this section in regulations made by the Lord Chancellor,

        (b) subject to subsections (8) and (9), the death or bankruptcy of the donee or, if the donee is a trust corporation, its winding-up or dissolution,

        (c) subject to subsection (11), the dissolution or annulment of a marriage or civil partnership between the donor and the donee,

        (d) the lack of capacity of the donee.

    (7) The cases are –

        (a) the donee is replaced under the terms of the instrument,

        (b) he is one of two or more persons appointed to act as donees jointly and severally in respect of any matter and, after the event, there is at least one remaining donee.

    (8) The bankruptcy of a donee does not terminate his appointment, or revoke the power, in so far as his authority relates to P's personal welfare.

(9) Where the donee is bankrupt merely because an interim bankruptcy restrictions order has effect in respect of him, his appointment and the power are suspended, so far as they relate to P's property and affairs, for so long as the order has effect.

(10) Where the donee is one of two or more appointed to act jointly and severally under the power in respect of any matter, the reference in subsection (9) to the suspension of the power is to its suspension in so far as it relates to that donee.

(11) The dissolution or annulment of a marriage or civil partnership does not terminate the appointment of a donee, or revoke the power, if the instrument provided that it was not to do so.

14 Protection of donee and others if no power created or power revoked
(1) Subsections (2) and (3) apply if –
  (a) an instrument has been registered under Schedule 1 as a lasting power of attorney, but
  (b) a lasting power of attorney was not created, whether or not the registration has been cancelled at the time of the act or transaction in question.
(2) A donee who acts in purported exercise of the power does not incur any liability (to P or any other person) because of the non-existence of the power unless at the time of acting he –
  (a) knows that a lasting power of attorney was not created, or
  (b) is aware of circumstances which, if a lasting power of attorney had been created, would have terminated his authority to act as a donee.
(3) Any transaction between the donee and another person is, in favour of that person, as valid as if the power had been in existence, unless at the time of the transaction that person has knowledge of a matter referred to in subsection (2).
(4) If the interest of a purchaser depends on whether a transaction between the donee and the other person was valid by virtue of subsection (3), it is conclusively presumed in favour of the purchaser that the transaction was valid if –
  (a) the transaction was completed within 12 months of the date on which the instrument was registered, or
  (b) the other person makes a statutory declaration, before or within 3 months after the completion of the purchase, that he had no reason at the time of the transaction to doubt that the donee had authority to dispose of the property which was the subject of the transaction.
(5) In its application to a lasting power of attorney which relates to matters in addition to P's property and affairs, section 5 of the Powers of Attorney Act 1971 (c. 27) (protection where power is revoked) has effect as if references to revocation included the cessation of the power in relation to P's property and affairs.
(6) Where two or more donees are appointed under a lasting power of attorney, this section applies as if references to the donee were to all or any of them.

General powers of the court and appointment of deputies

15 Power to make declarations
(1) The court may make declarations as to –
  (a) whether a person has or lacks capacity to make a decision specified in the declaration;

(b) whether a person has or lacks capacity to make decisions on such matters as are described in the declaration;

(c) the lawfulness or otherwise of any act done, or yet to be done, in relation to that person.

(2) 'Act' includes an omission and a course of conduct.

16 Powers to make decisions and appoint deputies: general

(1) This section applies if a person ('P') lacks capacity in relation to a matter or matters concerning –

(a) P's personal welfare, or

(b) P's property and affairs.

(2) The court may –

(a) by making an order, make the decision or decisions on P's behalf in relation to the matter or matters, or

(b) appoint a person (a 'deputy') to make decisions on P's behalf in relation to the matter or matters.

(3) The powers of the court under this section are subject to the provisions of this Act and, in particular, to sections 1 (the principles) and 4 (best interests).

(4) When deciding whether it is in P's best interests to appoint a deputy, the court must have regard (in addition to the matters mentioned in section 4) to the principles that

(a) a decision by the court is to be preferred to the appointment of a deputy to make a decision, and

(b) the powers conferred on a deputy should be as limited in scope and duration as is reasonably practicable in the circumstances.

(5) The court may make such further orders or give such directions, and confer on a deputy such powers or impose on him such duties, as it thinks necessary or expedient for giving effect to, or otherwise in connection with, an order or appointment made by it under subsection (2).

(6) Without prejudice to section 4, the court may make the order, give the directions or make the appointment on such terms as it considers are in P's best interests, even though no application is before the court for an order, directions or an appointment on those terms.

(7) An order of the court may be varied or discharged by a subsequent order.

(8) The court may, in particular, revoke the appointment of a deputy or vary the powers conferred on him if it is satisfied that the deputy –

(a) has behaved, or is behaving, in a way that contravenes the authority conferred on him by the court or is not in P's best interests, or

(b) proposes to behave in a way that would contravene that authority or would not be in P's best interests.

16A Section 16 powers: Mental Health Act patients etc.

(1) If a person is ineligible to be deprived of liberty by this Act, the court may not include in a welfare order provision which authorises the person to be deprived of his liberty.

(2) If –

(a) a welfare order includes provision which authorises a person to be deprived of his liberty, and

(b) that person becomes ineligible to be deprived of liberty by this Act, the provision ceases to have effect for as long as the person remains ineligible.

(3) Nothing in subsection (2) affects the power of the court under section 16(7) to vary or discharge the welfare order.

(4) For the purposes of this section –

    (a) Schedule 1A applies for determining whether or not P is ineligible to be deprived of liberty by this Act;

    (b) 'welfare order' means an order under section 16(2)(a).

17 Section 16 powers: personal welfare

(1) The powers under section 16 as respects P's personal welfare extend in particular to –

    (a) deciding where P is to live;

    (b) deciding what contact, if any, P is to have with any specified persons;

    (c) making an order prohibiting a named person from having contact with P;

    (d) giving or refusing consent to the carrying out or continuation of a treatment by a person providing health care for P;

    (e) giving a direction that a person responsible for P's health care allow a different person to take over that responsibility.

(2) Subsection (1) is subject to section 20 (restrictions on deputies).

18 Section 16 powers: property and affairs

(1) The powers under section 16 as respects P's property and affairs extend in particular to –

    (a) the control and management of P's property;

    (b) the sale, exchange, charging, gift or other disposition of P's property;

    (c) the acquisition of property in P's name or on P's behalf;

    (d) the carrying on, on P's behalf, of any profession, trade or business;

    (e) the taking of a decision which will have the effect of dissolving a partnership of which P is a member;

    (f) the carrying out of any contract entered into by P;

    (g) the discharge of P's debts and of any of P's obligations, whether legally enforceable or not;

    (h) the settlement of any of P's property, whether for P's benefit or for the benefit of others;

    (i) the execution for P of a will;

    (j) the exercise of any power (including a power to consent) vested in P whether beneficially or as trustee or otherwise;

    (k) the conduct of legal proceedings in P's name or on P's behalf.

(2) No will may be made under subsection (1)(i) at a time when P has not reached 18.

(3) The powers under section 16 as respects any other matter relating to P's property and affairs may be exercised even though P has not reached 16, if the court considers it likely that P will still lack capacity to make decisions in respect of that matter when he reaches 18.

(4) Schedule 2 supplements the provisions of this section.

(5) Section 16(7) (variation and discharge of court orders) is subject to paragraph 6 of Schedule 2.

(6) Subsection (1) is subject to section 20 (restrictions on deputies).

19   Appointment of deputies

(1) A deputy appointed by the court must be –
  (a) an individual who has reached 18, or
  (b) as respects powers in relation to property and affairs, an individual who has reached 18 or a trust corporation.

(2) The court may appoint an individual by appointing the holder for the time being of a specified office or position.

(3) A person may not be appointed as a deputy without his consent.

(4) The court may appoint two or more deputies to act –
  (a) jointly,
  (b) jointly and severally, or
  (c) jointly in respect of some matters and jointly and severally in respect of others.

(5) When appointing a deputy or deputies, the court may at the same time appoint one or more other persons to succeed the existing deputy or those deputies –
  (a) in such circumstances, or on the happening of such events, as may be specified by the court;
  (b) for such period as may be so specified.

(6) A deputy is to be treated as P's agent in relation to anything done or decided by him within the scope of his appointment and in accordance with this Part.

(7) The deputy is entitled –
  (a) to be reimbursed out of P's property for his reasonable expenses in discharging his functions, and
  (b) if the court so directs when appointing him, to remuneration out of P's property for discharging them.

(8) The court may confer on a deputy powers to –
  (a) take possession or control of all or any specified part of P's property;
  (b) exercise all or any specified powers in respect of it, including such powers of investment as the court may determine.

(9) The court may require a deputy –
  (a) to give to the Public Guardian such security as the court thinks fit for the due discharge of his functions, and
  (b) to submit to the Public Guardian such reports at such times or at such intervals as the court may direct.

20   Restrictions on deputies

(1) A deputy does not have power to make a decision on behalf of P in relation to a matter if he knows or has reasonable grounds for believing that P has capacity in relation to the matter.

(2) Nothing in section 16(5) or 17 permits a deputy to be given power –
  (a) to prohibit a named person from having contact with P;
  (b) to direct a person responsible for P's health care to allow a different person to take over that responsibility.

(3) A deputy may not be given powers with respect to –
  (a) the settlement of any of P's property, whether for P's benefit or for the benefit of others,

(b) the execution for P of a will, or

(c) the exercise of any power (including a power to consent) vested in P whether beneficially or as trustee or otherwise.

(4) A deputy may not be given power to make a decision on behalf of P which is inconsistent with a decision made, within the scope of his authority and in accordance with this Act, by the donee of a lasting power of attorney granted by P (or, if there is more than one donee, by any of them).

(5) A deputy may not refuse consent to the carrying out or continuation of life-sustaining treatment in relation to P.

(6) The authority conferred on a deputy is subject to the provisions of this Act and, in particular, sections 1 (the principles) and 4 (best interests).

(7) A deputy may not do an act that is intended to restrain P unless four conditions are satisfied.

(8) The first condition is that, in doing the act, the deputy is acting within the scope of an authority expressly conferred on him by the court.

(9) The second is that P lacks, or the deputy reasonably believes that P lacks, capacity in relation to the matter in question.

(10) The third is that the deputy reasonably believes that it is necessary to do the act in order to prevent harm to P.

(11) The fourth is that the act is a proportionate response to –

(a) the likelihood of P's suffering harm, and

(b) the seriousness of that harm.

(12) For the purposes of this section, a deputy restrains P if he –

(a) uses, or threatens to use, force to secure the doing of an act which P resists, or

(b) restricts P's liberty of movement, whether or not P resists, or if he authorises another person to do any of those things.

(13) . . .

21 Transfer of proceedings relating to people under 18

(1) The Lord Chief Justice, with the concurrence of the Lord Chancellor, may by order make provision as to the transfer of proceedings relating to a person under 18, in such circumstances as are specified in the order –

(a) from the Court of Protection to a court having jurisdiction under the Children Act 1989 (c. 41), or

(b) from a court having jurisdiction under that Act to the Court of Protection.

(2) The Lord Chief Justice may nominate any of the following to exercise his functions under this section –

(a) the President of the Court of Protection;

(b) a judicial officer holder (as defined in section 109(4) of the Constitutional Reform Act 2005).

Powers of court in relation to Schedule A1

21A Powers of court in relation to Schedule A1

(1) This section applies if either of the following has been given under Schedule A1 –

(a) a standard authorisation;

(b) an urgent authorisation.

(2) Where a standard authorisation has been given, the court may determine any question relating to any of the following matters –
  (a) whether the relevant person meets one or more of the qualifying requirements;
  (b) the period during which the standard authorisation is to be in force;
  (c) the purpose for which the standard authorisation is given;
  (d) the conditions subject to which the standard authorisation is given.
(3) If the court determines any question under subsection (2), the court may make an order –
  (a) varying or terminating the standard authorisation, or
  (b) directing the supervisory body to vary or terminate the standard authorisation.
(4) Where an urgent authorisation has been given, the court may determine any question relating to any of the following matters –
  (a) whether the urgent authorisation should have been given;
  (b) the period during which the urgent authorisation is to be in force;
  (c) the purpose for which the urgent authorisation is given.
(5) Where the court determines any question under subsection (4), the court may make an order –
  (a) varying or terminating the urgent authorisation, or
  (b) directing the managing authority of the relevant hospital or care home to vary or terminate the urgent authorisation.
(6) Where the court makes an order under subsection (3) or (5), the court may make an order about a person's liability for any act done in connection with the standard or urgent authorisation before its variation or termination.
(7) An order under subsection (6) may, in particular, exclude a person from liability.

Powers of the court in relation to lasting powers of attorney

22 Powers of court in relation to validity of lasting powers of attorney
(1) This section and section 23 apply if –
  (a) a person ('P') has executed or purported to execute an instrument with a view to creating a lasting power of attorney, or
  (b) an instrument has been registered as a lasting power of attorney conferred by P.
(2) The court may determine any question relating to –
  (a) whether one or more of the requirements for the creation of a lasting power of attorney have been met;
  (b) whether the power has been revoked or has otherwise come to an end.
(3) Subsection (4) applies if the court is satisfied –
  (a) that fraud or undue pressure was used to induce P –
    (i) to execute an instrument for the purpose of creating a lasting power of attorney, or
    (ii) to create a lasting power of attorney, or
  (b) that the donee (or, if more than one, any of them) of a lasting power of attorney –
    (i) has behaved, or is behaving, in a way that contravenes his authority or is not in P's best interests, or
    (ii) proposes to behave in a way that would contravene his authority or would not be in P's best interests.

(4) The court may –
- (a) direct that an instrument purporting to create the lasting power of attorney is not to be registered, or
- (b) if P lacks capacity to do so, revoke the instrument or the lasting power of attorney.

(5) If there is more than one donee, the court may under subsection (4)(b) revoke the instrument or the lasting power of attorney so far as it relates to any of them.

(6) 'Donee' includes an intended donee.

23 Powers of court in relation to operation of lasting powers of attorney

(1) The court may determine any question as to the meaning or effect of a lasting power of attorney or an instrument purporting to create one.

(2) The court may –
- (a) give directions with respect to decisions –
  - (i) which the donee of a lasting power of attorney has authority to make, and
  - (ii) which P lacks capacity to make;
- (b) give any consent or authorisation to act which the donee would have to obtain from P if P had capacity to give it.

(3) The court may, if P lacks capacity to do so –
- (a) give directions to the donee with respect to the rendering by him of reports or accounts and the production of records kept by him for that purpose;
- (b) require the donee to supply information or produce documents or things in his possession as donee;
- (c) give directions with respect to the remuneration or expenses of the donee;
- (d) relieve the donee wholly or partly from any liability which he has or may have incurred on account of a breach of his duties as donee.

(4) The court may authorise the making of gifts which are not within section 12(2) (permitted gifts).

(5) Where two or more donees are appointed under a lasting power of attorney, this section applies as if references to the donee were to all or any of them.

Advance decisions to refuse treatment

24 Advance decisions to refuse treatment: general

(1) 'Advance decision' means a decision made by a person ('P'), after he has reached 18 and when he has capacity to do so, that if –
- (a) at a later time and in such circumstances as he may specify, a specified treatment is proposed to be carried out or continued by a person providing health care for him, and
- (b) at that time he lacks capacity to consent to the carrying out or continuation of the treatment, the specified treatment is not to be carried out or continued.

(2) For the purposes of subsection (1)(a), a decision may be regarded as specifying a treatment or circumstances even though expressed in layman's terms.

(3) P may withdraw or alter an advance decision at any time when he has capacity to do so.

(4) A withdrawal (including a partial withdrawal) need not be in writing.

(5) An alteration of an advance decision need not be in writing (unless section 25(5) applies in relation to the decision resulting from the alteration).

25 Validity and applicability of advance decisions

(1) An advance decision does not affect the liability which a person may incur for carrying out or continuing a treatment in relation to P unless the decision is at the material time –

    (a) valid, and

    (b) applicable to the treatment.

(2) An advance decision is not valid if P –

    (a) has withdrawn the decision at a time when he had capacity to do so,

    (b) has, under a lasting power of attorney created after the advance decision was made, conferred authority on the donee (or, if more than one, any of them) to give or refuse consent to the treatment to which the advance decision relates, or

    (c) has done anything else clearly inconsistent with the advance decision remaining his fixed decision.

(3) An advance decision is not applicable to the treatment in question if at the material time P has capacity to give or refuse consent to it.

(4) An advance decision is not applicable to the treatment in question if –

    (a) that treatment is not the treatment specified in the advance decision,

    (b) any circumstances specified in the advance decision are absent, or

    (c) there are reasonable grounds for believing that circumstances exist which P did not anticipate at the time of the advance decision and which would have affected his decision had he anticipated them.

(5) An advance decision is not applicable to life-sustaining treatment unless –

    (a) the decision is verified by a statement by P to the effect that it is to apply to that treatment even if life is at risk, and

    (b) the decision and statement comply with subsection (6).

(6) A decision or statement complies with this subsection only if –

    (a) it is in writing,

    (b) it is signed by P or by another person in P's presence and by P's direction,

    (c) the signature is made or acknowledged by P in the presence of a witness, and

    (d) the witness signs it, or acknowledges his signature, in P's presence.

(7) The existence of any lasting power of attorney other than one of a description mentioned in subsection (2)(b) does not prevent the advance decision from being regarded as valid and applicable.

26 Effect of advance decisions

(1) If P has made an advance decision which is –

    (a) valid, and

    (b) applicable to a treatment, the decision has effect as if he had made it, and had had capacity to make it, at the time when the question arises whether the treatment should be carried out or continued.

(2) A person does not incur liability for carrying out or continuing the treatment unless, at the time, he is satisfied that an advance decision exists which is valid and applicable to the treatment.

(3) A person does not incur liability for the consequences of withholding or withdrawing a treatment from P if, at the time, he reasonably believes that an advance decision exists which is valid and applicable to the treatment.

(4) The court may make a declaration as to whether an advance decision –

(a) exists;

(b) is valid;

(c) is applicable to a treatment.

(5) Nothing in an apparent advance decision stops a person –

(a) providing life-sustaining treatment, or

(b) doing any act he reasonably believes to be necessary to prevent a serious deterioration in P's condition, while a decision as respects any relevant issue is sought from the court.

Excluded decisions

27 Family relationships etc.

(1) Nothing in this Act permits a decision on any of the following matters to be made on behalf of a person –

(a) consenting to marriage or a civil partnership,

(b) consenting to have sexual relations,

(c) consenting to a decree of divorce being granted on the basis of two years' separation,

(d) consenting to a dissolution order being made in relation to a civil partnership on the basis of two years' separation,

(e) consenting to a child's being placed for adoption by an adoption agency,

(f) consenting to the making of an adoption order,

(g) discharging parental responsibilities in matters not relating to a child's property,

(h) giving a consent under the Human Fertilisation and Embryology Act 1990 (c. 37).

(2) 'Adoption order' means –

(a) an adoption order within the meaning of the Adoption and Children Act 2002 (c. 38) (including a future adoption order), and

(b) an order under section 84 of that Act (parental responsibility prior to adoption abroad).

28 Mental Health Act matters

(1) Nothing in this Act authorises anyone –

(a) to give a patient medical treatment for mental disorder, or

(b) to consent to a patient's being given medical treatment for mental disorder, if, at the time when it is proposed to treat the patient, his treatment is regulated by Part 4 of the Mental Health Act.

(1A) Subsection (1) does not apply in relation to any form of treatment to which section 58A of that Act (electro-convulsive therapy, etc.) applies if the patient comes within subsection (7) of that section (informal patient under 18 who cannot give consent).

(1B) Section 5 does not apply to an act to which section 64B of the Mental Health Act applies (treatment of community patients not recalled to hospital).

(2) 'Medical treatment', 'mental disorder' and 'patient' have the same meaning as in that Act.

29   Voting rights

(1) Nothing in this Act permits a decision on voting at an election for any public office, or at a referendum, to be made on behalf of a person.

(2) 'Referendum' has the same meaning as in section 101 of the Political Parties, Elections and Referendums Act 2000 (c. 41).

Research

30   Research

(1) Intrusive research carried out on, or in relation to, a person who lacks capacity to consent to it is unlawful unless it is carried out –
  (a) as part of a research project which is for the time being approved by the appropriate body for the purposes of this Act in accordance with section 31, and
  (b) in accordance with sections 32 and 33.

(2) Research is intrusive if it is of a kind that would be unlawful if it was carried out –
  (a) on or in relation to a person who had capacity to consent to it, but
  (b) without his consent.

(3) A clinical trial which is subject to the provisions of clinical trials regulations is not to be treated as research for the purposes of this section.

(4) 'Appropriate body', in relation to a research project, means the person, committee or other body specified in regulations made by the appropriate authority as the appropriate body in relation to a project of the kind in question.

(5) 'Clinical trials regulations' means –
  (a) the Medicines for Human Use (Clinical Trials) Regulations 2004 (S.I. 2004/1031) and any other regulations replacing those regulations or amending them, and
  (b) any other regulations relating to clinical trials and designated by the Secretary of State as clinical trials regulations for the purposes of this section.

(6) In this section, section 32 and section 34, 'appropriate authority' means –
  (a) in relation to the carrying out of research in England, the Secretary of State, and
  (b) in relation to the carrying out of research in Wales, the National Assembly for Wales.

31   Requirements for approval

(1) The appropriate body may not approve a research project for the purposes of this Act unless satisfied that the following requirements will be met in relation to research carried out as part of the project on, or in relation to, a person who lacks capacity to consent to taking part in the project ('P').

(2) The research must be connected with –
  (a) an impairing condition affecting P, or
  (b) its treatment.

(3) 'Impairing condition' means a condition which is (or may be) attributable to, or which causes or contributes to (or may cause or contribute to), the impairment of, or disturbance in the functioning of, the mind or brain.

(4) There must be reasonable grounds for believing that research of comparable effectiveness cannot be carried out if the project has to be confined to, or relate only to, persons who have capacity to consent to taking part in it.

(5) The research must –

    (a) have the potential to benefit P without imposing on P a burden that is disproportionate to the potential benefit to P, or

    (b) be intended to provide knowledge of the causes or treatment of, or of the care of persons affected by, the same or a similar condition.

(6) If the research falls within paragraph (b) of subsection (5) but not within paragraph (a), there must be reasonable grounds for believing –

    (a) that the risk to P from taking part in the project is likely to be negligible, and

    (b) that anything done to, or in relation to, P will not –

        (i) interfere with P's freedom of action or privacy in a significant way, or

        (ii) be unduly invasive or restrictive.

(7) There must be reasonable arrangements in place for ensuring that the requirements of sections 32 and 33 will be met.

32 Consulting carers etc.

(1) This section applies if a person ('R') –

    (a) is conducting an approved research project, and

    (b) wishes to carry out research, as part of the project, on or in relation to a person ('P') who lacks capacity to consent to taking part in the project.

(2) R must take reasonable steps to identify a person who –

    (a) otherwise than in a professional capacity or for remuneration, is engaged in caring for P or is interested in P's welfare, and

    (b) is prepared to be consulted by R under this section.

(3) If R is unable to identify such a person he must, in accordance with guidance issued by the appropriate authority, nominate a person who –

    (a) is prepared to be consulted by R under this section, but

    (b) has no connection with the project.

(4) R must provide the person identified under subsection (2), or nominated under subsection (3), with information about the project and ask him –

    (a) for advice as to whether P should take part in the project, and

    (b) what, in his opinion, P's wishes and feelings about taking part in the project would be likely to be if P had capacity in relation to the matter.

(5) If, at any time, the person consulted advises R that in his opinion P's wishes and feelings would be likely to lead him to decline to take part in the project (or to wish to withdraw from it) if he had capacity in relation to the matter, R must ensure –

    (a) if P is not already taking part in the project, that he does not take part in it;

    (b) if P is taking part in the project, that he is withdrawn from it.

(6) But subsection (5)(b) does not require treatment that P has been receiving as part of the project to be discontinued if R has reasonable grounds for believing that there would be a significant risk to P's health if it were discontinued.

(7) The fact that a person is the donee of a lasting power of attorney given by P, or is P's deputy, does not prevent him from being the person consulted under this section.

(8) Subsection (9) applies if treatment is being, or is about to be, provided for P as a matter of urgency and R considers that, having regard to the nature of the research and of the particular circumstances of the case –

    (a) it is also necessary to take action for the purposes of the research as a matter of urgency, but

    (b) it is not reasonably practicable to consult under the previous provisions of this section.

(9) R may take the action if –

    (a) he has the agreement of a registered medical practitioner who is not involved in the organisation or conduct of the research project, or

    (b) where it is not reasonably practicable in the time available to obtain that agreement, he acts in accordance with a procedure approved by the appropriate body at the time when the research project was approved under section 31.

(10) But R may not continue to act in reliance on subsection (9) if he has reasonable grounds for believing that it is no longer necessary to take the action as a matter of urgency.

33 Additional safeguards

(1) This section applies in relation to a person who is taking part in an approved research project even though he lacks capacity to consent to taking part.

(2) Nothing may be done to, or in relation to, him in the course of the research –

    (a) to which he appears to object (whether by showing signs of resistance or otherwise) except where what is being done is intended to protect him from harm or to reduce or prevent pain or discomfort, or

    (b) which would be contrary to –

     (i) an advance decision of his which has effect, or

    (ii) any other form of statement made by him and not subsequently withdrawn, of which R is aware.

(3) The interests of the person must be assumed to outweigh those of science and society.

(4) If he indicates (in any way) that he wishes to be withdrawn from the project he must be withdrawn without delay.

(5) P must be withdrawn from the project, without delay, if at any time the person conducting the research has reasonable grounds for believing that one or more of the requirements set out in section 31(2) to (7) is no longer met in relation to research being carried out on, or in relation to, P.

(6) But neither subsection (4) nor subsection (5) requires treatment that P has been receiving as part of the project to be discontinued if R has reasonable grounds for believing that there would be a significant risk to P's health if it were discontinued.

34 Loss of capacity during research project

(1) This section applies where a person ('P') –

    (a) has consented to take part in a research project begun before the commencement of section 30, but

    (b) before the conclusion of the project, loses capacity to consent to continue to take part in it.

(2) The appropriate authority may by regulations provide that, despite P's loss of capacity, research of a prescribed kind may be carried out on, or in relation to, P if –
  (a) the project satisfies prescribed requirements,
  (b) any information or material relating to P which is used in the research is of a prescribed description and was obtained before P's loss of capacity, and
  (c) the person conducting the project takes in relation to P such steps as may be prescribed for the purpose of protecting him.

(3) The regulations may, in particular, –
  (a) make provision about when, for the purposes of the regulations, a project is to be treated as having begun;
  (b) include provision similar to any made by section 31, 32 or 33.

Independent mental capacity advocate service

35   Appointment of independent mental capacity advocates

(1) The appropriate authority must make such arrangements as it considers reasonable to enable persons ('independent mental capacity advocates') to be available to represent and support persons to whom acts or decisions proposed under sections 37, 38 and 39 relate or persons who fall within section 39A, 39C or 39D.

(2) The appropriate authority may make regulations as to the appointment of independent mental capacity advocates.

(3) The regulations may, in particular, provide –
  (a) that a person may act as an independent mental capacity advocate only in such circumstances, or only subject to such conditions, as may be prescribed;
  (b) for the appointment of a person as an independent mental capacity advocate to be subject to approval in accordance with the regulations.

(4) In making arrangements under subsection (1), the appropriate authority must have regard to the principle that a person to whom a proposed act or decision relates should, so far as practicable, be represented and supported by a person who is independent of any person who will be responsible for the act or decision.

(5) The arrangements may include provision for payments to be made to, or in relation to, persons carrying out functions in accordance with the arrangements.

(6) For the purpose of enabling him to carry out his functions, an independent mental capacity advocate –
  (a) may interview in private the person whom he has been instructed to represent, and
  (b) may, at all reasonable times, examine and take copies of –
    (i) any health record,
    (ii) any record of, or held by, a local authority and compiled in connection with a social services function, and
    (iii) any record held by a person registered under Part 2 of the Care Standards Act 2000 (c. 14), which the person holding the record considers may be relevant to the independent mental capacity advocate's investigation.

(7) In this section, section 36 and section 37, 'the appropriate authority' means –
  (a) in relation to the provision of the services of independent mental capacity advocates in England, the Secretary of State, and
  (b) in relation to the provision of the services of independent mental capacity advocates in Wales, the National Assembly for Wales.

36   Functions of independent mental capacity advocates

(1) The appropriate authority may make regulations as to the functions of independent mental capacity advocates.

(2) The regulations may, in particular, make provision requiring an advocate to take such steps as may be prescribed for the purpose of –

(a) providing support to the person whom he has been instructed to represent ('P') so that P may participate as fully as possible in any relevant decision;

(b) obtaining and evaluating relevant information;

(c) ascertaining what P's wishes and feelings would be likely to be, and the beliefs and values that would be likely to influence P, if he had capacity;

(d) ascertaining what alternative courses of action are available in relation to P;

(e) obtaining a further medical opinion where treatment is proposed and the advocate thinks that one should be obtained.

(3) The regulations may also make provision as to circumstances in which the advocate may challenge, or provide assistance for the purpose of challenging, any relevant decision.

37   Provision of serious medical treatment by NHS body

(1) This section applies if an NHS body –

(a) is proposing to provide, or secure the provision of, serious medical treatment for a person ('P') who lacks capacity to consent to the treatment, and

(b) is satisfied that there is no person, other than one engaged in providing care or treatment for P in a professional capacity or for remuneration, whom it would be appropriate to consult in determining what would be in P's best interests.

(2) But this section does not apply if P's treatment is regulated by Part 4 or 4A of the Mental Health Act.

(3) Before the treatment is provided, the NHS body must instruct an independent mental capacity advocate to represent P.

(4) If the treatment needs to be provided as a matter of urgency, it may be provided even though the NHS body has not been able to comply with subsection (3).

(5) The NHS body must, in providing or securing the provision of treatment for P, take into account any information given, or submissions made, by the independent mental capacity advocate.

(6) 'Serious medical treatment' means treatment which involves providing, withholding or withdrawing treatment of a kind prescribed by regulations made by the appropriate authority.

(7) 'NHS body' has such meaning as may be prescribed by regulations made for the purposes of this section by –

(a) the Secretary of State, in relation to bodies in England, or

(b) the National Assembly for Wales, in relation to bodies in Wales.

38   Provision of accommodation by NHS body

(1) This section applies if an NHS body proposes to make arrangements –

(a) for the provision of accommodation in a hospital or care home for a person ('P') who lacks capacity to agree to the arrangements, or

(b) for a change in P's accommodation to another hospital or care home, and is satisfied that there is no person, other than one engaged in providing care or treatment for P in a professional capacity or for remuneration, whom it would be appropriate for it to consult in determining what would be in P's best interests.

(2) But this section does not apply if P is accommodated as a result of an obligation imposed on him under the Mental Health Act.

(2A) And this section does not apply if –

(a) an independent mental capacity advocate must be appointed under section 39A or 39C (whether or not by the NHS body) to represent P, and

(b) the hospital or care home in which P is to be accommodated under the arrangements referred to in this section is the relevant hospital or care home under the authorisation referred to in that section.

(3) Before making the arrangements, the NHS body must instruct an independent mental capacity advocate to represent P unless it is satisfied that –

(a) the accommodation is likely to be provided for a continuous period which is less than the applicable period, or

(b) the arrangements need to be made as a matter of urgency.

(4) If the NHS body –

(a) did not instruct an independent mental capacity advocate to represent P before making the arrangements because it was satisfied that subsection (3)(a) or (b) applied, but

(b) subsequently has reason to believe that the accommodation is likely to be provided for a continuous period –

(i) beginning with the day on which accommodation was first provided in accordance with the arrangements, and

(ii) ending on or after the expiry of the applicable period, it must instruct an independent mental capacity advocate to represent P.

(5) The NHS body must, in deciding what arrangements to make for P, take into account any information given, or submissions made, by the independent mental capacity advocate.

(6) 'Care home' has the meaning given in section 3 of the Care Standards Act 2000 (c. 14).

(7) 'Hospital' means –

(a) a health service hospital as defined by section 128 of the National Health Service Act 1977 (c. 49), or

(b) an independent hospital as defined by section 2 of the Care Standards Act 2000.

(8) 'NHS body' has such meaning as may be prescribed by regulations made for the purposes of this section by –

(a) the Secretary of State, in relation to bodies in England, or

(b) the National Assembly for Wales, in relation to bodies in Wales.

(9) 'Applicable period' means –

(a) in relation to accommodation in a hospital, 28 days, and

(b) in relation to accommodation in a care home, 8 weeks.

(10) For the purposes of subsection (1), a person appointed under Part 10 of Schedule A1 to be P's representative is not, by virtue of that appointment, engaged in providing care or treatment for P in a professional capacity or for remuneration.

39 Provision of accommodation by local authority

(1) This section applies if a local authority propose to make arrangements –

(a) for the provision of residential accommodation for a person ('P') who lacks capacity to agree to the arrangements, or

(b) for a change in P's residential accommodation, and are satisfied that there is no person, other than one engaged in providing care or treatment for P in a professional capacity or for remuneration, whom it would be appropriate for them to consult in determining what would be in P's best interests.

(2) But this section applies only if the accommodation is to be provided in accordance with –

    (a) section 21 or 29 of the National Assistance Act 1948 (c. 29), or

    (b) section 117 of the Mental Health Act, as the result of a decision taken by the local authority under section 47 of the National Health Service and Community Care Act 1990 (c. 19).

(3) This section does not apply if P is accommodated as a result of an obligation imposed on him under the Mental Health Act.

(3A) And this section does not apply if –

    (a) an independent mental capacity advocate must be appointed under section 39A or 39C (whether or not by the local authority) to represent P, and

    (b) the place in which P is to be accommodated under the arrangements referred to in this section is the relevant hospital or care home under the authorisation referred to in that section.

(4) Before making the arrangements, the local authority must instruct an independent mental capacity advocate to represent P unless they are satisfied that –

    (a) the accommodation is likely to be provided for a continuous period of less than 8 weeks, or

    (b) the arrangements need to be made as a matter of urgency.

(5) If the local authority –

    (a) did not instruct an independent mental capacity advocate to represent P before making the arrangements because they were satisfied that subsection (4)(a) or (b) applied, but

    (b) subsequently have reason to believe that the accommodation is likely to be provided for a continuous period that will end 8 weeks or more after the day on which accommodation was first provided in accordance with the arrangements, they must instruct an independent mental capacity advocate to represent P.

(6) The local authority must, in deciding what arrangements to make for P, take into account any information given, or submissions made, by the independent mental capacity advocate.

(7) For the purposes of subsection (1), a person appointed under Part 10 of Schedule A1 to be P's representative is not, by virtue of that appointment, engaged in providing care or treatment for P in a professional capacity or for remuneration.

39A Person becomes subject to Schedule A1

(1) This section applies if –

    (a) a person ('P') becomes subject to Schedule A1, and

    (b) the managing authority of the relevant hospital or care home are satisfied that there is no person, other than one engaged in providing care or treatment for P in a professional capacity or for remuneration, whom it would be appropriate to consult in determining what would be in P's best interests.

(2) The managing authority must notify the supervisory body that this section applies.

(3) The supervisory body must instruct an independent mental capacity advocate to represent P.

(4) Schedule A1 makes provision about the role of an independent mental capacity advocate appointed under this section.

(5) This section is subject to paragraph 161 of Schedule A1.

(6) For the purposes of subsection (1), a person appointed under Part 10 of Schedule A1 to be P's representative is not, by virtue of that appointment, engaged in providing care or treatment for P in a professional capacity or for remuneration.

39B Section 39A: supplementary provision

(1) This section applies for the purposes of section 39A.

(2) P becomes subject to Schedule A1 in any of the following cases.

(3) The first case is where an urgent authorisation is given in relation to P under paragraph 76(2) of Schedule A1 (urgent authorisation given before request made for standard authorisation).

(4) The second case is where the following conditions are met.

(5) The first condition is that a request is made under Schedule A1 for a standard authorisation to be given in relation to P ('the requested authorisation').

(6) The second condition is that no urgent authorisation was given under paragraph 76(2) of Schedule A1 before that request was made.

(7) The third condition is that the requested authorisation will not be in force on or before, or immediately after, the expiry of an existing standard authorisation.

(8) The expiry of a standard authorisation is the date when the authorisation is expected to cease to be in force.

(9) The third case is where, under paragraph 69 of Schedule 6, the supervisory body select a person to carry out an assessment of whether or not the relevant person is a detained resident.

39C Person unrepresented whilst subject to Schedule A1

(1) This section applies if –
   (a) an authorisation under Schedule A1 is in force in relation to a person ('P'),
   (b) the appointment of a person as P's representative ends in accordance with regulations made under Part 10 of Schedule A1, and
   (c) the managing authority of the relevant hospital or care home are satisfied that there is no person, other than one engaged in providing care or treatment for P in a professional capacity or for remuneration, whom it would be appropriate to consult in determining what would be in P's best interests.

(2) The managing authority must notify the supervisory body that this section applies.

(3) The supervisory body must instruct an independent mental capacity advocate to represent P.

(4) Paragraph 159 of Schedule A1 makes provision about the role of an independent mental capacity advocate appointed under this section.

(5) The appointment of an independent mental capacity advocate under this section ends when a new appointment of a person as P's representative is made in accordance with Part 10 of Schedule A1.

(6) For the purposes of subsection (1), a person appointed under Part 10 of Schedule A1 to be P's representative is not, by virtue of that appointment, engaged in providing care or treatment for P in a professional capacity or for remuneration.

39D   Person subject to Schedule A1 without paid representative

(1) This section applies if –

    (a) an authorisation under Schedule A1 is in force in relation to a person ('P'),

    (b) P has a representative ('R') appointed under Part 10 of Schedule A1, and

    (c) R is not being paid under regulations under Part 10 of Schedule A1 for acting as P's representative.

(2) The supervisory body must instruct an independent mental capacity advocate to represent P in any of the following cases.

(3) The first case is where P makes a request to the supervisory body to instruct an advocate.

(4) The second case is where R makes a request to the supervisory body to instruct an advocate.

(5) The third case is where the supervisory body have reason to believe one or more of the following –

    (a) that, without the help of an advocate, P and R would be unable to exercise one or both of the relevant rights;

    (b) that P and R have each failed to exercise a relevant right when it would have been reasonable to exercise it;

    (c) that P and R are each unlikely to exercise a relevant right when it would be reasonable to exercise it.

(6) The duty in subsection (2) is subject to section 39E.

(7) If an advocate is appointed under this section, the advocate is, in particular, to take such steps as are practicable to help P and R to understand the following matters –

    (a) the effect of the authorisation;

    (b) the purpose of the authorisation;

    (c) the duration of the authorisation;

    (d) any conditions to which the authorisation is subject;

    (e) the reasons why each assessor who carried out an assessment in connection with the request for the authorisation, or in connection with a review of the authorisation, decided that P met the qualifying requirement in question;

    (f) the relevant rights;

    (g) how to exercise the relevant rights.

(8) The advocate is, in particular, to take such steps as are practicable to help P or R –

    (a) to exercise the right to apply to court, if it appears to the advocate that P or R wishes to exercise that right, or

    (b) to exercise the right of review, if it appears to the advocate that P or R wishes to exercise that right.

(9) If the advocate helps P or R to exercise the right of review –

    (a) the advocate may make submissions to the supervisory body on the question of whether a qualifying requirement is reviewable;

    (b) the advocate may give information, or make submissions, to any assessor carrying out a review assessment.

(10) In this section –

'relevant rights' means –

    (a) the right to apply to court, and

    (b) the right of review;

'right to apply to court' means the right to make an application to the court to exercise its jurisdiction under section 21A;

'right of review' means the right under Part 8 of Schedule A1 to request a review.

39E   Limitation on duty to instruct advocate under section 39D

(1) This section applies if an advocate is already representing P in accordance with an instruction under section 39D.

(2) Section 39D(2) does not require another advocate to be instructed, unless the following conditions are met.

(3) The first condition is that the existing advocate was instructed –

    (a) because of a request by R, or

    (b) because the supervisory body had reason to believe one or more of the things in section 39D(5).

(4) The second condition is that the other advocate would be instructed because of a request by P.

40   Exceptions

(1) The duty imposed by section 37(3), 38(3) or (4), 39(4) or 39(5), 39A(3), 39C(3) or 39D(2) does not apply where there is –

    (a) a person nominated by P (in whatever manner) as a person to be consulted on matters to which that duty relates,

    (b) a donee of a lasting power of attorney created by P who is authorised to make decisions in relation to those matters, or

    (c) a deputy appointed by the court for P with power to make decisions in relation to those matters.

(2) A person appointed under Part 10 of Schedule A1 to be P's representative is not, by virtue of that appointment, a person nominated by P as a person to be consulted in matters to which a duty mentioned in subsection (1) relates.

41   Power to adjust role of independent mental capacity advocate

(1) The appropriate authority may make regulations –

    (a) expanding the role of independent mental capacity advocates in relation to persons who lack capacity, and

    (b) adjusting the obligation to make arrangements imposed by section 35.

(2) The regulations may, in particular –

    (a) prescribe circumstances (different to those set out in sections 37, 38 and 39) in which an independent mental capacity advocate must, or circumstances in which one may, be instructed by a person of a prescribed description to represent a person who lacks capacity, and

    (b) include provision similar to any made by section 37, 38, 39 or 40.

(3) 'Appropriate authority' has the same meaning as in section 35.

Miscellaneous and supplementary

42   Codes of practice

(1) The Lord Chancellor must prepare and issue one or more codes of practice –

(a) for the guidance of persons assessing whether a person has capacity in relation to any matter,

(b) for the guidance of persons acting in connection with the care or treatment of another person (see section 5),

(c) for the guidance of donees of lasting powers of attorney,

(d) for the guidance of deputies appointed by the court,

(e) for the guidance of persons carrying out research in reliance on any provision made by or under this Act (and otherwise with respect to sections 30 to 34),

(f) for the guidance of independent mental capacity advocates,

    (fa) for the guidance of persons exercising functions under Schedule A1,

    (fb) for the guidance of representatives appointed under Part 10 of Schedule A1,

(g) with respect to the provisions of sections 24 to 26 (advance decisions and apparent advance decisions), and

(h) with respect to such other matters concerned with this Act as he thinks fit.

(2) The Lord Chancellor may from time to time revise a code.

(3) The Lord Chancellor may delegate the preparation or revision of the whole or any part of a code so far as he considers expedient.

(4) It is the duty of a person to have regard to any relevant code if he is acting in relation to a person who lacks capacity and is doing so in one or more of the following ways –

(a) as the donee of a lasting power of attorney,

(b) as a deputy appointed by the court,

(c) as a person carrying out research in reliance on any provision made by or under this Act (see sections 30 to 34),

(d) as an independent mental capacity advocate,

    (da) in the exercise of functions under Schedule A1,

    (db) as a representative appointed under Part 10 of Schedule A1,

(e) in a professional capacity,

(f) for remuneration.

(5) If it appears to a court or tribunal conducting any criminal or civil proceedings that –

(a) a provision of a code, or

(b) a failure to comply with a code, is relevant to a question arising in the proceedings, the provision or failure must be taken into account in deciding the question.

(6) A code under subsection (1)(d) may contain separate guidance for deputies appointed by virtue of paragraph 1(2) of Schedule 5 (functions of deputy conferred on receiver appointed under the Mental Health Act).

(7) In this section and in section 43, 'code' means a code prepared or revised under this section.

43 Codes of practice: procedure

(1) Before preparing or revising a code, the Lord Chancellor must consult –

(a) the National Assembly for Wales, and

(b) such other persons as he considers appropriate.

(2) The Lord Chancellor may not issue a code unless –

(a) a draft of the code has been laid by him before both Houses of Parliament, and

(b) the 40 day period has elapsed without either House resolving not to approve the draft.

(3) The Lord Chancellor must arrange for any code that he has issued to be published in such a way as he considers appropriate for bringing it to the attention of persons likely to be concerned with its provisions.

(4) '40 day period', in relation to the draft of a proposed code, means –

   (a) if the draft is laid before one House on a day later than the day on which it is laid before the other House, the period of 40 days beginning with the later of the two days;

   (b) in any other case, the period of 40 days beginning with the day on which it is laid before each House.

(5) In calculating the period of 40 days, no account is to be taken of any period during which Parliament is dissolved or prorogued or during which both Houses are adjourned for more than 4 days.

44   Ill-treatment or neglect

(1) Subsection (2) applies if a person ('D') –

   (a) has the care of a person ('P') who lacks, or whom D reasonably believes to lack, capacity,

   (b) is the donee of a lasting power of attorney, or an enduring power of attorney (within the meaning of Schedule 4), created by P, or

   (c) is a deputy appointed by the court for P.

(2) D is guilty of an offence if he ill-treats or wilfully neglects P.

(3) A person guilty of an offence under this section is liable –

   (a) on summary conviction, to imprisonment for a term not exceeding 12 months or a fine not exceeding the statutory maximum or both;

   (b) on conviction on indictment, to imprisonment for a term not exceeding 5 years or a fine or both.

Part 2   The court of protection and the public guardian

The Court of Protection

45   The Court of Protection

(1) There is to be a superior court of record known as the Court of Protection.

(2) The court is to have an official seal.

(3) The court may sit at any place in England and Wales, on any day and at any time.

(4) The court is to have a central office and registry at a place appointed by the Lord Chancellor, after consulting the Lord Chief Justice.

(5) The Lord Chancellor may, after consulting the Lord Chief Justice, designate as additional registries of the court any district registry of the High Court and any county court office.

(5A)   The Lord Chief Justice may nominate any of the following to exercise his functions under this section –

   (a) the President of the Court of Protection;

   (b) a judicial officer holder (as defined in section 109(4) of the Constitutional Reform Act 2005).

(6) The office of the Supreme Court called the Court of Protection ceases to exist.

46 The judges of the Court of Protection

(1) Subject to Court of Protection Rules under section 51(2)(d), the jurisdiction of the court is exercisable by a judge nominated for that purpose by –

    (a) the Lord Chief Justice, or

    (b) where nominated by the Lord Chief Justice to act on his behalf under this subsection –

        (i) the President of the Court of Protection;

        (ii) a judicial officer holder (as defined in section 109(4) of the Constitutional Reform Act 2005).

(2) To be nominated, a judge must be –

    (a) the President of the Family Division,

    (b) the Vice-Chancellor,

    (c) a puisne judge of the High Court,

    (d) a circuit judge, or

    (e) a district judge.

(3) The Lord Chief Justice, after consulting the Lord Chancellor, must –

    (a) appoint one of the judges nominated by virtue of subsection (2)(a) to (c) to be President of the Court of Protection, and

    (b) appoint another of those judges to be Vice-President of the Court of Protection.

(4) The Chief Justice, after consulting the Lord Chancellor, must appoint one of the judges nominated by virtue of subsection (2)(d) or (e) to be Senior Judge of the Court of Protection, having such administrative functions in relation to the court as the Lord Chancellor, after consulting the Lord Chief Justice, may direct.

Supplementary powers

47 General powers and effect of orders etc.

(1) The court has in connection with its jurisdiction the same powers, rights, privileges and authority as the High Court.

(2) Section 204 of the Law of Property Act 1925 (c. 20) (orders of High Court conclusive in favour of purchasers) applies in relation to orders and directions of the court as it applies to orders of the High Court.

(3) Office copies of orders made, directions given or other instruments issued by the court and sealed with its official seal are admissible in all legal proceedings as evidence of the originals without any further proof.

48 Interim orders and directions

The court may, pending the determination of an application to it in relation to a person ('P'), make an order or give directions in respect of any matter if –

    (a) there is reason to believe that P lacks capacity in relation to the matter,

    (b) the matter is one to which its powers under this Act extend, and

    (c) it is in P's best interests to make the order, or give the directions, without delay.

49 Power to call for reports

(1) This section applies where, in proceedings brought in respect of a person ('P') under Part 1, the court is considering a question relating to P.

(2) The court may require a report to be made to it by the Public Guardian or by a Court of Protection Visitor.

(3) The court may require a local authority, or an NHS body, to arrange for a report to be made –

    (a) by one of its officers or employees, or

    (b) by such other person (other than the Public Guardian or a Court of Protection Visitor) as the authority, or the NHS body, considers appropriate.

(4) The report must deal with such matters relating to P as the court may direct.

(5) Court of Protection Rules may specify matters which, unless the court directs otherwise, must also be dealt with in the report.

(6) The report may be made in writing or orally, as the court may direct.

(7) In complying with a requirement, the Public Guardian or a Court of Protection Visitor may, at all reasonable times, examine and take copies of –

    (a) any health record,

    (b) any record of, or held by, a local authority and compiled in connection with a social services function, and

    (c) any record held by a person registered under Part 2 of the Care Standards Act 2000 (c. 14), so far as the record relates to P.

(8) If the Public Guardian or a Court of Protection Visitor is making a visit in the course of complying with a requirement, he may interview P in private.

(9) If a Court of Protection Visitor who is a Special Visitor is making a visit in the course of complying with a requirement, he may if the court so directs carry out in private a medical, psychiatric or psychological examination of P's capacity and condition.

(10) 'NHS body' has the meaning given in section 148 of the Health and Social Care (Community Health and Standards) Act 2003 (c. 43).

(11) 'Requirement' means a requirement imposed under subsection (2) or (3).

Practice and procedure

50 Applications to the Court of Protection

(1) No permission is required for an application to the court for the exercise of any of its powers under this Act –

    (a) by a person who lacks, or is alleged to lack, capacity,

    (b) if such a person has not reached 18, by anyone with parental responsibility for him,

    (c) by the donor or a donee of a lasting power of attorney to which the application relates,

    (d) by a deputy appointed by the court for a person to whom the application relates, or

    (e) by a person named in an existing order of the court, if the application relates to the order.

(1A) Nor is permission required for an application to the court under section 21A by the relevant person's representative.

(2) But, subject to Court of Protection Rules and to paragraph 20(2) of Schedule 3 (declarations relating to private international law), permission is required for any other application to the court.

(3) In deciding whether to grant permission the court must, in particular, have regard to –

(a) the applicant's connection with the person to whom the application relates,

(b) the reasons for the application,

(c) the benefit to the person to whom the application relates of a proposed order or directions, and

(d) whether the benefit can be achieved in any other way.

(4) 'Parental responsibility' has the same meaning as in the Children Act 1989 (c. 41).

51 Court of Protection Rules

(1) Rules of court with respect to the practice and procedure of the court (to be called 'Court of Protection Rules') may be made in accordance with Part 1 of Schedule 1 to the Constitutional Reform Act 2003.

(2) Court of Protection Rules may, in particular, make provision –

(a) as to the manner and form in which proceedings are to be commenced;

(b) as to the persons entitled to be notified of, and be made parties to, the proceedings;

(c) for the allocation, in such circumstances as may be specified, of any specified description of proceedings to a specified judge or to specified descriptions of judges;

(d) for the exercise of the jurisdiction of the court, in such circumstances as may be specified, by its officers or other staff;

(e) for enabling the court to appoint a suitable person (who may, with his consent, be the Official Solicitor) to act in the name of, or on behalf of, or to represent the person to whom the proceedings relate;

(f) for enabling an application to the court to be disposed of without a hearing;

(g) for enabling the court to proceed with, or with any part of, a hearing in the absence of the person to whom the proceedings relate;

(h) for enabling or requiring the proceedings or any part of them to be conducted in private and for enabling the court to determine who is to be admitted when the court sits in private and to exclude specified persons when it sits in public;

(i) as to what may be received as evidence (whether or not admissible apart from the rules) and the manner in which it is to be presented;

(j) for the enforcement of orders made and directions given in the proceedings.

(3) Court of Protection Rules may, instead of providing for any matter, refer to provision made or to be made about that matter by directions.

(4) Court of Protection Rules may make different provision for different areas.

52 Practice directions

(1) Directions as to the practice and procedure of the court may be given in accordance with Part 1 of Schedule 2 to the Constitutional Reform Act 2005.

(2) Practice directions given otherwise than under subsection (1) may not be given without the approval of –

(a) the Lord Chancellor, and

(b) the Lord Chief Justice.

(3) The Lord Chief Justice may nominate any of the following to exercise his functions under this section –

(a) the President of the Court of Protection;

(b) a judicial office holder (as defined in section 109(4) of the Constitutional Reform Act 2005).

177

53 Rights of appeal

(1) Subject to the provisions of this section, an appeal lies to the Court of Appeal from any decision of the court.

(2) Court of Protection Rules may provide that where a decision of the court is made by –

  (a) a person exercising the jurisdiction of the court by virtue of rules made under section 51(2)(d),

  (b) a district judge, or

  (c) a circuit judge, an appeal from that decision lies to a prescribed higher judge of the court and not to the Court of Appeal.

(3) For the purposes of this section the higher judges of the court are –

  (a) in relation to a person mentioned in subsection (2)(a), a circuit judge or a district judge;

  (b) in relation to a person mentioned in subsection (2)(b), a circuit judge;

  (c) in relation to any person mentioned in subsection (2), one of the judges nominated by virtue of section 46(2)(a) to (c).

(4) Court of Protection Rules may make provision –

  (a) that, in such cases as may be specified, an appeal from a decision of the court may not be made without permission;

  (b) as to the person or persons entitled to grant permission to appeal;

  (c) as to any requirements to be satisfied before permission is granted;

  (d) that where a higher judge of the court makes a decision on an appeal, no appeal may be made to the Court of Appeal from that decision unless the Court of Appeal considers that –

   (i) the appeal would raise an important point of principle or practice, or

   (ii) there is some other compelling reason for the Court of Appeal to hear it;

  (e) as to any considerations to be taken into account in relation to granting or refusing permission to appeal.

Fees and costs

54 Fees

(1) The Lord Chancellor may with the consent of the Treasury by order prescribe fees payable in respect of anything dealt with by the court.

(2) An order under this section may in particular contain provision as to –

  (a) scales or rates of fees;

  (b) exemptions from and reductions in fees;

  (c) remission of fees in whole or in part.

(3) Before making an order under this section, the Lord Chancellor must consult –

  (a) the President of the Court of Protection,

  (b) the Vice-President of the Court of Protection, and

  (c) the Senior Judge of the Court of Protection.

(4) The Lord Chancellor must take such steps as are reasonably practicable to bring information about fees to the attention of persons likely to have to pay them.

(5) Fees payable under this section are recoverable summarily as a civil debt.

55 Costs

(1) Subject to Court of Protection Rules, the costs of and incidental to all proceedings in the court are in its discretion.

(2) The rules may in particular make provision for regulating matters relating to the costs of those proceedings, including prescribing scales of costs to be paid to legal or other representatives.

(3) The court has full power to determine by whom and to what extent the costs are to be paid.

(4) The court may, in any proceedings –

    (a) disallow, or

    (b) order the legal or other representatives concerned to meet, the whole of any wasted costs or such part of them as may be determined in accordance with the rules.

(5) 'Legal or other representative', in relation to a party to proceedings, means any person exercising a right of audience or right to conduct litigation on his behalf.

(6) 'Wasted costs' means any costs incurred by a party –

    (a) as a result of any improper, unreasonable or negligent act or omission on the part of any legal or other representative or any employee of such a representative, or

    (b) which, in the light of any such act or omission occurring after they were incurred, the court considers it is unreasonable to expect that party to pay.

56 Fees and costs: supplementary

(1) Court of Protection Rules may make provision –

    (a) as to the way in which, and funds from which, fees and costs are to be paid;

    (b) for charging fees and costs upon the estate of the person to whom the proceedings relate;

    (c) for the payment of fees and costs within a specified time of the death of the person to whom the proceedings relate or the conclusion of the proceedings.

(2) A charge on the estate of a person created by virtue of subsection (1)(b) does not cause any interest of the person in any property to fail or determine or to be prevented from recommencing.

The Public Guardian

57 The Public Guardian

(1) For the purposes of this Act, there is to be an officer, to be known as the Public Guardian.

(2) The Public Guardian is to be appointed by the Lord Chancellor.

(3) There is to be paid to the Public Guardian out of money provided by Parliament such salary as the Lord Chancellor may determine.

(4) The Lord Chancellor may, after consulting the Public Guardian –

    (a) provide him with such officers and staff, or

    (b) enter into such contracts with other persons for the provision (by them or their sub-contractors) of officers, staff or services, as the Lord Chancellor thinks necessary for the proper discharge of the Public Guardian's functions.

(5) Any functions of the Public Guardian may, to the extent authorised by him, be performed by any of his officers.

58 Functions of the Public Guardian

(1) The Public Guardian has the following functions –

    (a) establishing and maintaining a register of lasting powers of attorney,

    (b) establishing and maintaining a register of orders appointing deputies,

    (c) supervising deputies appointed by the court,

    (d) directing a Court of Protection Visitor to visit –

        (i) a donee of a lasting power of attorney,

        (ii) a deputy appointed by the court, or

        (iii) the person granting the power of attorney or for whom the deputy is appointed ('P'), and to make a report to the Public Guardian on such matters as he may direct,

    (e) receiving security which the court requires a person to give for the discharge of his functions,

    (f) receiving reports from donees of lasting powers of attorney and deputies appointed by the court,

    (g) reporting to the court on such matters relating to proceedings under this Act as the court requires,

    (h) dealing with representations (including complaints) about the way in which a donee of a lasting power of attorney or a deputy appointed by the court is exercising his powers,

    (i) publishing, in any manner the Public Guardian thinks appropriate, any information he thinks appropriate about the discharge of his functions.

(2) The functions conferred by subsection (1)(c) and (h) may be discharged in co-operation with any other person who has functions in relation to the care or treatment of P.

(3) The Lord Chancellor may by regulations make provision –

    (a) conferring on the Public Guardian other functions in connection with this Act;

    (b) in connection with the discharge by the Public Guardian of his functions.

(4) Regulations made under subsection (3)(b) may in particular make provision as to –

    (a) the giving of security by deputies appointed by the court and the enforcement and discharge of security so given;

    (b) the fees which may be charged by the Public Guardian;

    (c) the way in which, and funds from which, such fees are to be paid;

    (d) exemptions from and reductions in such fees;

    (e) remission of such fees in whole or in part;

    (f) the making of reports to the Public Guardian by deputies appointed by the court and others who are directed by the court to carry out any transaction for a person who lacks capacity.

(5) For the purpose of enabling him to carry out his functions, the Public Guardian may, at all reasonable times, examine and take copies of –

    (a) any health record,

    (b) any record of, or held by, a local authority and compiled in connection with a social services function, and

    (c) any record held by a person registered under Part 2 of the Care Standards Act 2000 (c. 14), so far as the record relates to P.

(6) The Public Guardian may also for that purpose interview P in private.

59 Public Guardian Board (repealed)

60 Annual report

(1) The Public Guardian must make an annual report to the Lord Chancellor about the discharge of his functions.

(2) The Lord Chancellor must, within one month of receiving the report, lay a copy of it before Parliament.

Court of Protection Visitors

61 Court of Protection Visitors

(1) A Court of Protection Visitor is a person who is appointed by the Lord Chancellor to –
   (a) a panel of Special Visitors, or
   (b) a panel of General Visitors.
(2) A person is not qualified to be a Special Visitor unless he –
   (a) is a registered medical practitioner or appears to the Lord Chancellor to have other suitable qualifications or training, and
   (b) appears to the Lord Chancellor to have special knowledge of and experience in cases of impairment of or disturbance in the functioning of the mind or brain.
(3) A General Visitor need not have a medical qualification.
(4) A Court of Protection Visitor –
   (a) may be appointed for such term and subject to such conditions, and
   (b) may be paid such remuneration and allowances, as the Lord Chancellor may determine.
(5) For the purpose of carrying out his functions under this Act in relation to a person who lacks capacity ('P'), a Court of Protection Visitor may, at all reasonable times, examine and take copies of –
   (a) any health record,
   (b) any record of, or held by, a local authority and compiled in connection with a social services function, and
   (c) any record held by a person registered under Part 2 of the Care Standards Act 2000 (c. 14), so far as the record relates to P.
(6) A Court of Protection Visitor may also for that purpose interview P in private.

Part 3   Miscellaneous and general

Declaratory provision

62 Scope of the Act

For the avoidance of doubt, it is hereby declared that nothing in this Act is to be taken to affect the law relating to murder or manslaughter or the operation of section 2 of the Suicide Act 1961 (c. 60) (assisting suicide).

Private international law

63 International protection of adults

Schedule 3 –
   (a) gives effect in England and Wales to the Convention on the International Protection of Adults signed at the Hague on 13th January 2000 (Cm. 5881) (in so far as this Act does not otherwise do so), and
   (b) makes related provision as to the private international law of England and Wales.

General

64 Interpretation

(1) In this Act –

'the 1985 Act' means the Enduring Powers of Attorney Act 1985 (c. 29),

'advance decision' has the meaning given in section 24(1),

'authorisation under Schedule A1' means either –

(a) a standard authorisation under that Schedule, or

(b) an urgent authorisation under that Schedule.

'the court' means the Court of Protection established by section 45,

'Court of Protection Rules' has the meaning given in section 51(1),

'Court of Protection Visitor' has the meaning given in section 61,

'deputy' has the meaning given in section 16(2)(b),

'enactment' includes a provision of subordinate legislation (within the meaning of the Interpretation Act 1978 (c. 30)),

'health record' has the meaning given in section 68 of the Data Protection Act 1998 (c. 29) (as read with section 69 of that Act),

'the Human Rights Convention' has the same meaning as 'the Convention' in the Human Rights Act 1998 (c. 42),

'independent mental capacity advocate' has the meaning given in section 35(1),

'lasting power of attorney' has the meaning given in section 9,

'life-sustaining treatment' has the meaning given in section 4(10),

'local authority', except in Schedule A1, means –

(a) the council of a county in England in which there are no district councils,

(b) the council of a district in England,

(c) the council of a county or county borough in Wales,

(d) the council of a London borough,

(e) the Common Council of the City of London, or

(f) the Council of the Isles of Scilly,

'Mental Health Act' means the Mental Health Act 1983 (c. 20),

'prescribed', in relation to regulations made under this Act, means prescribed by those regulations,

'property' includes any thing in action and any interest in real or personal property,

'public authority' has the same meaning as in the Human Rights Act 1998,

'Public Guardian' has the meaning given in section 57,

'purchaser' and 'purchase' have the meaning given in section 205(1) of the Law of Property Act 1925 (c. 20),

'social services function' has the meaning given in section 1A of the Local Authority Social Services Act 1970 (c. 42),

'treatment' includes a diagnostic or other procedure,

'trust corporation' has the meaning given in section 68(1) of the Trustee Act 1925 (c. 19), and 'will' includes codicil.

(2) In this Act, references to making decisions, in relation to a donee of a lasting power of attorney or a deputy appointed by the court, include, where appropriate, acting on decisions made.

(3) In this Act, references to the bankruptcy of an individual include a case where a bankruptcy restrictions order under the Insolvency Act 1986 (c. 45) has effect in respect of him.

(4) 'Bankruptcy restrictions order' includes an interim bankruptcy restrictions order.

(5) In this Act, references to deprivation of a person's liberty have the same meaning as in Article 5(1) of the Human Rights Convention.

(6) For the purposes of such references, it does not matter whether a person is deprived of his liberty by a public authority or not.

65   Rules, regulations and orders

(1) Any power to make rules, regulations or orders under this Act, other than the power in section 21 –
   (a) is exercisable by statutory instrument;
   (b) includes power to make supplementary, incidental, consequential, transitional or saving provision;
   (c) includes power to make different provision for different cases.

(2) Any statutory instrument containing rules, regulations or orders made by the Lord Chancellor or the Secretary of State under this Act, other than –
   (a) regulations under section 34 (loss of capacity during research project),
   (b) regulations under section 41 (adjusting role of independent mental capacity advocacy service),
   (c) regulations under paragraph 32(1)(b) of Schedule 3 (private international law relating to the protection of adults),
   (d) an order of the kind mentioned in section 67(6) (consequential amendments of primary legislation), or
   (e) an order under section 68 (commencement), is subject to annulment in pursuance of a resolution of either House of Parliament.

(3) A statutory instrument containing an Order in Council under paragraph 31 of Schedule 3 (provision to give further effect to Hague Convention) is subject to annulment in pursuance of a resolution of either House of Parliament.

(4) A statutory instrument containing regulations made by the Secretary of State under section 34 or 41 or by the Lord Chancellor under paragraph 32(1)(b) of Schedule 3 may not be made unless a draft has been laid before and approved by resolution of each House of Parliament.

(4A) Subsection (2) does not apply to a statutory instrument containing regulations made by the Secretary of State under Schedule A1.

(4B) If such a statutory instrument contains regulations under paragraph 42(2)(b), 129, 162 or 164 of Schedule A1 (whether or not it also contains other regulations), the instrument may not be made unless a draft has been laid before and approved by resolution of each House of Parliament.

(4C) Subject to that, such a statutory instrument is subject to annulment in pursuance of a resolution of either House of Parliament.

(5) An order under section 21 –
   (a) may include supplementary, incidental, consequential, transitional or saving provision;
   (b) may make different provision for different cases;
   (c) is to be made in the form of a statutory instrument to which the Statutory Instruments Act 1946 applies as if the order were made by a Minister of the Crown; and
   (d) is subject to annulment in pursuance of a resolution of either House of Parliament.

66   Existing receivers and enduring powers of attorney etc.

(1) The following provisions cease to have effect –

  (a) Part 7 of the Mental Health Act,

  (b) the Enduring Powers of Attorney Act 1985 (c. 29).

(2) No enduring power of attorney within the meaning of the 1985 Act is to be created after the commencement of subsection (1)(b).

(3) Schedule 4 has effect in place of the 1985 Act in relation to any enduring power of attorney created before the commencement of subsection (1)(b).

(4) Schedule 5 contains transitional provisions and savings in relation to Part 7 of the Mental Health Act and the 1985 Act.

67   Minor and consequential amendments and repeals

(1) Schedule 6 contains minor and consequential amendments.

(2) Schedule 7 contains repeals.

(3) The Lord Chancellor may by order make supplementary, incidental, consequential, transitional or saving provision for the purposes of, in consequence of, or for giving full effect to a provision of this Act.

(4) An order under subsection (3) may, in particular –

  (a) provide for a provision of this Act which comes into force before another provision of this Act has come into force to have effect, until the other provision has come into force, with specified modifications;

  (b) amend, repeal or revoke an enactment, other than one contained in an Act or Measure passed in a Session after the one in which this Act is passed.

(5) The amendments that may be made under subsection (4)(b) are in addition to those made by or under any other provision of this Act.

(6) An order under subsection (3) which amends or repeals a provision of an Act or Measure may not be made unless a draft has been laid before and approved by resolution of each House of Parliament.

68   Commencement and extent

(1) This Act, other than sections 30 to 41, comes into force in accordance with provision made by order by the Lord Chancellor.

(2) Sections 30 to 41 come into force in accordance with provision made by order by –

  (a) the Secretary of State, in relation to England, and

  (b) the National Assembly for Wales, in relation to Wales.

(3) An order under this section may appoint different days for different provisions and different purposes.

(4) Subject to subsections (5) and (6), this Act extends to England and Wales only.

(5) The following provisions extend to the United Kingdom –

  (a) paragraph 16(1) of Schedule 1 (evidence of instruments and of registration of lasting powers of attorney),

  (b) paragraph 15(3) of Schedule 4 (evidence of instruments and of registration of enduring powers of attorney).

(6) Subject to any provision made in Schedule 6, the amendments and repeals made by Schedules 6 and 7 have the same extent as the enactments to which they relate.

69   Short title

This Act may be cited as the Mental Capacity Act 2005.

Schedule A1

Hospital and care home residents: deprivation of liberty

Part 1   Authorisation to deprive residents of liberty etc.

Application of Part

1. (1) This Part applies if the following conditions are met.

(2) The first condition is that a person ('P') is detained in a hospital or care home – for the purpose of being given care or treatment – in circumstances which amount to deprivation of the person's liberty.

(3) The second condition is that a standard or urgent authorisation is in force.

(4) The third condition is that the standard or urgent authorisation relates –

(a) to P, and

(b) to the hospital or care home in which P is detained.

Authorisation to deprive P of liberty

2. The managing authority of the hospital or care home may deprive P of his liberty by detaining him as mentioned in paragraph 1(2).

No liability for acts done for purpose of depriving P of liberty

3. (1) This paragraph applies to any act which a person ('D') does for the purpose of detaining P as mentioned in paragraph 1(2).

(2) D does not incur any liability in relation to the act that he would not have incurred if P –

(a) had had capacity to consent in relation to D's doing the act, and

(b) had consented to D's doing the act.

No protection for negligent acts etc.

4. (1) Paragraphs 2 and 3 do not exclude a person's civil liability for loss or damage, or his criminal liability, resulting from his negligence in doing any thing.

(2) Paragraphs 2 and 3 do not authorise a person to do anything otherwise than for the purpose of the standard or urgent authorisation that is in force.

(3) In a case where a standard authorisation is in force, paragraphs 2 and 3 do not authorise a person to do anything which does not comply with the conditions (if any) included in the authorisation.

Part 2   Interpretation: main terms

Introduction

5. This Part applies for the purposes of this Schedule.

Detained resident

6. 'Detained resident' means a person detained in a hospital or care home – for the purpose of being given care or treatment – in circumstances which amount to deprivation of the person's liberty.

Relevant person etc.

7. In relation to a person who is, or is to be, a detained resident –

'relevant person' means the person in question;

'relevant hospital or care home' means the hospital or care home in question;

'relevant care or treatment' means the care or treatment in question.

Authorisations

8. 'Standard authorisation' means an authorisation given under Part 4.

9. 'Urgent authorisation' means an authorisation given under Part 5.

10. 'Authorisation under this Schedule' means either of the following –

    (a) a standard authorisation;

    (b) an urgent authorisation.

11. (1) The purpose of a standard authorisation is the purpose which is stated in the authorisation in accordance with paragraph 55(1)(d).

(2) The purpose of an urgent authorisation is the purpose which is stated in the authorisation in accordance with paragraph 80(d).

Part 3   The qualifying requirement

The qualifying requirements

12. (1) These are the qualifying requirements referred to in this Schedule –

    (a) the age requirement;

    (b) the mental health requirement;

    (c) the mental capacity requirement;

    (d) the best interests requirement;

    (e) the eligibility requirement;

    (f) the no refusals requirement.

(2) Any question of whether a person who is, or is to be, a detained resident meets the qualifying requirements is to be determined in accordance with this Part.

(3) In a case where –

    (a) the question of whether a person meets a particular qualifying requirement arises in relation to the giving of a standard authorisation, and

    (b) any circumstances relevant to determining that question are expected to change between the time when the determination is made and the time when the authorisation is expected to come into force, those circumstances are to be taken into account as they are expected to be at the later time.

The age requirement

13. The relevant person meets the age requirement if he has reached 18.

The mental health requirement

14. (1) The relevant person meets the mental health requirement if he is suffering from mental disorder (within the meaning of the Mental Health Act, but disregarding any exclusion for persons with learning disability).

(2) An exclusion for persons with learning disability is any provision of the Mental Health Act which provides for a person with learning disability not to be regarded as suffering from mental disorder for one or more purposes of that Act.

The mental capacity requirement

15. The relevant person meets the mental capacity requirement if he lacks capacity in relation to the question whether or not he should be accommodated in the relevant hospital or care home for the purpose of being given the relevant care or treatment.

The best interests requirement

16. (1) The relevant person meets the best interests requirement if all of the following conditions are met.

(2) The first condition is that the relevant person is, or is to be, a detained resident.

(3) The second condition is that it is in the best interests of the relevant person for him to be a detained resident.

(4) The third condition is that, in order to prevent harm to the relevant person, it is necessary for him to be a detained resident.

(5) The fourth condition is that it is a proportionate response to –
    (a) the likelihood of the relevant person suffering harm, and
    (b) the seriousness of that harm, for him to be a detained resident.

The eligibility requirement

17. (1) The relevant person meets the eligibility requirement unless he is ineligible to be deprived of liberty by this Act.

(2) Schedule 1A applies for the purpose of determining whether or not P is ineligible to be deprived of liberty by this Act.

The no refusals requirement

18. The relevant person meets the no refusals requirement unless there is a refusal within the meaning of paragraph 19 or 20.

19. (1) There is a refusal if these conditions are met –
    (a) the relevant person has made an advance decision;
    (b) the advance decision is valid;
    (c) the advance decision is applicable to some or all of the relevant treatment.

(2) Expressions used in this paragraph and any of sections 24, 25 or 26 have the same meaning in this paragraph as in that section.

20. (1) There is a refusal if it would be in conflict with a valid decision of a donee or deputy for the relevant person to be accommodated in the relevant hospital or care home for the purpose of receiving some or all of the relevant care or treatment –
    (a) in circumstances which amount to deprivation of the person's liberty, or
    (b) at all.

(2) A donee is a donee of a lasting power of attorney granted by the relevant person.

(3) A decision of a donee or deputy is valid if it is made –

    (a) within the scope of his authority as donee or deputy, and

    (b) in accordance with Part 1 of this Act.

Part 4   Standard authorisations

Supervisory body to give authorisation

21. Only the supervisory body may give a standard authorisation.

22. The supervisory body may not give a standard authorisation unless –

    (a) the managing authority of the relevant hospital or care home have requested it, or

    (b) paragraph 71 applies (right of third party to require consideration of whether authorisation needed).

23. The managing authority may not make a request for a standard authorisation unless

    (a) they are required to do so by paragraph 24 (as read with paragraphs 27 to 29),

    (b) they are required to do so by paragraph 25 (as read with paragraph 28), or

    (c) they are permitted to do so by paragraph 30.

Duty to request authorisation: basic cases

24. (1) The managing authority must request a standard authorisation in any of the following cases.

(2) The first case is where it appears to the managing authority that the relevant person

    (a) is not yet accommodated in the relevant hospital or care home,

    (b) is likely – at some time within the next 28 days – to be a detained resident in the relevant hospital or care home, and

    (c) is likely –

        (i) at that time, or

        (ii) at some later time within the next 28 days, to meet all of the qualifying requirements.

(3) The second case is where it appears to the managing authority that the relevant person –

    (a) is already accommodated in the relevant hospital or care home,

    (b) is likely – at some time within the next 28 days – to be a detained resident in the relevant hospital or care home, and

    (c) is likely –

        (i) at that time, or

        (ii) at some later time within the next 28 days, to meet all of the qualifying requirements.

(4) The third case is where it appears to the managing authority that the relevant person –

    (a) is a detained resident in the relevant hospital or care home, and

    (b) meets all of the qualifying requirements, or is likely to do so at some time within the next 28 days. (5) This paragraph is subject to paragraphs 27 to 29.

Duty to request authorisation: change in place of detention

25. (1) The relevant managing authority must request a standard authorisation if it appears to them that these conditions are met.

(2) The first condition is that a standard authorisation –
   (a) has been given, and
   (b) has not ceased to be in force.

(3) The second condition is that there is, or is to be, a change in the place of detention.

(4) This paragraph is subject to paragraph 28.

26. (1) This paragraph applies for the purposes of paragraph 25.

(2) There is a change in the place of detention if the relevant person –
   (a) ceases to be a detained resident in the stated hospital or care home, and
   (b) becomes a detained resident in a different hospital or care home ('the new hospital or care home').

(3) The stated hospital or care home is the hospital or care home to which the standard authorisation relates.

(4) The relevant managing authority are the managing authority of the new hospital or care home.

Other authority for detention: request for authorisation

27. (1) This paragraph applies if, by virtue of section 4A(3), a decision of the court authorises the relevant person to be a detained resident.

(2) Paragraph 24 does not require a request for a standard authorisation to be made in relation to that detention unless these conditions are met.

(3) The first condition is that the standard authorisation would be in force at a time immediately after the expiry of the other authority.

(4) The second condition is that the standard authorisation would not be in force at any time on or before the expiry of the other authority.

(5) The third condition is that it would, in the managing authority's view, be unreasonable to delay making the request until a time nearer the expiry of the other authority.

(6) In this paragraph –
   (a) the other authority is –
      (i) the decision mentioned in sub-paragraph (1), or
      (ii) any further decision of the court which, by virtue of section 4A(3), authorises, or is expected to authorise, the relevant person to be a detained resident;
   (b) the expiry of the other authority is the time when the other authority is expected to cease to authorise the relevant person to be a detained resident.

Request refused: no further request unless change of circumstances

28. (1) This paragraph applies if –
   (a) a managing authority request a standard authorisation under paragraph 24 or 25, and
   (b) the supervisory body are prohibited by paragraph 50(2) from giving the authorisation.

(2) Paragraph 24 or 25 does not require that managing authority to make a new request for a standard authorisation unless it appears to the managing authority that –
   (a) there has been a change in the relevant person's case, and
   (b) because of that change, the supervisory body are likely to give a standard authorisation if requested.

Authorisation given: request for further authorisation

29. (1) This paragraph applies if a standard authorisation –

(a) has been given in relation to the detention of the relevant person, and

(b) that authorisation ('the existing authorisation') has not ceased to be in force.

(2) Paragraph 24 does not require a new request for a standard authorisation ('the new authorisation') to be made unless these conditions are met.

(3) The first condition is that the new authorisation would be in force at a time immediately after the expiry of the existing authorisation.

(4) The second condition is that the new authorisation would not be in force at any time on or before the expiry of the existing authorisation.

(5) The third condition is that it would, in the managing authority's view, be unreasonable to delay making the request until a time nearer the expiry of the existing authorisation.

(6) The expiry of the existing authorisation is the time when it is expected to cease to be in force.

Power to request authorisation

30. (1) This paragraph applies if –

(a) a standard authorisation has been given in relation to the detention of the relevant person,

(b) that authorisation ('the existing authorisation') has not ceased to be in force,

(c) the requirement under paragraph 24 to make a request for a new standard authorisation does not apply, because of paragraph 29, and

(d) a review of the existing authorisation has been requested, or is being carried out, in accordance with Part 8.

(2) The managing authority may request a new standard authorisation which would be in force on or before the expiry of the existing authorisation; but only if it would also be in force immediately after that expiry.

(3) The expiry of the existing authorisation is the time when it is expected to cease to be in force.

(4) Further provision relating to cases where a request is made under this paragraph can be found in –

(a) paragraph 62 (effect of decision about request), and

(b) paragraph 134 (effect of request on Part 8 review).

Information included in request

31. A request for a standard authorisation must include the information (if any) required by regulations.

Records of requests

32. (1) The managing authority of a hospital or care home must keep a written record of –

(a) each request that they make for a standard authorisation, and

(b) the reasons for making each request.

(2) A supervisory body must keep a written record of each request for a standard authorisation that is made to them.

Relevant person must be assessed

33. (1) This paragraph applies if the supervisory body are requested to give a standard authorisation.

(2) The supervisory body must secure that all of these assessments are carried out in relation to the relevant person –
    (a) an age assessment;
    (b) a mental health assessment;
    (c) a mental capacity assessment;
    (d) a best interests assessment;
    (e) an eligibility assessment;
    (f) a no refusals assessment.
(3) The person who carries out any such assessment is referred to as the assessor.
(4) Regulations may be made about the period (or periods) within which assessors must carry out assessments.
(5) This paragraph is subject to paragraphs 49 and 133.

Age assessment
34. An age assessment is an assessment of whether the relevant person meets the age requirement.

Mental health assessment
35. A mental health assessment is an assessment of whether the relevant person meets the mental health requirement.
36. When carrying out a mental health assessment, the assessor must also –
    (a) consider how (if at all) the relevant person's mental health is likely to be affected by his being a detained resident, and
    (b) notify the best interests assessor of his conclusions.

Mental capacity assessment
37. A mental capacity assessment is an assessment of whether the relevant person meets the mental capacity requirement.

Best interests assessment
38. A best interests assessment is an assessment of whether the relevant person meets the best interests requirement.
39. (1) In carrying out a best interests assessment, the assessor must comply with the duties in sub-paragraphs (2) and (3).
(2) The assessor must consult the managing authority of the relevant hospital or care home.
(3) The assessor must have regard to all of the following –
    (a) the conclusions which the mental health assessor has notified to the best interests assessor in accordance with paragraph 36(b);
    (b) any relevant needs assessment;
    (c) any relevant care plan.
(4) A relevant needs assessment is an assessment of the relevant person's needs which –
    (a) was carried out in connection with the relevant person being accommodated in the relevant hospital or care home, and
    (b) was carried out by or on behalf of –
      (i) the managing authority of the relevant hospital or care home, or
      (ii) the supervisory body.

(5) A relevant care plan is a care plan which –
   (a) sets out how the relevant person's needs are to be met whilst he is accommodated in the relevant hospital or care home, and
   (b) was drawn up by or on behalf of –
      (i) the managing authority of the relevant hospital or care home, or
      (ii) the supervisory body.
(6) The managing authority must give the assessor a copy of –
   (a) any relevant needs assessment carried out by them or on their behalf, or
   (b) any relevant care plan drawn up by them or on their behalf.
(7) The supervisory body must give the assessor a copy of –
   (a) any relevant needs assessment carried out by them or on their behalf, or
   (b) any relevant care plan drawn up by them or on their behalf.
(8) The duties in sub-paragraphs (2) and (3) do not affect any other duty to consult or to take the views of others into account.

40. (1) This paragraph applies whatever conclusion the best interests assessment comes to.
(2) The assessor must state in the best interests assessment the name and address of every interested person whom he has consulted in carrying out the assessment.

41. Paragraphs 42 and 43 apply if the best interests assessment comes to the conclusion that the relevant person meets the best interests requirement.

42. (1) The assessor must state in the assessment the maximum authorisation period.
(2) The maximum authorisation period is the shorter of these periods –
   (a) the period which, in the assessor's opinion, would be the appropriate maximum period for the relevant person to be a detained resident under the standard authorisation that has been requested;
   (b) 1 year, or such shorter period as may be prescribed in regulations.
(3) Regulations under sub-paragraph (2)(b) –
   (a) need not provide for a shorter period to apply in relation to all standard authorisations;
   (b) may provide for different periods to apply in relation to different kinds of standard authorisations.
(4) Before making regulations under sub-paragraph (2)(b) the Secretary of State must consult all of the following –
   (a) each body required by regulations under paragraph 162 to monitor and report on the operation of this Schedule in relation to England;
   (b) such other persons as the Secretary of State considers it appropriate to consult.
(5) Before making regulations under sub-paragraph (2)(b) the National Assembly for Wales must consult all of the following –
   (a) each person or body directed under paragraph 163(2) to carry out any function of the Assembly of monitoring and reporting on the operation of this Schedule in relation to Wales;
   (b) such other persons as the Assembly considers it appropriate to consult.

43. The assessor may include in the assessment recommendations about conditions to which the standard authorisation is, or is not, to be subject in accordance with paragraph 53.

44. (1) This paragraph applies if the best interests assessment comes to the conclusion that the relevant person does not meet the best interests requirement.

(2) If, on the basis of the information taken into account in carrying out the assessment, it appears to the assessor that there is an unauthorised deprivation of liberty, he must include a statement to that effect in the assessment.

(3) There is an unauthorised deprivation of liberty if the managing authority of the relevant hospital or care home are already depriving the relevant person of his liberty without authority of the kind mentioned in section 4A.

45. The duties with which the best interests assessor must comply are subject to the provision included in appointment regulations under Part 10 (in particular, provision made under paragraph 146).

Eligibility assessment

46. An eligibility assessment is an assessment of whether the relevant person meets the eligibility requirement.

47. (1) Regulations may –

    (a) require an eligibility assessor to request a best interests assessor to provide relevant eligibility information, and

    (b) require the best interests assessor, if such a request is made, to provide such relevant eligibility information as he may have.

(2) In this paragraph –

'best interests assessor' means any person who is carrying out, or has carried out, a best interests assessment in relation to the relevant person;

'eligibility assessor' means a person carrying out an eligibility assessment in relation to the relevant person;

'relevant eligibility information' is information relevant to assessing whether or not the relevant person is ineligible by virtue of paragraph 5 of Schedule 1A.

No refusals assessment

48. A no refusals assessment is an assessment of whether the relevant person meets the no refusals requirement.

Equivalent assessment already carried out

49. (1) The supervisory body are not required by paragraph 33 to secure that a particular kind of assessment ('the required assessment') is carried out in relation to the relevant person if the following conditions are met.

(2) The first condition is that the supervisory body have a written copy of an assessment of the relevant person ('the existing assessment') that has already been carried out.

(3) The second condition is that the existing assessment complies with all requirements under this Schedule with which the required assessment would have to comply (if it were carried out).

(4) The third condition is that the existing assessment was carried out within the previous 12 months; but this condition need not be met if the required assessment is an age assessment.

(5) The fourth condition is that the supervisory body are satisfied that there is no reason why the existing assessment may no longer be accurate.

(6) If the required assessment is a best interests assessment, in satisfying themselves as mentioned in sub-paragraph (5), the supervisory body must take into account any information given, or submissions made, by –

  (a) the relevant person's representative,

  (b) any section 39C IMCA or

  (c) any section 39D IMCA.

(7) It does not matter whether the existing assessment was carried out in connection with a request for a standard authorisation or for some other purpose.

(8) If, because of this paragraph, the supervisory body are not required by paragraph 33 to secure that the required assessment is carried out, the existing assessment is to be treated for the purposes of this Schedule –

  (a) as an assessment of the same kind as the required assessment, and

  (b) as having been carried out under paragraph 33 in connection with the request for the standard authorisation.

Duty to give authorisation

50. (1) The supervisory body must give a standard authorisation if –

  (a) all assessments are positive, and

  (b) the supervisory body have written copies of all those assessments.

(2) The supervisory body must not give a standard authorisation except in accordance with sub-paragraph (1).

(3) All assessments are positive if each assessment carried out under paragraph 33 has come to the conclusion that the relevant person meets the qualifying requirement to which the assessment relates.

Terms of authorisation

51. (1) If the supervisory body are required to give a standard authorisation, they must decide the period during which the authorisation is to be in force.

(2) That period must not exceed the maximum authorisation period stated in the best interests assessment.

52. A standard authorisation may provide for the authorisation to come into force at a time after it is given.

53. (1) A standard authorisation may be given subject to conditions.

(2) Before deciding whether to give the authorisation subject to conditions, the supervisory body must have regard to any recommendations in the best interests assessment about such conditions.

(3) The managing authority of the relevant hospital or care home must ensure that any conditions are complied with.

Form of authorisation

54. A standard authorisation must be in writing.

55. (1) A standard authorisation must state the following things –

  (a) the name of the relevant person;

  (b) the name of the relevant hospital or care home;

  (c) the period during which the authorisation is to be in force;

  (d) the purpose for which the authorisation is given;

  (e) any conditions subject to which the authorisation is given;

  (f) the reason why each qualifying requirement is met.

(2) The statement of the reason why the eligibility requirement is met must be framed by reference to the cases in the table in paragraph 2 of Schedule 1A.

56. (1) If the name of the relevant hospital or care home changes, the standard authorisation is to be read as if it stated the current name of the hospital or care home.

(2) But sub-paragraph (1) is subject to any provision relating to the change of name which is made in any enactment or in any instrument made under an enactment.

Duty to give information about decision

57. (1) This paragraph applies if –
  (a) a request is made for a standard authorisation, and
  (b) the supervisory body are required by paragraph 50(1) to give the standard authorisation.

(2) The supervisory body must give a copy of the authorisation to each of the following
  (a) the relevant person's representative;
  (b) the managing authority of the relevant hospital or care home;
  (c) the relevant person;
  (d) any section 39A IMCA;
  (e) every interested person consulted by the best interests assessor.

(3) The supervisory body must comply with this paragraph as soon as practicable after they give the standard authorisation.

58. (1) This paragraph applies if –
  (a) a request is made for a standard authorisation, and
  (b) the supervisory body are prohibited by paragraph 50(2) from giving the standard authorisation.

(2) The supervisory body must give notice, stating that they are prohibited from giving the authorisation, to each of the following –
  (a) the managing authority of the relevant hospital or care home;
  (b) the relevant person;
  (c) any section 39A IMCA;
  (d) every interested person consulted by the best interests assessor.

(3) The supervisory body must comply with this paragraph as soon as practicable after it becomes apparent to them that they are prohibited from giving the authorisation.

Duty to give information about effect of authorisation

59. (1) This paragraph applies if a standard authorisation is given.

(2) The managing authority of the relevant hospital or care home must take such steps as are practicable to ensure that the relevant person understands all of the following –
  (a) the effect of the authorisation;
  (b) the right to make an application to the court to exercise its jurisdiction under section 21A;
  (c) the right under Part 8 to request a review
  (d) the right to have a section 39D IMCA appointed;
  (e) how to have a section 39D IMCA appointed.

(3) Those steps must be taken as soon as is practicable after the authorisation is given.

(4) Those steps must include the giving of appropriate information both orally and in writing.

(5) Any written information given to the relevant person must also be given by the managing authority to the relevant person's representative.

(6) They must give the information to the representative as soon as is practicable after it is given to the relevant person.

(7) Sub-paragraph (8) applies if the managing authority is notified that a section 39D IMCA has been appointed.

(8) As soon as is practicable after being notified, the managing authority must give the section 39D IMCA a copy of the written information given in accordance with sub-paragraph (4).

Records of authorisations

60. A supervisory body must keep a written record of all of the following information –
 (a) the standard authorisations that they have given;
 (b) the requests for standard authorisations in response to which they have not given an authorisation;
 (c) in relation to each standard authorisation given: the matters stated in the authorisation in accordance with paragraph 55.

Variation of an authorisation

61. (1) A standard authorisation may not be varied except in accordance with Part 7 or 8.

(2) This paragraph does not affect the powers of the Court of Protection or of any other court.

Effect of decision about request made under paragraph 25 or 30

62. (1) This paragraph applies where the managing authority request a new standard authorisation under either of the following –
 (a) paragraph 25 (change in place of detention);
 (b) paragraph 30 (existing authorisation subject to review).

(2) If the supervisory body are required by paragraph 50(1) to give the new authorisation, the existing authorisation terminates at the time when the new authorisation comes into force.

(3) If the supervisory body are prohibited by paragraph 50(2) from giving the new authorisation, there is no effect on the existing authorisation's continuation in force.

When an authorisation is in force

63. (1) A standard authorisation comes into force when it is given.

(2) But if the authorisation provides for it to come into force at a later time, it comes into force at that time.

64. (1) A standard authorisation ceases to be in force at the end of the period stated in the authorisation in accordance with paragraph 55(1)(c).

(2) But if the authorisation terminates before then in accordance with paragraph 62(2) or any other provision of this Schedule, it ceases to be in force when the termination takes effect.

(3) This paragraph does not affect the powers of the Court of Protection or of any other court.

65. (1) This paragraph applies if a standard authorisation ceases to be in force.

(2) The supervisory body must give notice that the authorisation has ceased to be in force.

(3) The supervisory body must give that notice to all of the following –
 (a) the managing authority of the relevant hospital or care home;
 (b) the relevant person;

(c) the relevant person's representative;

(d) every interested person consulted by the best interests assessor.

(4) The supervisory body must give that notice as soon as practicable after the authorisation ceases to be in force.

When a request for a standard authorisation is 'disposed of'

66. A request for a standard authorisation is to be regarded for the purposes of this Schedule as disposed of if the supervisory body have given –

(a) a copy of the authorisation in accordance with paragraph 57, or

(b) notice in accordance with paragraph 58.

Right of third party to require consideration of whether authorisation needed

67. For the purposes of paragraphs 68 to 73 there is an unauthorised deprivation of liberty if –

(a) a person is already a detained resident in a hospital or care home, and

(b) the detention of the person is not authorised as mentioned in section 4A

68. (1) If the following conditions are met, an eligible person may request the supervisory body to decide whether or not there is an unauthorised deprivation of liberty.

(2) The first condition is that the eligible person has notified the managing authority of the relevant hospital or care home that it appears to the eligible person that there is an unauthorised deprivation of liberty.

(3) The second condition is that the eligible person has asked the managing authority to request a standard authorisation in relation to the detention of the relevant person.

(4) The third condition is that the managing authority has not requested a standard authorisation within a reasonable period after the eligible person asks it to do so.

(5) In this paragraph 'eligible person' means any person other than the managing authority of the relevant hospital or care home.

69. (1) This paragraph applies if an eligible person requests the supervisory body to decide whether or not there is an unauthorised deprivation of liberty.

(2) The supervisory body must select and appoint a person to carry out an assessment of whether or not the relevant person is a detained resident.

(3) But the supervisory body need not select and appoint a person to carry out such an assessment in either of these cases.

(4) The first case is where it appears to the supervisory body that the request by the eligible person is frivolous or vexatious.

(5) The second case is where it appears to the supervisory body that –

(a) the question of whether or not there is an unauthorised deprivation of liberty has already been decided, and

(b) since that decision, there has been no change of circumstances which would merit the question being decided again.

(6) The supervisory body must not select and appoint a person to carry out an assessment under this paragraph unless it appears to the supervisory body that the person would be –

(a) suitable to carry out a best interests assessment (if one were obtained in connection with a request for a standard authorisation relating to the relevant person), and

(b) eligible to carry out such a best interests assessment.

(7) The supervisory body must notify the persons specified in sub-paragraph (8) –

(a) that the supervisory body have been requested to decide whether or not there is an unauthorised deprivation of liberty;

(b) of their decision whether or not to select and appoint a person to carry out an assessment under this paragraph;

(c) if their decision is to select and appoint a person, of the person appointed.

(8) The persons referred to in sub-paragraph (7) are –

(a) the eligible person who made the request under paragraph 68;

(b) the person to whom the request relates;

(c) the managing authority of the relevant hospital or care home;

(d) any section 39A IMCA.

70. (1) Regulations may be made about the period within which an assessment under paragraph 69 must be carried out.

(2) Regulations made under paragraph 129(3) apply in relation to the selection and appointment of a person under paragraph 69 as they apply to the selection of a person under paragraph 129 to carry out a best interests assessment.

(3) The following provisions apply to an assessment under paragraph 69 as they apply to an assessment carried out in connection with a request for a standard authorisation –

(a) paragraph 131 (examination and copying of records);

(b) paragraph 132 (representations);

(c) paragraphs 134 and 135(1) and (2) (duty to keep records and give copies).

(4) The copies of the assessment which the supervisory body are required to give under paragraph 135(2) must be given as soon as practicable after the supervisory body are themselves given a copy of the assessment.

71. (1) This paragraph applies if –

(a) the supervisory body obtain an assessment under paragraph 69,

(b) the assessment comes to the conclusion that the relevant person is a detained resident, and

(c) it appears to the supervisory body that the detention of the person is not authorised as mentioned in section 4A.

(2) This Schedule (including Part 5) applies as if the managing authority of the relevant hospital or care home had, in accordance with Part 4, requested the supervisory body to give a standard authorisation in relation to the relevant person.

(3) The managing authority of the relevant hospital or care home must supply the supervisory body with the information (if any) which the managing authority would, by virtue of paragraph 31, have had to include in a request for a standard authorisation.

(4) The supervisory body must notify the persons specified in paragraph 69(8) –

(a) of the outcome of the assessment obtained under paragraph 69, and

(b) that this Schedule applies as mentioned in sub-paragraph (2).

72. (1) This paragraph applies if –

(a) the supervisory body obtain an assessment under paragraph 69, and

(b) the assessment comes to the conclusion that the relevant person is not a detained resident.

(2) The supervisory body must notify the persons specified in paragraph 69(8) of the outcome of the assessment.

73. (1) This paragraph applies if –

(a) the supervisory body obtain an assessment under paragraph 69,

(b) the assessment comes to the conclusion that the relevant person is a detained resident, and

(c) it appears to the supervisory body that the detention of the person is authorised as mentioned in section 4A.

(2) The supervisory body must notify the persons specified in paragraph 69(8) –

(a) of the outcome of the assessment, and

(b) that it appears to the supervisory body that the detention is authorised.

Part 5 Urgent authorisations

Managing authority to give authorisation

74. Only the managing authority of the relevant hospital or care home may give an urgent authorisation.

75. The managing authority may give an urgent authorisation only if they are required to do so by paragraph 76 (as read with paragraph 77).

Duty to give authorisation

76. (1) The managing authority must give an urgent authorisation in either of the following cases.

(2) The first case is where –

(a) the managing authority are required to make a request under paragraph 24 or 25 for a standard authorisation, and

(b) they believe that the need for the relevant person to be a detained resident is so urgent that it is appropriate for the detention to begin before they make the request.

(3) The second case is where –

(a) the managing authority have made a request under paragraph 24 or 25 for a standard authorisation, and

(b) they believe that the need for the relevant person to be a detained resident is so urgent that it is appropriate for the detention to begin before the request is disposed of.

(4) References in this paragraph to the detention of the relevant person are references to the detention to which paragraph 24 or 25 relates.

(5) This paragraph is subject to paragraph 77.

77. (1) This paragraph applies where the managing authority have given an urgent authorisation ('the original authorisation') in connection with a case where a person is, or is to be, a detained resident ('the existing detention').

(2) No new urgent authorisation is to be given under paragraph 76 in connection with the existing detention.

(3) But the managing authority may request the supervisory body to extend the duration of the original authorisation.

(4) Only one request under sub-paragraph (3) may be made in relation to the original authorisation.

(5) Paragraphs 84 to 86 apply to any request made under sub-paragraph (3).

Terms of authorisation

78. (1) If the managing authority decide to give an urgent authorisation, they must decide the period during which the authorisation is to be in force.

(2) That period must not exceed 7 days.

Form of authorisation

79. An urgent authorisation must be in writing.

80. An urgent authorisation must state the following things –
   (a) the name of the relevant person;
   (b) the name of the relevant hospital or care home;
   (c) the period during which the authorisation is to be in force;
   (d) the purpose for which the authorisation is given.

81. (1) If the name of the relevant hospital or care home changes, the urgent authorisation is to be read as if it stated the current name of the hospital or care home.

(2) But sub-paragraph (1) is subject to any provision relating to the change of name which is made in any enactment or in any instrument made under an enactment.

Duty to keep records and give copies

82. (1) This paragraph applies if an urgent authorisation is given.

(2) The managing authority must keep a written record of why they have given the urgent authorisation.

(3) As soon as practicable after giving the authorisation, the managing authority must give a copy of the authorisation to all of the following –
   (a) the relevant person;
   (b) any section 39A IMCA.

Duty to give information about authorisation

83. (1) This paragraph applies if an urgent authorisation is given.

(2) The managing authority of the relevant hospital or care home must take such steps as are practicable to ensure that the relevant person understands all of the following –
   (a) the effect of the authorisation;
   (b) the right to make an application to the court to exercise its jurisdiction under section 21A.

(3) Those steps must be taken as soon as is practicable after the authorisation is given.

(4) Those steps must include the giving of appropriate information both orally and in writing.

Request for extension of duration

84. (1) This paragraph applies if the managing authority make a request under paragraph 77 for the supervisory body to extend the duration of the original authorisation.

(2) The managing authority must keep a written record of why they have made the request.

(3) The managing authority must give the relevant person notice that they have made the request.

(4) The supervisory body may extend the duration of the original authorisation if it appears to them that –
   (a) the managing authority have made the required request for a standard authorisation,
   (b) there are exceptional reasons why it has not yet been possible for that request to be disposed of, and
   (c) it is essential for the existing detention to continue until the request is disposed of.

(5) The supervisory body must keep a written record that the request has been made to them.

(6) In this paragraph and paragraphs 85 and 86 –
   (a) 'original authorisation' and 'existing detention' have the same meaning as in paragraph 77;
   (b) the required request for a standard authorisation is the request that is referred to in paragraph 76(2) or (3).

85. (1) This paragraph applies if, under paragraph 84, the supervisory body decide to extend the duration of the original authorisation.

(2) The supervisory body must decide the period of the extension.

(3) That period must not exceed 7 days.

(4) The supervisory body must give the managing authority notice stating the period of the extension.

(5) The managing authority must then vary the original authorisation so that it states the extended duration.

(6) Paragraphs 82(3) and 83 apply (with the necessary modifications) to the variation of the original authorisation as they apply to the giving of an urgent authorisation.

(7) The supervisory body must keep a written record of –
   (a) the outcome of the request, and
   (b) the period of the extension.

86. (1) This paragraph applies if, under paragraph 84, the supervisory body decide not to extend the duration of the original authorisation.

(2) The supervisory body must give the managing authority notice stating –
   (a) the decision, and
   (b) their reasons for making it.

(3) The managing authority must give a copy of that notice to all of the following –
   (a) the relevant person;
   (b) any section 39A IMCA.

(4) The supervisory body must keep a written record of the outcome of the request.

No variation

87. (1) An urgent authorisation may not be varied except in accordance with paragraph 85.

(2) This paragraph does not affect the powers of the Court of Protection or of any other court.

When an authorisation is in force

88. An urgent authorisation comes into force when it is given.

89. (1) An urgent authorisation ceases to be in force at the end of the period stated in the authorisation in accordance with paragraph 80(c) (subject to any variation in accordance with paragraph 85).

(2) But if the required request is disposed of before the end of that period, the urgent authorisation ceases to be in force as follows.

(3) If the supervisory body are required by paragraph 50(1) to give the requested authorisation, the urgent authorisation ceases to be in force when the requested authorisation comes into force.

(4) If the supervisory body are prohibited by paragraph 50(2) from giving the requested authorisation, the urgent authorisation ceases to be in force when the managing authority receive notice under paragraph 58.

(5) In this paragraph –

'required request' means the request referred to in paragraph 76(2) or (3);

'requested authorisation' means the standard authorisation to which the required request relates.

(6) This paragraph does not affect the powers of the Court of Protection or of any other court.

90. (1) This paragraph applies if an urgent authorisation ceases to be in force.

(2) The supervisory body must give notice that the authorisation has ceased to be in force.

(3) The supervisory body must give that notice to all of the following –

(a) the relevant person;

(b) any section 39A IMCA.

(4) The supervisory body must give that notice as soon as practicable after the authorisation ceases to be in force.

Part 6   Eligibility requirement not met: suspension of standard authorisation

91. (1) This Part applies if the following conditions are met.

(2) The first condition is that a standard authorisation –

(a) has been given, and

(b) has not ceased to be in force.

(3) The second condition is that the managing authority of the relevant hospital or care home are satisfied that the relevant person has ceased to meet the eligibility requirement.

(4) But this Part does not apply if the relevant person is ineligible by virtue of paragraph 5 of Schedule 1A (in which case see Part 8).

92. The managing authority of the relevant hospital or care home must give the supervisory body notice that the relevant person has ceased to meet the eligibility requirement.

93. (1) This paragraph applies if the managing authority give the supervisory body notice under paragraph 92.

(2) The standard authorisation is suspended from the time when the notice is given.

(3) The supervisory body must give notice that the standard authorisation has been suspended to the following persons –

(a) the relevant person;

(b) the relevant person's representative;

(c) the managing authority of the relevant hospital or care home.

94. (1) This paragraph applies if, whilst the standard authorisation is suspended, the managing authority are satisfied that the relevant person meets the eligibility requirement again.

(2) The managing authority must give the supervisory body notice that the relevant person meets the eligibility requirement again.

95. (1) This paragraph applies if the managing authority give the supervisory body notice under paragraph 94.

(2) The standard authorisation ceases to be suspended from the time when the notice is given.

(3) The supervisory body must give notice that the standard authorisation has ceased to be suspended to the following persons –

    (a) the relevant person;

    (b) the relevant person's representative;

    (c) any section 39D IMCA;

    (d) the managing authority of the relevant hospital or care home.

(4) The supervisory body must give notice under this paragraph as soon as practicable after they are given notice under paragraph 94.

96. (1) This paragraph applies if no notice is given under paragraph 94 before the end of the relevant 28 day period.

(2) The standard authorisation ceases to have effect at the end of the relevant 28 day period.

(3) The relevant 28 day period is the period of 28 days beginning with the day on which the standard authorisation is suspended under paragraph 93.

97. The effect of suspending the standard authorisation is that Part 1 ceases to apply for as long as the authorisation is suspended.

Part 7 Standard authorisations: change in supervisory responsibility

Application of this Part

98. (1) This Part applies if these conditions are met.

(2) The first condition is that a standard authorisation –

    (a) has been given, and

    (b) has not ceased to be in force.

(3) The second condition is that there is a change in supervisory responsibility.

(4) The third condition is that there is not a change in the place of detention (within the meaning of paragraph 25).

99. For the purposes of this Part there is a change in supervisory responsibility if –

    (a) one body ('the old supervisory body') have ceased to be supervisory body in relation to the standard authorisation, and

    (b) a different body ('the new supervisory body') have become supervisory body in relation to the standard authorisation.

Effect of change in supervisory responsibility

100. (1) The new supervisory body becomes the supervisory body in relation to the authorisation.

(2) Anything done by or in relation to the old supervisory body in connection with the authorisation has effect, so far as is necessary for continuing its effect after the change, as if done by or in relation to the new supervisory body.

(3) Anything which relates to the authorisation and which is in the process of being done by or in relation to the old supervisory body at the time of the change may be continued by or in relation to the new supervisory body.

(4) But –

(a) the old supervisory body do not, by virtue of this paragraph, cease to be liable for anything done by them in connection with the authorisation before the change; and

(b) the new supervisory body do not, by virtue of this paragraph, become liable for any such thing.

Part 8   Standard authorisations: Review

Application of this Part

101. (1) This Part applies if a standard authorisation –

(a) has been given, and

(b) has not ceased to be in force.

(2) Paragraphs 102 to 122 are subject to paragraphs 123 to 125.

Review by supervisory body

102. (1) The supervisory body may at any time carry out a review of the standard authorisation in accordance with this Part.

(2) The supervisory body must carry out such a review if they are requested to do so by an eligible person.

(3) Each of the following is an eligible person –

(a) the relevant person;

(b) the relevant person's representative;

(c) the managing authority of the relevant hospital or care home.

Request for review

103. (1) An eligible person may, at any time, request the supervisory body to carry out a review of the standard authorisation in accordance with this Part.

(2) The managing authority of the relevant hospital or care home must make such a request if one or more of the qualifying requirements appear to them to be reviewable.

Grounds for review

104. (1) Paragraphs 105 to 107 set out the grounds on which the qualifying requirements are reviewable.

(2) A qualifying requirement is not reviewable on any other ground.

Non-qualification ground

105. (1) Any of the following qualifying requirements is reviewable on the ground that the relevant person does not meet the requirement –

(a) the age requirement;

(b) the mental health requirement;

(c) the mental capacity requirement;

(d) the best interests requirement;

(e) the no refusals requirement.

(2) The eligibility requirement is reviewable on the ground that the relevant person is ineligible by virtue of paragraph 5 of Schedule 1A.

(3) The ground in sub-paragraph (1) and the ground in sub-paragraph (2) are referred to as the non-qualification ground.

Change of reason ground

106. (1) Any of the following qualifying requirements is reviewable on the ground set out in sub-paragraph (2) –

(a) the mental health requirement;

(b) the mental capacity requirement;

(c) the best interests requirement;

(d) the eligibility requirement;

(e) the no refusals requirement.

(2) The ground is that the reason why the relevant person meets the requirement is not the reason stated in the standard authorisation.

(3) This ground is referred to as the change of reason ground.

Variation of conditions ground

107. (1) The best interests requirement is reviewable on the ground that –

(a) there has been a change in the relevant person's case, and

(b) because of that change, it would be appropriate to vary the conditions to which the standard authorisation is subject.

(2) This ground is referred to as the variation of conditions ground.

(3) A reference to varying the conditions to which the standard authorisation is subject is a reference to –

(a) amendment of an existing condition,

(b) omission of an existing condition, or

(c) inclusion of a new condition (whether or not there are already any existing conditions).

Notice that review to be carried out

108. (1) If the supervisory body are to carry out a review of the standard authorisation, they must give notice of the review to the following persons –

(a) the relevant person;

(b) the relevant person's representative;

(c) the managing authority of the relevant hospital or care home.

(2) The supervisory body must give the notice –

(a) before they begin the review, or

(b) if that is not practicable, as soon as practicable after they have begun it.

(3) This paragraph does not require the supervisory body to give notice to any person who has requested the review.

Starting a review

109. To start a review of the standard authorisation, the supervisory body must decide which, if any, of the qualifying requirements appear to be reviewable.

No reviewable qualifying requirements

110. (1) This paragraph applies if no qualifying requirements appear to be reviewable.

(2) This Part does not require the supervisory body to take any action in respect of the standard authorisation.

One or more reviewable qualifying requirements

111. (1) This paragraph applies if one or more qualifying requirements appear to be reviewable.

(2) The supervisory body must secure that a separate review assessment is carried out in relation to each qualifying requirement which appears to be reviewable.

(3) But sub-paragraph (2) does not require the supervisory body to secure that a best interests review assessment is carried out in a case where the best interests requirement appears to the supervisory body to be non-assessable.

(4) The best interests requirement is non-assessable if –
(a) the requirement is reviewable only on the variation of conditions ground, and
(b) the change in the relevant person's case is not significant.

(5) In making any decision whether the change in the relevant person's case is significant, regard must be had to –
(a) the nature of the change, and
(b) the period that the change is likely to last for.

Review assessments

112. (1) A review assessment is an assessment of whether the relevant person meets a qualifying requirement.

(2) In relation to a review assessment –
(a) a negative conclusion is a conclusion that the relevant person does not meet the qualifying requirement to which the assessment relates;
(b) a positive conclusion is a conclusion that the relevant person meets the qualifying requirement to which the assessment relates.

(3) An age review assessment is a review assessment carried out in relation to the age requirement.

(4) A mental health review assessment is a review assessment carried out in relation to the mental health requirement.

(5) A mental capacity review assessment is a review assessment carried out in relation to the mental capacity requirement.

(6) A best interests review assessment is a review assessment carried out in relation to the best interests requirement.

(7) An eligibility review assessment is a review assessment carried out in relation to the eligibility requirement.

(8) A no refusals review assessment is a review assessment carried out in relation to the no refusals requirement.

113. (1) In carrying out a review assessment, the assessor must comply with any duties which would be imposed upon him under Part 4 if the assessment were being carried out in connection with a request for a standard authorisation.

(2) But in the case of a best interests review assessment, paragraphs 43 and 44 do not apply.

(3) Instead of what is required by paragraph 43, the best interests review assessment must include recommendations about whether – and, if so, how – it would be appropriate to vary the conditions to which the standard authorisation is subject.

Best interests requirement reviewable but non-assessable

114. (1) This paragraph applies in a case where –
(a) the best interests requirement appears to be reviewable, but
(b) in accordance with paragraph 111(3), the supervisory body are not required to secure that a best interests review assessment is carried out.

(2) The supervisory body may vary the conditions to which the standard authorisation is subject in such ways (if any) as the supervisory body think are appropriate in the circumstances.

Best interests review assessment positive

115. (1) This paragraph applies in a case where –
  (a) a best interests review assessment is carried out, and
  (b) the assessment comes to a positive conclusion.
(2) The supervisory body must decide the following questions –
  (a) whether or not the best interests requirement is reviewable on the change of reason ground;
  (b) whether or not the best interests requirement is reviewable on the variation of conditions ground;
  (c) if so, whether or not the change in the person's case is significant.
(3) If the supervisory body decide that the best interests requirement is reviewable on the change of reason ground, they must vary the standard authorisation so that it states the reason why the relevant person now meets that requirement
(4) If the supervisory body decide that –
  (a) the best interests requirement is reviewable on the variation of conditions ground, and
  (b) the change in the relevant person's case is not significant, they may vary the conditions to which the standard authorisation is subject in such ways (if any) as they think are appropriate in the circumstances.
(5) If the supervisory body decide that –
  (a) the best interests requirement is reviewable on the variation of conditions ground, and
  (b) the change in the relevant person's case is significant, they must vary the conditions to which the standard authorisation is subject in such ways as they think are appropriate in the circumstances.
(6) If the supervisory body decide that the best interests requirement is not reviewable on –
  (a) the change of reason ground, or
  (b) the variation of conditions ground, this Part does not require the supervisory body to take any action in respect of the standard authorisation so far as the best interests requirement relates to it.

Mental health, mental capacity, eligibility or no refusals review assessment positive

116. (1) This paragraph applies if the following conditions are met.
(2) The first condition is that one or more of the following are carried out –
  (a) a mental health review assessment;
  (b) a mental capacity review assessment;
  (c) an eligibility review assessment;
  (d) a no refusals review assessment.
(3) The second condition is that each assessment carried out comes to a positive conclusion.
(4) The supervisory body must decide whether or not each of the assessed qualifying requirements is reviewable on the change of reason ground.
(5) If the supervisory body decide that any of the assessed qualifying requirements is reviewable on the change of reason ground, they must vary the standard authorisation so that it states the reason why the relevant person now meets the requirement or requirements in question.

(6) If the supervisory body decide that none of the assessed qualifying requirements are reviewable on the change of reason ground, this Part does not require the supervisory body to take any action in respect of the standard authorisation so far as those requirements relate to it.

(7) An assessed qualifying requirement is a qualifying requirement in relation to which a review assessment is carried out.

One or more review assessments negative

117. (1) This paragraph applies if one or more of the review assessments carried out comes to a negative conclusion.

(2) The supervisory body must terminate the standard authorisation with immediate effect.

Completion of a review

118. (1) The review of the standard authorisation is complete in any of the following cases.

(2) The first case is where paragraph 110 applies.

(3) The second case is where –
   (a) paragraph 111 applies, and
   (b) paragraph 117 requires the supervisory body to terminate the standard authorisation.

(4) In such a case, the supervisory body need not comply with any of the other provisions of paragraphs 114 to 116 which would be applicable to the review (were it not for this sub-paragraph).

(5) The third case is where –
   (a) paragraph 111 applies,
   (b) paragraph 117 does not require the supervisory body to terminate the standard authorisation, and
   (c) the supervisory body comply with all of the provisions of paragraphs 114 to 116 (so far as they are applicable to the review).

Variations under this Part

119. Any variation of the standard authorisation made under this Part must be in writing.

Notice of outcome of review

120. (1) When the review of the standard authorisation is complete, the supervisory body must give notice to all of the following –
   (a) the managing authority of the relevant hospital or care home;
   (b) the relevant person;
   (c) the relevant person's representative;
   (d) any section 39D IMCA.

(20) That notice must state –
   (a) the outcome of the review, and
   (b) what variation (if any) has been made to the authorisation under this Part.

Records

121. A supervisory body must keep a written record of the following information –
   (a) each request for a review that is made to them;
   (b) the outcome of each request;
   (c) each review which they carry out;

(d) the outcome of each review which they carry out;

(e) any variation of an authorisation made in consequence of a review.

Relationship between review and suspension under Part 6

122. (1) This paragraph applies if a standard authorisation is suspended in accordance with Part 6.

(2) No review may be requested under this Part whilst the standard authorisation is suspended.

(3) If a review has already been requested, or is being carried out, when the standard authorisation is suspended, no steps are to be taken in connection with that review whilst the authorisation is suspended.

Relationship between review and request for new authorisation

123. (1) This paragraph applies if, in accordance with paragraph 24 (as read with paragraph 29), the managing authority of the relevant hospital or care home make a request for a new standard authorisation which would be in force after the expiry of the existing authorisation.

(2) No review may be requested under this Part until the request for the new standard authorisation has been disposed of.

(3) If a review has already been requested, or is being carried out, when the new standard authorisation is requested, no steps are to be taken in connection with that review until the request for the new standard authorisation has been disposed of.

124. (1) This paragraph applies if –

(a) a review under this Part has been requested, or is being carried out, and

(b) the managing authority of the relevant hospital or care home make a request under paragraph 30 for a new standard authorisation which would be in force on or before, and after, the expiry of the existing authorisation.

(2) No steps are to be taken in connection with the review under this Part until the request for the new standard authorisation has been disposed of.

125. In paragraphs 123 and 124 –

(a) the existing authorisation is the authorisation referred to in paragraph 101;

(b) the expiry of the existing authorisation is the time when it is expected to cease to be in force.

Part 9 Assessments under this schedule

Introduction

126. This Part contains provision about assessments under this Schedule.

127. An assessment under this Schedule is either of the following –

(a) an assessment carried out in connection with a request for a standard authorisation under Part 4;

(b) a review assessment carried out in connection with a review of a standard authorisation under Part 8.

128. In this Part, in relation to an assessment under this Schedule –

'assessor' means the person carrying out the assessment;

'relevant procedure' means –

(a) the request for the standard authorisation, or

(b) the review of the standard authorisation;

'supervisory body' means the supervisory body responsible for securing that the assessment is carried out.

Supervisory body to select assessor

129. (1) It is for the supervisory body to select a person to carry out an assessment under this Schedule.

(2) The supervisory body must not select a person to carry out an assessment unless the person –

    (a) appears to the supervisory body to be suitable to carry out the assessment (having regard, in particular, to the type of assessment and the person to be assessed), and

    (b) is eligible to carry out the assessment.

(3) Regulations may make provision about the selection, and eligibility, of persons to carry out assessments under this Schedule.

(4) Sub-paragraphs (5) and (6) apply if two or more assessments are to be obtained for the purposes of the relevant procedure.

(5) In a case where the assessments to be obtained include a mental health assessment and a best interests assessment, the supervisory body must not select the same person to carry out both assessments.

(6) Except as prohibited by sub-paragraph (5), the supervisory body may select the same person to carry out any number of the assessments which the person appears to be suitable, and is eligible, to carry out.

130. (1) This paragraph applies to regulations under paragraph 129(3).

(2) The regulations may make provision relating to a person's –

    (a) qualifications,

    (b) skills,

    (c) training,

    (d) experience,

    (e) relationship to, or connection with, the relevant person or any other person,

    (f) involvement in the care or treatment of the relevant person,

    (g) connection with the supervisory body, or

    (h) connection with the relevant hospital or care home, or with any other establishment or undertaking.

(3) The provision that the regulations may make in relation to a person's training may provide for particular training to be specified by the appropriate authority otherwise than in the regulations.

(4) In sub-paragraph (3) the 'appropriate authority' means –

    (a) in relation to England: the Secretary of State;

    (b) in relation to Wales: the National Assembly for Wales.

(5) The regulations may make provision requiring a person to be insured in respect of liabilities that may arise in connection with the carrying out of an assessment.

(6) In relation to cases where two or more assessments are to be obtained for the purposes of the relevant procedure, the regulations may limit the number, kind or combination of assessments which a particular person is eligible to carry out.

(7) Sub-paragraphs (2) to (6) do not limit the generality of the provision that may be made in the regulations.

Examination and copying of records

131. An assessor may, at all reasonable times, examine and take copies of –
   (a) any health record,
   (b) any record of, or held by, a local authority and compiled in accordance with a social services function, and
   (c) any record held by a person registered under Part 2 of the Care Standards Act 2000, which the assessor considers may be relevant to the assessment which is being carried out.

Representations

132. In carrying out an assessment under this Schedule, the assessor must take into account any information given, or submissions made, by any of the following –
   (a) the relevant person's representative;
   (b) any section 39A IMCA;
   (c) any section 39C IMCA
   (d) any section 39D IMCA.

Assessments to stop if any comes to negative conclusion

133. (1) This paragraph applies if an assessment under this Schedule comes to the conclusion that the relevant person does not meet one of the qualifying requirements.

(2) This Schedule does not require the supervisory body to secure that any other assessments under this Schedule are carried out in relation to the relevant procedure.

(3) The supervisory body must give notice to any assessor who is carrying out another assessment in connection with the relevant procedure that they are to cease carrying out that assessment.

(4) If an assessor receives such notice, this Schedule does not require the assessor to continue carrying out that assessment.

Duty to keep records and give copies

134. (1) This paragraph applies if an assessor has carried out an assessment under this Schedule (whatever conclusions the assessment has come to).

(2) The assessor must keep a written record of the assessment.

(3) As soon as practicable after carrying out the assessment, the assessor must give copies of the assessment to the supervisory body.

135. (1) This paragraph applies to the supervisory body if they are given a copy of an assessment under this Schedule.

(2) The supervisory body must give copies of the assessment to all of the following –
   (a) the managing authority of the relevant hospital or care home;
   (b) the relevant person;
   (c) any section 39A IMCA;
   (d) the relevant person's representative.

(3) If –
   (a) the assessment is obtained in relation to a request for a standard authorisation, and
   (b) the supervisory body are required by paragraph 50(1) to give the standard authorisation, the supervisory body must give the copies of the assessment when they give copies of the authorisation in accordance with paragraph 57.

(4) If –
   (a) the assessment is obtained in relation to a request for a standard authorisation, and

(b) the supervisory body are prohibited by paragraph 50(2) from giving the standard authorisation, the supervisory body must give the copies of the assessment when they give notice in accordance with paragraph 58.

(5) If the assessment is obtained in connection with the review of a standard authorisation, the supervisory body must give the copies of the assessment when they give notice in accordance with paragraph 120.

136. (1) This paragraph applies to the supervisory body if –

(a) they are given a copy of a best interests assessment, and

(b) the assessment includes, in accordance with paragraph 44(2), a statement that it appears to the assessor that there is an unauthorised deprivation of liberty.

(2) The supervisory body must notify all of the persons listed in sub-paragraph (3) that the assessment includes such a statement.

(3) Those persons are –

(a) the managing authority of the relevant hospital or care home;

(b) the relevant parties;

(c) any section 39A IMCA;

(d) any interested person consulted by the best interests assessor.

(4) The supervisory body must comply with this paragraph when (or at some time before) they comply with paragraph 135.

Part 10   Relevant person's representative

The representative

137. In this Schedule the relevant person's representative is the person appointed as such in accordance with this Part.

138. (1) Regulations may make provision about the selection and appointment of representatives.

(2) In this Part such regulations are referred to as 'appointment regulations'.

Supervisory body to appoint representative

139. (1) The supervisory body must appoint a person to be the relevant person's representative as soon as practicable after a standard authorisation is given.

(2) The supervisory body must appoint a person to be the relevant person's representative if a vacancy arises whilst a standard authorisation is in force.

(3) Where a vacancy arises, the appointment under sub-paragraph (2) is to be made as soon as practicable after the supervisory body becomes aware of the vacancy.

140. (1) The selection of a person for appointment under paragraph 139 must not be made unless it appears to the person making the selection that the prospective representative would, if appointed –

(a) maintain contact with the relevant person,

(b) represent the relevant person in matters relating to or connected with this Schedule, and

(c) support the relevant person in matters relating to or connected with this Schedule.

141. (1) Any appointment of a representative for a relevant person is in addition to, and does not affect, any appointment of a donee or deputy.

(2) The functions of any representative are in addition to, and do not affect –

(a) the authority of any donee,

(b) the powers of any deputy, or

(c) any powers of the court.

Appointment regulations

142. Appointment regulations may provide that the procedure for appointing a representative may begin at any time after a request for a standard authorisation is made (including a time before the request has been disposed of).

143. (1) Appointment regulations may make provision about who is to select a person for appointment as a representative.

(2) But regulations under this paragraph may only provide for the following to make a selection –

(a) the relevant person, if he has capacity in relation to the question of which person should be his representative;

(b) a donee of a lasting power of attorney granted by the relevant person, if it is within the scope of his authority to select a person;

(c) a deputy, if it is within the scope of his authority to select a person;

(d) a best interests assessor;

(e) the supervisory body.

(3) Regulations under this paragraph may provide that a selection by the relevant person, a donee or a deputy is subject to approval by a best interests assessor or the supervisory body.

(4) Regulations under this paragraph may provide that, if more than one selection is necessary in connection with the appointment of a particular representative –

(a) the same person may make more than one selection;

(b) different persons may make different selections.

(5) For the purposes of this paragraph a best interests assessor is a person carrying out a best interests assessment in connection with the standard authorisation in question (including the giving of that authorisation).

144. (1) Appointment regulations may make provision about who may, or may not, be –

(a) selected for appointment as a representative, or

(b) appointed as a representative.

(2) Regulations under this paragraph may relate to any of the following matters –

(a) a person's age;

(b) a person's suitability;

(c) a person's independence;

(d) a person's willingness;

(e) a person's qualifications.

145. Appointment regulations may make provision about the formalities of appointing a person as a representative.

146. In a case where a best interests assessor is to select a person to be appointed as a representative, appointment regulations may provide for the variation of the assessor's duties in relation to the assessment which he is carrying out.

Monitoring of representatives

147. Regulations may make provision requiring the managing authority of the relevant hospital or care home to –

(a) monitor, and

(b) report to the supervisory body on, the extent to which a representative is maintaining contact with the relevant person.

Termination

148. Regulations may make provision about the circumstances in which the appointment of a person as the relevant person's representative ends or may be ended.

149. Regulations may make provision about the formalities of ending the appointment of a person as a representative.

Suspension of representative's functions

150. (1) Regulations may make provision about the circumstances in which functions exercisable by, or in relation to, the relevant person's representative (whether under this Schedule or not) may be –

(a) suspended, and

(b) if suspended, revived.

(2) The regulations may make provision about the formalities for giving effect to the suspension or revival of a function.

(3) The regulations may make provision about the effect of the suspension or revival of a function.

Payment of representative

151. Regulations may make provision for payments to be made to, or in relation to, persons exercising functions as the relevant person's representative.

Regulations under this Part

152. The provisions of this Part which specify provision that may be made in regulations under this Part do not affect the generality of the power to make such regulations.

Effect of appointment of section 39C IMCA

153. Paragraphs 159 and 160 make provision about the exercise of functions by, or towards, the relevant person's representative during periods when

(a) no person is appointed as the relevant person's representative, but

(b) a person is appointed as a section 39C IMCA.

Part 11   Imcas

Application of Part

154. This Part applies for the purposes of this Schedule.

The IMCAs

155. A section 39A IMCA is an independent mental capacity advocate appointed under section 39A.

156. A section 39C IMCA is an independent mental capacity advocate appointed under section 39C.

157. A section 39D IMCA is an independent mental capacity advocate appointed under section 39D.

158. An IMCA is a section 39A IMCA or a section 39C IMCA or a section 39D IMCA.

Section 39C IMCA: functions

159. (1) This paragraph applies if, and for as long as, there is a section 39C IMCA.

(2) In the application of the relevant provisions, references to the relevant person's representative are to be read as references to the section 39C IMCA.

(3) But sub-paragraph (2) does not apply to any function under the relevant provisions for as long as the function is suspended in accordance with provision made under Part 10.

(4) In this paragraph and paragraph 160 the relevant provisions are –

  (a) paragraph 102(3)(b) (request for review under Part 8);

  (b) paragraph 108(1)(b) (notice of review under Part 8);

  (c) paragraph 120(1)(c) (notice of outcome of review under Part 8).

160. (1) This paragraph applies if –

  (a) a person is appointed as the relevant person's representative, and

  (b) a person accordingly ceases to hold an appointment as a section 39C IMCA.

(2) Where a function under a relevant provision has been exercised by, or towards, the section 39C IMCA, there is no requirement for that function to be exercised again by, or towards, the relevant person's representative.

Section 39A IMCA: restriction of functions

161. (1) This paragraph applies if –

  (a) there is a section 39A IMCA, and

  (b) a person is appointed under Part 10 to be the relevant person's representative (whether or not that person, or any person subsequently appointed, is currently the relevant person's representative).

(2) The duties imposed on, and the powers exercisable by, the section 39A IMCA do not apply.

(3) The duties imposed on, and the powers exercisable by, any other person do not apply, so far as they fall to be performed or exercised towards the section 39A IMCA.

(4) But sub-paragraph (2) does not apply to any power of challenge exercisable by the section 39A IMCA.

(5) And sub-paragraph (3) does not apply to any duty or power of any other person so far as it relates to any power of challenge exercisable by the section 39A IMCA.

(6) Before exercising any power of challenge, the section 39A IMCA must take the views of the relevant person's representative into account.

(7) A power of challenge is a power to make an application to the court to exercise its jurisdiction under section 21A in connection with the giving of the standard authorisation.

Part 12   Miscellaneous

Monitoring of operation of Schedule

162. (1) Regulations may make provision for, and in connection with, requiring one or more prescribed bodies to monitor, and report on, the operation of this Schedule in relation to England.

(2) The regulations may, in particular, give a prescribed body authority to do one or more of the following things –

  (a) to visit hospitals and care homes;

    (b) to visit and interview persons accommodated in hospitals and care homes;

    (c) to require the production of, and to inspect, records relating to the care or treatment of persons.

(3) 'Prescribed' means prescribed in regulations under this paragraph.

163. (1) Regulations may make provision for, and in connection with, enabling the National Assembly for Wales to monitor, and report on, the operation of this Schedule in relation to Wales.

(2) The National Assembly may direct one or more persons or bodies to carry out the Assembly's functions under regulations under this paragraph.

Disclosure of information

164. (1) Regulations may require either or both of the following to disclose prescribed information to prescribed bodies –

    (a) supervisory bodies;

    (b) managing authorities of hospitals or care homes.

(2) 'Prescribed' means prescribed in regulations under this paragraph.

(3) Regulations under this paragraph may only prescribe information relating to matters with which this Schedule is concerned.

Directions by National Assembly in relation to supervisory functions

165. (1) The National Assembly for Wales may direct a Local Health Board to exercise in relation to its area any supervisory functions which are specified in the direction.

(2) Directions under this paragraph must not preclude the National Assembly from exercising the functions specified in the directions.

(3) In this paragraph 'supervisory functions' means functions which the National Assembly have as supervisory body, so far as they are exercisable in relation to hospitals (whether NHS or independent hospitals, and whether in Wales or England).

166. (1) This paragraph applies where, under paragraph 165, a Local Health Board ('the specified LHB') is directed to exercise supervisory functions ('delegated functions').

(2) The National Assembly for Wales may give directions to the specified LHB about the Board's exercise of delegated functions.

(3) The National Assembly may give directions for any delegated functions to be exercised, on behalf of the specified LHB, by a committee, subcommittee or officer of that Board.

(4) The National Assembly may give directions providing for any delegated functions to be exercised by the specified LHB jointly with one or more other Local Health Boards.

(5) Where, under sub-paragraph (4), delegated functions are exercisable jointly, the National Assembly may give directions providing for the functions to be exercised, on behalf of the Local Health Boards in question, by a joint committee or joint subcommittee.

167. (1) Directions under paragraph 165 must be given in regulations. (2) Directions under paragraph 166 may be given –

    (a) in regulations, or

    (b) by instrument in writing.

168. The power under paragraph 165 or paragraph 166 to give directions includes power to vary or revoke directions given under that paragraph.

Notices

169. Any notice under this Schedule must be in writing.

Regulations

170. (1) This paragraph applies to all regulations under this Schedule, except regulations under paragraph 162, 163, 167 or 183.

(2) It is for the Secretary of State to make such regulations in relation to authorisations under this Schedule which relate to hospitals and care homes situated in England.

(3) It is for the National Assembly for Wales to make such regulations in relation to authorisations under this Schedule which relate to hospitals and care homes situated in Wales.

171. It is for the Secretary of State to make regulations under paragraph 162.

172. It is for the National Assembly for Wales to make regulations under paragraph 163 or 167.

173. (1) This paragraph applies to regulations under paragraph 183.

(2) It is for the Secretary of State to make such regulations in relation to cases where a question as to the ordinary residence of a person is to be determined by the Secretary of State.

(3) It is for the National Assembly for Wales to make such regulations in relation to cases where a question as to the ordinary residence of a person is to be determined by the National Assembly.

Part 13   Interpretation

Introduction

174. This Part applies for the purposes of this Schedule.

Hospitals and their managing authorities

175. (1) 'Hospital' means –
   (a) an NHS hospital, or
   (b) an independent hospital.

(2) 'NHS hospital' means –
   (a) a health service hospital as defined by section 275 of the National Health Service Act 2006 or section 206 of the National Health Service (Wales) Act 2006, or
   (b) a hospital as defined by section 206 of the National Health Service (Wales) Act 2006 vested in a Local Health Board.

(3) 'Independent hospital' means a hospital as defined by section 2 of the Care Standards Act 2000 which is not an NHS hospital.

176. (1) 'Managing authority', in relation to an NHS hospital, means –
   (a) if the hospital –
      (i) is vested in the appropriate national authority for the purposes of its functions under the National Health Service Act 2006 or of the National Health Service (Wales) Act 2006, or
      (ii) consists of any accommodation provided by a local authority and used as a hospital by or on behalf of the appropriate national authority under either of those Acts, the Primary Care Trust, Strategic Health Authority, Local Health Board or Special Health Authority responsible for the administration of the hospital;
   (b) if the hospital is vested in a Primary Care Trust, National Health Service trust or NHS foundation trust, that trust;
   (c) if the hospital is vested in a Local Health Board, that Board.

(2) For this purpose the appropriate national authority is –

    (a) in relation to England: the Secretary of State;

    (b) in relation to Wales: the National Assembly for Wales;

    (c) in relation to England and Wales: the Secretary of State and the National Assembly acting jointly.

177. 'Managing authority', in relation to an independent hospital, means the person registered, or required to be registered, under Part 2 of the Care Standards Act 2000 in respect of the hospital.

Care homes and their managing authorities

178. 'Care home' has the meaning given by section 3 of the Care Standards Act 2000.

179. 'Managing authority', in relation to a care home, means the person registered, or required to be registered, under Part 2 of the Care Standards Act 2000 in respect of the care home.

Supervisory bodies: hospitals

180. (1) The identity of the supervisory body is determined under this paragraph in cases where the relevant hospital is situated in England.

(2) If a Primary Care Trust commissions the relevant care or treatment, that Trust is the supervisory body.

(3) If the National Assembly for Wales or a Local Health Board commission the relevant care or treatment, the National Assembly are the supervisory body.

(4) In any other case, the supervisory body are the Primary Care Trust for the area in which the relevant hospital is situated.

(5) If a hospital is situated in the areas of two (or more) Primary Care Trusts, it is to be regarded for the purposes of sub-paragraph (4) as situated in whichever of the areas the greater (or greatest) part of the hospital is situated.

181. (1) The identity of the supervisory body is determined under this paragraph in cases where the relevant hospital is situated in Wales.

(2) The National Assembly for Wales are the supervisory body.

(3) But if a Primary Care Trust commissions the relevant care or treatment, that Trust is the supervisory body.

Supervisory bodies: care homes

182. (1) The identity of the supervisory body is determined under this paragraph in cases where the relevant care home is situated in England or in Wales.

(2) The supervisory body are the local authority for the area in which the relevant person is ordinarily resident.

(3) But if the relevant person is not ordinarily resident in the area of a local authority, the supervisory body are the local authority for the area in which the care home is situated.

(4) In relation to England 'local authority' means –

    (a) the council of a county;

    (b) the council of a district for which there is no county council;

    (c) the council of a London borough;

    (d) the Common Council of the City of London;

    (e) the Council of the Isles of Scilly.

(5) In relation to Wales 'local authority' means the council of a county or county borough.

(6) If a care home is situated in the areas of two (or more) local authorities, it is to be regarded for the purposes of sub-paragraph (3) as situated in whichever of the areas the greater (or greatest) part of the care home is situated.

183. (1) Subsections (5) and (6) of section 24 of the National Assistance Act 1948 (deemed place of ordinary residence) apply to any determination of where a person is ordinarily resident for the purposes of paragraph 182 as those subsections apply to such a determination for the purposes specified in those subsections.

(2) In the application of section 24(6) of the 1948 Act by virtue of subsection (1), section 24(6) is to be read as if it referred to a hospital vested in a Local Health Board as well as to hospitals vested in the Secretary of State and the other bodies mentioned in section 24(6).

(3) Any question arising as to the ordinary residence of a person is to be determined by the Secretary of State or by the National Assembly for Wales.

(4) The Secretary of State and the National Assembly must make and publish arrangements for determining which cases are to be dealt with by the Secretary of State and which are to be dealt with by the National Assembly.

(5) Those arrangements may include provision for the Secretary of State and the National Assembly to agree, in relation to any question that has arisen, which of them is to deal with the case.

(6) Regulations may make provision about arrangements that are to have effect before, upon, or after the determination of any question as to the ordinary residence of a person.

(7) The regulations may, in particular, authorise or require a local authority to do any or all of the following things –

    (a) to act as supervisory body even though it may wish to dispute that it is the supervisory body;

    (b) to become the supervisory body in place of another local authority;

    (c) to recover from another local authority expenditure incurred in exercising functions as the supervisory body.

Same body managing authority and supervisory body

184. (1) This paragraph applies if, in connection with a particular person's detention as a resident in a hospital or care home, the same body are both –

    (a) the managing authority of the relevant hospital or care home, and

    (b) the supervisory body.

(2) The fact that a single body are acting in both capacities does not prevent the body from carrying out functions under this Schedule in each capacity.

(3) But, in such a case, this Schedule has effect subject to any modifications contained in regulations that may be made for this purpose.

Interested persons

185. Each of the following is an interested person –

    (a) the relevant person's spouse or civil partner;

    (b) where the relevant person and another person of the opposite sex are not married to each other but are living together as husband and wife: the other person;

    (c) where the relevant person and another person of the same sex are not civil partners of each other but are living together as if they were civil partners: the other person;

    (d) the relevant person's children and step-children;

    (e) the relevant person's parents and step-parents;

(f) the relevant person's brothers and sisters, half-brothers and half-sisters, and stepbrothers and stepsisters;

(g) the relevant person's grandparents;

(h) a deputy appointed for the relevant person by the court;

(i) a donee of a lasting power of attorney granted by the relevant person.

186. (1) An interested person consulted by the best interests assessor is any person whose name is stated in the relevant best interests assessment in accordance with paragraph 40 (interested persons whom the assessor consulted in carrying out the assessment).

(2) The relevant best interests assessment is the most recent best interests assessment carried out in connection with the standard authorisation in question (whether the assessment was carried out under Part 4 or Part 8).

187. Where this Schedule imposes on a person a duty towards an interested person, the duty does not apply if the person on whom the duty is imposed –

(a) is not aware of the interested person's identity or of a way of contacting him, and

(b) cannot reasonably ascertain it.

188. The following table contains an index of provisions defining or otherwise explaining expressions used in this Schedule –

[Schedule A1 inserted by section 50(5) and Schedule 7 to the 2007 Act.]

Schedule 1 (section 9)

Lasting Powers of Attorney: formalities

Part 1   Making instruments

General requirements as to making instruments

1. (1) An instrument is not made in accordance with this Schedule unless –
   (a) it is in the prescribed form,
   (b) it complies with paragraph 2, and
   (c) any prescribed requirements in connection with its execution are satisfied.
   (2) Regulations may make different provision according to whether –
   (a) the instrument relates to personal welfare or to property and affairs (or to both);
   (b) only one or more than one donee is to be appointed (and if more than one, whether jointly or jointly and severally).
   (3) In this Schedule –
   (a) 'prescribed' means prescribed by regulations, and
   (b) 'regulations' means regulations made for the purposes of this Schedule by the Lord Chancellor.

Requirements as to content of instruments

2. (1) The instrument must include –
   (a) the prescribed information about the purpose of the instrument and the effect of a lasting power of attorney,
   (b) a statement by the donor to the effect that he –
   (i) has read the prescribed information or a prescribed part of it (or has had it read to him), and
   (ii) intends the authority conferred under the instrument to include authority to make decisions on his behalf in circumstances where he no longer has capacity,
   (c) a statement by the donor –
   (i) naming a person or persons whom the donor wishes to be notified of any application for the registration of the instrument, or
   (ii) stating that there are no persons whom he wishes to be notified of any such application,
   (d) a statement by the donee (or, if more than one, each of them) to the effect that he –
   (i) has read the prescribed information or a prescribed part of it (or has had it read to him), and
   (ii) understands the duties imposed on a donee of a lasting power of attorney under sections 1 (the principles) and 4 (best interests), and

(e) a certificate by a person of a prescribed description that, in his opinion, at the time when the donor executes the instrument –
  (i) the donor understands the purpose of the instrument and the scope of the authority conferred under it,
  (ii) no fraud or undue pressure is being used to induce the donor to create a lasting power of attorney, and
  (iii) there is nothing else which would prevent a lasting power of attorney from being created by the instrument.
(2) Regulations may –
  (a) prescribe a maximum number of named persons;
  (b) provide that, where the instrument includes a statement under sub-paragraph (1)(c)(ii), two persons of a prescribed description must each give a certificate under sub-paragraph (1)(e).
(3) The persons who may be named persons do not include a person who is appointed as donee under the instrument.
(4) In this Schedule, 'named person' means a person named under sub-paragraph (1)(c).
(5) A certificate under sub-paragraph (1)(e) –
  (a) must be made in the prescribed form, and
  (b) must include any prescribed information.
(6) The certificate may not be given by a person appointed as donee under the instrument.

Failure to comply with prescribed form

3. (1) If an instrument differs in an immaterial respect in form or mode of expression from the prescribed form, it is to be treated by the Public Guardian as sufficient in point of form and expression.

(2) The court may declare that an instrument which is not in the prescribed form is to be treated as if it were, if it is satisfied that the persons executing the instrument intended it to create a lasting power of attorney.

Part 2   Registration

Applications and procedure for registration

4. (1) An application to the Public Guardian for the registration of an instrument intended to create a lasting power of attorney –
  (a) must be made in the prescribed form, and
  (b) must include any prescribed information.
(2) The application may be made –
  (a) by the donor,
  (b) by the donee or donees, or
  (c) if the instrument appoints two or more donees to act jointly and severally in respect of any matter, by any of the donees.
(3) The application must be accompanied by –
  (a) the instrument, and
  (b) any fee provided for under section 58(4)(b).
(4) A person who, in an application for registration, makes a statement which he knows to be false in a material particular is guilty of an offence and is liable –

    (a) on summary conviction, to imprisonment for a term not exceeding 12 months or a fine not exceeding the statutory maximum or both;

    (b) on conviction on indictment, to imprisonment for a term not exceeding 2 years or a fine or both.

5. Subject to paragraphs 11 to 14, the Public Guardian must register the instrument as a lasting power of attorney at the end of the prescribed period.

Notification requirements

6. (1) A donor about to make an application under paragraph 4(2)(a) must notify any named persons that he is about to do so.

(2) The donee (or donees) about to make an application under paragraph 4(2)(b) or (c) must notify any named persons that he is (or they are) about to do so.

7. As soon as is practicable after receiving an application by the donor under paragraph 4(2)(a), the Public Guardian must notify the donee (or donees) that the application has been received.

8. (1) As soon as is practicable after receiving an application by a donee (or donees) under paragraph 4(2)(b), the Public Guardian must notify the donor that the application has been received.

(2) As soon as is practicable after receiving an application by a donee under paragraph 4(2)(c), the Public Guardian must notify –

    (a) the donor, and

    (b) the donee or donees who did not join in making the application, that the application has been received.

9. (1) A notice under paragraph 6 must be made in the prescribed form.

(2) A notice under paragraph 6, 7 or 8 must include such information, if any, as may be prescribed.

Power to dispense with notification requirements

10. The court may –

    (a) on the application of the donor, dispense with the requirement to notify under paragraph 6(1), or

    (b) on the application of the donee or donees concerned, dispense with the requirement to notify under paragraph 6(2),

if satisfied that no useful purpose would be served by giving the notice.

Instrument not made properly or containing ineffective provision

11. (1) If it appears to the Public Guardian that an instrument accompanying an application under paragraph 4 is not made in accordance with this Schedule, he must not register the instrument unless the court directs him to do so.

(2) Sub-paragraph (3) applies if it appears to the Public Guardian that the instrument contains a provision which –

    (a) would be ineffective as part of a lasting power of attorney, or

    (b) would prevent the instrument from operating as a valid lasting power of attorney.

(3) The Public Guardian –

    (a) must apply to the court for it to determine the matter under section 23(1), and

    (b) pending the determination by the court, must not register the instrument.

(4) Sub-paragraph (5) applies if the court determines under section 23(1) (whether or not on an application by the Public Guardian) that the instrument contains a provision which –

    (a) would be ineffective as part of a lasting power of attorney, or

    (b) would prevent the instrument from operating as a valid lasting power of attorney.

(5) The court must –

    (a) notify the Public Guardian that it has severed the provision, or

    (b) direct him not to register the instrument.

(6) Where the court notifies the Public Guardian that it has severed a provision, he must register the instrument with a note to that effect attached to it.

Deputy already appointed

12. (1) Sub-paragraph (2) applies if it appears to the Public Guardian that –

    (a) there is a deputy appointed by the court for the donor, and

    (b) the powers conferred on the deputy would, if the instrument were registered, to any extent conflict with the powers conferred on the attorney.

(2) The Public Guardian must not register the instrument unless the court directs him to do so.

Objection by donee or named person

13. (1) Sub-paragraph (2) applies if a donee or a named person –

    (a) receives a notice under paragraph 6, 7 or 8 of an application for the registration of an instrument, and

    (b) before the end of the prescribed period, gives notice to the Public Guardian of an objection to the registration on the ground that an event mentioned in section 13(3) or (6)(a) to (d) has occurred which has revoked the instrument.

(2) If the Public Guardian is satisfied that the ground for making the objection is established, he must not register the instrument unless the court, on the application of the person applying for the registration –

    (a) is satisfied that the ground is not established, and

    (b) directs the Public Guardian to register the instrument.

(3) Sub-paragraph (4) applies if a donee or a named person –

    (a) receives a notice under paragraph 6, 7 or 8 of an application for the registration of an instrument, and

    (b) before the end of the prescribed period –

        (i) makes an application to the court objecting to the registration on a prescribed ground, and

        (ii) notifies the Public Guardian of the application.

(4) The Public Guardian must not register the instrument unless the court directs him to do so.

Objection by donor

14. (1) This paragraph applies if the donor –

    (a) receives a notice under paragraph 8 of an application for the registration of an instrument, and

    (b) before the end of the prescribed period, gives notice to the Public Guardian of an objection to the registration.

(2) The Public Guardian must not register the instrument unless the court, on the application of the donee or, if more than one, any of them –

    (a) is satisfied that the donor lacks capacity to object to the registration, and

    (b) directs the Public Guardian to register the instrument.

Notification of registration

15. Where an instrument is registered under this Schedule, the Public Guardian must give notice of the fact in the prescribed form to –

    (a) the donor, and

    (b) the donee or, if more than one, each of them.

Evidence of registration

16. (1) A document purporting to be an office copy of an instrument registered under this Schedule is, in any part of the United Kingdom, evidence of –

    (a) the contents of the instrument, and

    (b) the fact that it has been registered.

(2) Sub-paragraph (1) is without prejudice to –

    (a) section 3 of the Powers of Attorney Act 1971 (c. 27) (proof by certified copy), and

    (b) any other method of proof authorised by law.

Part 3   Cancellation of registration and notification of severance

17. (1) The Public Guardian must cancel the registration of an instrument as a lasting power of attorney on being satisfied that the power has been revoked –

    (a) as a result of the donor's bankruptcy, or

    (b) on the occurrence of an event mentioned in section 13(6)(a) to (d).

(2) If the Public Guardian cancels the registration of an instrument he must notify –

    (a) the donor, and

    (b) the donee or, if more than one, each of them.

18. The court must direct the Public Guardian to cancel the registration of an instrument as a lasting power of attorney if it –

    (a) determines under section 22(2)(a)that a requirement for creating the power was not met,

    (b) determines under section 22(2)(b)that the power has been revoked or has otherwise come to an end, or

    (c) revokes the power under section 22(4)(b) (fraud etc.).

19. (1) Sub-paragraph (2) applies if the court determines under section 23(1) that a lasting power of attorney contains a provision which –

    (a) is ineffective as part of a lasting power of attorney, or

    (b) prevents the instrument from operating as a valid lasting power of attorney.

(2) The court must –

    (a) notify the Public Guardian that it has severed the provision, or

    (b) direct him to cancel the registration of the instrument as a lasting power of attorney.

20. On the cancellation of the registration of an instrument, the instrument and any office copies of it must be delivered up to the Public Guardian to be cancelled.

Part 4   Records of alterations in registered powers

Partial revocation or suspension of power as a result of bankruptcy

21. If in the case of a registered instrument it appears to the Public Guardian that under section 13 a lasting power of attorney is revoked, or suspended, in relation to the donor's property and affairs (but not in relation to other matters), the Public Guardian must attach to the instrument a note to that effect.

Termination of appointment of donee which does not revoke power

22. If in the case of a registered instrument it appears to the Public Guardian that an event has occurred –
   (a) which has terminated the appointment of the donee, but
   (b) which has not revoked the instrument, the Public Guardian must attach to the instrument a note to that effect.

Replacement of donee

23. If in the case of a registered instrument it appears to the Public Guardian that the donee has been replaced under the terms of the instrument the Public Guardian must attach to the instrument a note to that effect.

Severance of ineffective provisions

24. If in the case of a registered instrument the court notifies the Public Guardian under paragraph 19(2)(a) that it has severed a provision of the instrument, the Public Guardian must attach to it a note to that effect.

Notification of alterations

25. If the Public Guardian attaches a note to an instrument under paragraph 21, 22, 23 or 24 he must give notice of the note to the donee or donees of the power (or, as the case may be, to the other donee or donees of the power).

Schedule 1A

Persons ineligible to be deprived of liberty by this Act

Part 1   Ineligible persons

Application
1. This Schedule applies for the purposes of –
    (a) section 16A, and
    (b) paragraph 17 of Schedule A1.
Determining ineligibility
2. A person ('P') is ineligible to be deprived of liberty by this Act ('ineligible') if –
    (a) P falls within one of the cases set out in the second column of the following table, and
    (b) the corresponding entry in the third column of the table – or the provision, or one of the provisions, referred to in that entry – provides that he is ineligible.

	Status of P	*Determination of ineligibility*
Case A	P is – (a) subject to the hospital treatment regime, and (b) detained in a hospital under that regime.	P is ineligible.
Case B	P is – (a) subject to the hospital treatment regime, but (b) not detained in a hospital under that regime.	See paragraphs 3 and 4.
Case C	P is subject to the community treatment regime.	See paragraphs 3 and 4.
Case D	P is subject to the guardianship regime.	See paragraphs 3 and 5.
Case E	P is – (a) within the scope of the Mental Health Act, but (b) not subject to any of the mental health regimes.	See paragraph 5.

Authorised course of action not in accordance with regime
3. (1) This paragraph applies in cases B, C and D in the table in paragraph 2.
(2) P is ineligible if the authorised course of action is not in accordance with a requirement which the relevant regime imposes.
(3) That includes any requirement as to where P is, or is not, to reside.
(4) The relevant regime is the mental health regime to which P is subject.

Treatment for mental disorder in a hospital
4. (1) This paragraph applies in cases B and C in the table in paragraph 2.
(2) P is ineligible if the relevant care or treatment consists in whole or in part of medical treatment for mental disorder in a hospital.

P objects to being a mental health patient etc.

5. (1) This paragraph applies in cases D and E in the table in paragraph 2.

(2) P is ineligible if the following conditions are met.

(3) The first condition is that the relevant instrument authorises P to be a mental health patient.

(4) The second condition is that P objects –

    (a) to being a mental health patient, or

    (b) to being given some or all of the mental health treatment.

(5) The third condition is that a donee or deputy has not made a valid decision to consent to each matter to which P objects.

(6) In determining whether or not P objects to something, regard must be had to all the circumstances (so far as they are reasonably ascertainable), including the following –

    (a) P's behaviour;

    (b) P's wishes and feelings;

    (c) P's views, beliefs and values.

(7) But regard is to be had to circumstances from the past only so far as it is still appropriate to have regard to them.

Part 2   Interpretation

Application

6. This Part applies for the purposes of this Schedule.

Mental health regimes

7. The mental health regimes are –

    (a) the hospital treatment regime,

    (b) the community treatment regime, and

    (c) the guardianship regime.

Hospital treatment regime

8. (1) P is subject to the hospital treatment regime if he is subject to –

    (a) a hospital treatment obligation under the relevant enactment, or

    (b) an obligation under another England and Wales enactment which has the same effect as a hospital treatment obligation.

(2) But where P is subject to any such obligation, he is to be regarded as not subject to the hospital treatment regime during any period when he is subject to the community treatment regime.

(3) A hospital treatment obligation is an application, order or direction of a kind listed in the first column of the following table.

(4) In relation to a hospital treatment obligation, the relevant enactment is the enactment in the Mental Health Act which is referred to in the corresponding entry in the second column of the following table.

Hospital treatment obligation	*Relevant enactment*
Application for admission for assessment	Section 2
Application for admission for assessment	Section 4

Community treatment regime

9. P is subject to the community treatment regime if he is subject to –
   (a) a community treatment order under section 17A of the Mental Health Act, or
   (b) an obligation under another England and Wales enactment which has the same effect as a community treatment order.

Guardianship regime

10. P is subject to the guardianship regime if he is subject to –
   (a) a guardianship application under section 7 of the Mental Health Act,
   (b) a guardianship order under section 37 of the Mental Health Act, or
   (c) an obligation under another England and Wales enactment which has the same effect as a guardianship application or guardianship order.

England and Wales enactments

11. (1) An England and Wales enactment is an enactment which extends to England and Wales (whether or not it also extends elsewhere).

(2) It does not matter if the enactment is in the Mental Health Act or not.

P within scope of Mental Health Act

12. (1) P is within the scope of the Mental Health Act if –
   (a) an application in respect of P could be made under section 2 or 3 of the Mental Health Act, and
   (b) P could be detained in a hospital in pursuance of such an application, were one made.

(2) The following provisions of this paragraph apply when determining whether an application in respect of P could be made under section 2 or 3 of the Mental Health Act.

(3) If the grounds in section 2(2) of the Mental Health Act are met in P's case, it is to be assumed that the recommendations referred to in section 2(3) of that Act have been given.

(4) If the grounds in section 3(2) of the Mental Health Act are met in P's case, it is to be assumed that the recommendations referred to in section 3(3) of that Act have been given.

(5) In determining whether the ground in section 3(2)(c) of the Mental Health Act is met in P's case, it is to be assumed that the treatment referred to in section 3(2)(c) cannot be provided under this Act.

Authorised course of action, relevant care or treatment & relevant instrument

13. In a case where this Schedule applies for the purposes of section 16A –
'authorised course of action' means any course of action amounting to deprivation of liberty which the order under section 16(2)(a) authorises;
'relevant care or treatment' means any care or treatment which –
  (a) comprises, or forms part of, the authorised course of action, or
  (b) is to be given in connection with the authorised course of action;
'relevant instrument' means the order under section 16(2)(a).

14. In a case where this Schedule applies for the purposes of paragraph 17 of Schedule A1 –
'authorised course of action' means the accommodation of the relevant person in the relevant hospital or care home for the purpose of being given the relevant care or treatment;
'relevant care or treatment' has the same meaning as in Schedule A1;
'relevant instrument' means the standard authorisation under Schedule A1.

15. (1) This paragraph applies where the question whether a person is ineligible to be deprived of liberty by this Act is relevant to either of these decisions –
  (a) whether or not to include particular provision ('the proposed provision') in an order under section 16(2)(a);
  (b) whether or not to give a standard authorisation under Schedule A1.
(2) A reference in this Schedule to the authorised course of action or the relevant care or treatment is to be read as a reference to that thing as it would be if –
  (a) the proposed provision were included in the order, or
  (b) the standard authorisation were given.
(3) A reference in this Schedule to the relevant instrument is to be read as follows –
  (a) where the relevant instrument is an order under section 16(2)(a): as a reference to the order as it would be if the proposed provision were included in it;
  (b) where the relevant instrument is a standard authorisation: as a reference to the standard authorisation as it would be if it were given.

Expressions used in paragraph 5

16. (1) These expressions have the meanings given –
'donee' means a donee of a lasting power of attorney granted by P;
'mental health patient' means a person accommodated in a hospital for the purpose of being given medical treatment for mental disorder;
'mental health treatment' means the medical treatment for mental disorder referred to in the definition of 'mental health patient'.
(2) A decision of a donee or deputy is valid if it is made –
  (a) within the scope of his authority as donee or deputy, and
  (b) in accordance with Part 1 of this Act.

Expressions with same meaning as in Mental Health Act

17. (1) 'Hospital' has the same meaning as in Part 2 of the Mental Health Act.
(2) 'Medical treatment' has the same meaning as in the Mental Health Act.
(3) 'Mental disorder' has the same meaning as in Schedule A1 (see paragraph 14).

[Schedule 1A inserted by section 50(6) and Schedule 8 to the 2007 Act.]

Schedule 2 (section 18(4))

Property and affairs: supplementary provisions

Wills: general

1. Paragraphs 2 to 4 apply in relation to the execution of a will, by virtue of section 18, on behalf of P.

Provision that may be made in will

2. The will may make any provision (whether by disposing of property or exercising a power or otherwise) which could be made by a will executed by P if he had capacity to make it.

Wills: requirements relating to execution

3. (1) Sub-paragraph (2) applies if under section 16 the court makes an order or gives directions requiring or authorising a person ('the authorised person') to execute a will on behalf of P.

(2) Any will executed in pursuance of the order or direction –
  (a) must state that it is signed by P acting by the authorised person,
  (b) must be signed by the authorised person with the name of P and his own name, in the presence of two or more witnesses present at the same time,
  (c) must be attested and subscribed by those witnesses in the presence of the authorised person, and
  (d) must be sealed with the official seal of the court.

Wills: effect of execution

4. (1) This paragraph applies where a will is executed in accordance with paragraph 3.

(2) The Wills Act 1837 (c. 26) has effect in relation to the will as if it were signed by P by his own hand, except that
  (a) section 9 of the 1837 Act (requirements as to signing and attestation) does not apply, and
  (b) in the subsequent provisions of the 1837 Act any reference to execution in the manner required by the previous provisions is to be read as a reference to execution in accordance with paragraph 3.

(3) The will has the same effect for all purposes as if –
  (a) P had had the capacity to make a valid will, and
  (b) the will had been executed by him in the manner required by the 1837 Act.

(4) But sub-paragraph (3) does not have effect in relation to the will –
  (a) in so far as it disposes of immovable property outside England and Wales, or
  (b) in so far as it relates to any other property or matter if, when the will is executed
    (i) P is domiciled outside England and Wales, and
    (ii) the condition in sub-paragraph (5) is met.

(5) The condition is that, under the law of P's domicile, any question of his testamentary capacity would fall to be determined in accordance with the law of a place outside England and Wales.

Vesting orders ancillary to settlement etc.
5. (1) If provision is made by virtue of section 18 for –
  (a) the settlement of any property of P, or
  (b) the exercise of a power vested in him of appointing trustees or retiring from a trust, the court may also make as respects the property settled or the trust property such consequential vesting or other orders as the case may require.

(2) The power under sub-paragraph (1) includes, in the case of the exercise of such a power, any order which could have been made in such a case under Part 4 of the Trustee Act 1925 (c. 19).

Variation of settlements
6. (1) If a settlement has been made by virtue of section 18, the court may by order vary or revoke the settlement if –
  (a) the settlement makes provision for its variation or revocation,
  (b) the court is satisfied that a material fact was not disclosed when the settlement was made, or
  (c) the court is satisfied that there has been a substantial change of circumstances.

(2) Any such order may give such consequential directions as the court thinks fit.
7. (1) Sub-paragraph (2) applies if the court is satisfied –
  (a) that under the law prevailing in a place outside England and Wales a person ('M') has been appointed to exercise powers in respect of the property or affairs of P on the ground (however formulated) that P lacks capacity to make decisions with respect to the management and administration of his property and affairs, and
  (b) that, having regard to the nature of the appointment and to the circumstances of the case, it is expedient that the court should exercise its powers under this paragraph.

(2) The court may direct –
  (a) any stocks standing in the name of P, or
  (b) the right to receive dividends from the stocks, to be transferred into M's name or otherwise dealt with as required by M, and may give such directions as the court thinks fit for dealing with accrued dividends from the stocks.

(3) 'Stocks' includes –
  (a) shares, and
  (b) any funds, annuity or security transferable in the books kept by any body corporate or unincorporated company or society or by an instrument of transfer either alone or accompanied by other formalities, and 'dividends' is to be construed accordingly.

Preservation of interests in property disposed of on behalf of person lacking capacity
8. (1) Sub-paragraphs (2) and (3) apply if –
  (a) P's property has been disposed of by virtue of section 18,

(b) under P's will or intestacy, or by a gift perfected or nomination taking effect on his death, any other person would have taken an interest in the property but for the disposal, and

(c) on P's death, any property belonging to P's estate represents the property disposed of.

(2) The person takes the same interest, if and so far as circumstances allow, in the property representing the property disposed of.

(3) If the property disposed of was real property, any property representing it is to be treated, so long as it remains part of P's estate, as if it were real property.

(4) The court may direct that, on a disposal of P's property –

(a) which is made by virtue of section 18, and

(b) which would apart from this paragraph result in the conversion of personal property into real property, property representing the property disposed of is to be treated, so long as it remains P's property or forms part of P's estate, as if it were personal property.

(5) References in sub-paragraphs (1) to (4) to the disposal of property are to –

(a) the sale, exchange, charging of or other dealing (otherwise than by will) with property other than money;

(b) the removal of property from one place to another;

(c) the application of money in acquiring property;

(d) the transfer of money from one account to another;

and references to property representing property disposed of are to be construed accordingly and as including the result of successive disposals.

(6) The court may give such directions as appear to it necessary or expedient for the purpose of facilitating the operation of sub-paragraphs (1) to (3), including the carrying of money to a separate account and the transfer of property other than money.

9. (1) Sub-paragraph (2) applies if the court has ordered or directed the expenditure of money –

(a) for carrying out permanent improvements on any of P's property, or

(b) otherwise for the permanent benefit of any of P's property.

(2) The court may order that –

(a) the whole of the money expended or to be expended, or

(b) any part of it, is to be a charge on the property either without interest or with interest at a specified rate.

(3) An order under sub-paragraph (2) may provide for excluding or restricting the operation of paragraph 8(1) to (3).

(4) A charge under sub-paragraph (2) may be made in favour of such person as may be just and, in particular, where the money charged is paid out of P's general estate, may be made in favour of a person as trustee for P.

(5) No charge under sub-paragraph (2) may confer any right of sale or foreclosure during P's lifetime.

Powers as patron of benefice

10. (1) Any functions which P has as patron of a benefice may be discharged only by a person ('R') appointed by the court.

(2) R must be an individual capable of appointment under section 8(1)(b) of the 1986 Measure (which provides for an individual able to make a declaration of communicant status, a clerk in Holy Orders, etc. to be appointed to discharge a registered patron's functions).

(3) The 1986 Measure applies to R as it applies to an individual appointed by the registered patron of the benefice under section 8(1)(b) or (3) of that Measure to discharge his functions as patron.

(4) 'The 1986 Measure' means the Patronage (Benefices) Measure 1986 (No. 3).

Schedule 3 (section 63)

International protection of adults

Part 1 Preliminary

Introduction

1. This Part applies for the purposes of this Schedule.

The Convention

2. (1) 'Convention' means the Convention referred to in section 63.

(2) 'Convention country' means a country in which the Convention is in force.

(3) A reference to an Article or Chapter is to an Article or Chapter of the Convention.

(4) An expression which appears in this Schedule and in the Convention is to be construed in accordance with the Convention.

Countries, territories and nationals

3. (1) 'Country' includes a territory which has its own system of law.

(2) Where a country has more than one territory with its own system of law, a reference to the country, in relation to one of its nationals, is to the territory with which the national has the closer, or the closest, connection.

Adults with incapacity

4. 'Adult' means a person who –

   (a) as a result of an impairment or insufficiency of his personal faculties, cannot protect his interests, and
   (b) has reached 16.

Protective measures

5. (1) 'Protective measure' means a measure directed to the protection of the person or property of an adult; and it may deal in particular with any of the following –

   (a) the determination of incapacity and the institution of a protective regime,
   (b) placing the adult under the protection of an appropriate authority,
   (c) guardianship, curatorship or any corresponding system,
   (d) the designation and functions of a person having charge of the adult's person or property, or representing or otherwise helping him,
   (e) placing the adult in a place where protection can be provided,
   (f) administering, conserving or disposing of the adult's property,
   (g) authorising a specific intervention for the protection of the person or property of the adult.

(2) Where a measure of like effect to a protective measure has been taken in relation to a person before he reaches 16, this Schedule applies to the measure in so far as it has effect in relation to him once he has reached 16.

Central Authority

6. (1) Any function under the Convention of a Central Authority is exercisable in England and Wales by the Lord Chancellor.

(2) A communication may be sent to the Central Authority in relation to England and Wales by sending it to the Lord Chancellor.

Part 2   Jurisdiction of competent authority

Scope of jurisdiction

7. (1) The court may exercise its functions under this Act (in so far as it cannot otherwise do so) in relation to –
   (a) an adult habitually resident in England and Wales,
   (b) an adult's property in England and Wales,
   (c) an adult present in England and Wales or who has property there, if the matter is urgent, or
   (d) an adult present in England and Wales, if a protective measure which is temporary and limited in its effect to England and Wales is proposed in relation to him.

(2) An adult present in England and Wales is to be treated for the purposes of this paragraph as habitually resident there if –
   (a) his habitual residence cannot be ascertained,
   (b) he is a refugee, or
   (c) he has been displaced as a result of disturbance in the country of his habitual residence.

8. (1) The court may also exercise its functions under this Act (in so far as it cannot otherwise do so) in relation to an adult if sub-paragraph (2) or (3) applies in relation to him.

(2) This sub-paragraph applies in relation to an adult if –
   (a) he is a British citizen,
   (b) he has a closer connection with England and Wales than with Scotland or Northern Ireland, and
   (c) Article 7 has, in relation to the matter concerned, been complied with.

(3) This sub-paragraph applies in relation to an adult if the Lord Chancellor, having consulted such persons as he considers appropriate, agrees to a request under Article 8 in relation to the adult.

Exercise of jurisdiction

9. (1) This paragraph applies where jurisdiction is exercisable under this Schedule in connection with a matter which involves a Convention country other than England and Wales.

(2) Any Article on which the jurisdiction is based applies in relation to the matter in so far as it involves the other country (and the court must, accordingly, comply with any duty conferred on it as a result).

(3) Article 12 also applies, so far as its provisions allow, in relation to the matter in so far as it involves the other country.

10. A reference in this Schedule to the exercise of jurisdiction under this Schedule is to the exercise of functions under this Act as a result of this Part of this Schedule.

Part 3 Applicable law

Applicable law

11. In exercising jurisdiction under this Schedule, the court may, if it thinks that the matter has a substantial connection with a country other than England and Wales, apply the law of that other country.

12. Where a protective measure is taken in one country but implemented in another, the conditions of implementation are governed by the law of the other country.

Lasting powers of attorney, etc.

13. (1) If the donor of a lasting power is habitually resident in England and Wales at the time of granting the power, the law applicable to the existence, extent, modification or extinction of the power is –

(a) the law of England and Wales, or

(b) if he specifies in writing the law of a connected country for the purpose, that law.

(2) If he is habitually resident in another country at that time, but England and Wales is a connected country, the law applicable in that respect is –

(a) the law of the other country, or

(b) if he specifies in writing the law of England and Wales for the purpose, that law.

(3) A country is connected, in relation to the donor, if it is a country –

(a) of which he is a national,

(b) in which he was habitually resident, or

(c) in which he has property.

(4) Where this paragraph applies as a result of sub-paragraph (3)(c), it applies only in relation to the property which the donor has in the connected country.

(5) The law applicable to the manner of the exercise of a lasting power is the law of the country where it is exercised.

(6) In this Part of this Schedule, 'lasting power' means –

(a) a lasting power of attorney (see section 9),

(b) an enduring power of attorney within the meaning of Schedule 4, or

(c) any other power of like effect.

14. (1) Where a lasting power is not exercised in a manner sufficient to guarantee the protection of the person or property of the donor, the court, in exercising jurisdiction under this Schedule, may disapply or modify the power.

(2) Where, in accordance with this Part of this Schedule, the law applicable to the power is, in one or more respects, that of a country other than England and Wales, the court must, so far as possible, have regard to the law of the other country in that respect (or those respects).

15. Regulations may provide for Schedule 1 (lasting powers of attorney: formalities) to apply with modifications in relation to a lasting power which comes within paragraph 13(6)(c) above.

Protection of third parties

16. (1) This paragraph applies where a person (a 'representative') in purported exercise of an authority to act on behalf of an adult enters into a transaction with a third party.

(2) The validity of the transaction may not be questioned in proceedings, nor may the third party be held liable, merely because –

(a) where the representative and third party are in England and Wales when entering into the transaction, sub-paragraph (3) applies;

(b) here they are in another country at that time, sub-paragraph (4) applies.

(3) This sub-paragraph applies if –

(a) the law applicable to the authority in one or more respects is, as a result of this Schedule, the law of a country other than England and Wales, and

(b) the representative is not entitled to exercise the authority in that respect (or those respects) under the law of that other country.

(4) This sub-paragraph applies if –

(a) the law applicable to the authority in one or more respects is, as a result of this Part of this Schedule, the law of England and Wales, and

(b) the representative is not entitled to exercise the authority in that respect (or those respects) under that law.

(5) This paragraph does not apply if the third party knew or ought to have known that the applicable law was –

(a) in a case within sub-paragraph (3), the law of the other country;

(b) in a case within sub-paragraph (4), the law of England and Wales.

Mandatory rules

17. Where the court is entitled to exercise jurisdiction under this Schedule, the mandatory provisions of the law of England and Wales apply, regardless of any system of law which would otherwise apply in relation to the matter.

Public policy

18. Nothing in this Part of this Schedule requires or enables the application in England and Wales of a provision of the law of another country if its application would be manifestly contrary to public policy.

Part 4   Recognition and enforcement

Recognition

19. (1)   A protective measure taken in relation to an adult under the law of a country other than England and Wales is to be recognised in England and Wales if it was taken on the ground that the adult is habitually resident in the other country.

(2) A protective measure taken in relation to an adult under the law of a Convention country other than England and Wales is to be recognised in England and Wales if it was taken on a ground mentioned in Chapter 2 (jurisdiction).

(3) But the court may disapply this paragraph in relation to a measure if it thinks that –

(a) the case in which the measure was taken was not urgent,

(b) the adult was not given an opportunity to be heard, and

(c) that omission amounted to a breach of natural justice.

(4) It may also disapply this paragraph in relation to a measure if it thinks that –

(a) recognition of the measure would be manifestly contrary to public policy,

(b) the measure would be inconsistent with a mandatory provision of the law of England and Wales, or

(c) the measure is inconsistent with one subsequently taken, or recognised, in England and Wales in relation to the adult.

(5) And the court may disapply this paragraph in relation to a measure taken under the law of a Convention country in a matter to which Article 33 applies, if the court thinks that that Article has not been complied with in connection with that matter.

20. (1) An interested person may apply to the court for a declaration as to whether a protective measure taken under the law of a country other than England and Wales is to be recognised in England and Wales.

(2) No permission is required for an application to the court under this paragraph.

21. For the purposes of paragraphs 19 and 20, any finding of fact relied on when the measure was taken is conclusive.

Enforcement

22. (1) An interested person may apply to the court for a declaration as to whether a protective measure taken under the law of, and enforceable in, a country other than England and Wales is enforceable, or to be registered, in England and Wales in accordance with Court of Protection Rules.

(2) The court must make the declaration if –
- (a) the measure comes within sub-paragraph (1) or (2) of paragraph 19, and
- (b) the paragraph is not disapplied in relation to it as a result of sub-paragraph (3), (4) or (5).

(3) A measure to which a declaration under this paragraph relates is enforceable in England and Wales as if it were a measure of like effect taken by the court.

Measures taken in relation to those aged under 16

23. (1) This paragraph applies where –
- (a) provision giving effect to, or otherwise deriving from, the Convention in a country other than England and Wales applies in relation to a person who has not reached 16, and
- (b) a measure is taken in relation to that person in reliance on that provision.

(2) This Part of this Schedule applies in relation to that measure as it applies in relation to a protective measure taken in relation to an adult under the law of a Convention country other than England and Wales.

Supplementary

24. The court may not review the merits of a measure taken outside England and Wales except to establish whether the measure complies with this Schedule in so far as it is, as a result of this Schedule, required to do so.

25. Court of Protection Rules may make provision about an application under paragraph 20 or 22.

Part 5 Co-operation

Proposal for cross-border placement

26. (1) This paragraph applies where a public authority proposes to place an adult in an establishment in a Convention country other than England and Wales.

(2) The public authority must consult an appropriate authority in that other country about the proposed placement and, for that purpose, must send it –
- (a) a report on the adult, and
- (b) a statement of its reasons for the proposed placement.

(3) If the appropriate authority in the other country opposes the proposed placement within a reasonable time, the public authority may not proceed with it.

27. A proposal received by a public authority under Article 33 in relation to an adult is to proceed unless the authority opposes it within a reasonable time.

Adult in danger etc.

28. (1)   This paragraph applies if a public authority is told that an adult –
    (a) who is in serious danger, and
    (b) in relation to whom the public authority has taken, or is considering taking, protective measures, is, or has become resident, in a Convention country other than England and Wales.

(2) The public authority must tell an appropriate authority in that other country about –
    (a) the danger, and
    (b) the measures taken or under consideration.

29. A public authority may not request from, or send to, an appropriate authority in a Convention country information in accordance with Chapter 5 (cooperation) in relation to an adult if it thinks that doing so –
    (a) would be likely to endanger the adult or his property, or
    (b) would amount to a serious threat to the liberty or life of a member of the adult's family.

Part 6   General

Certificates

30. A certificate given under Article 38 by an authority in a Convention country other than England and Wales is, unless the contrary is shown, proof of the matters contained in it.

Powers to make further provision as to private international law

31. Her Majesty may by Order in Council confer on the Lord Chancellor, the court or another public authority functions for enabling the Convention to be given effect in England and Wales.

32. (1)   Regulations may make provision –
    (a) giving further effect to the Convention, or
    (b) otherwise about the private international law of England and Wales in relation to the protection of adults.

(2) The regulations may –
    (a) confer functions on the court or another public authority;
    (b) amend this Schedule;
    (c) provide for this Schedule to apply with specified modifications;
    (d) make provision about countries other than Convention countries.

Exceptions

33. Nothing in this Schedule applies, and no provision made under paragraph 32 is to apply, to any matter to which the Convention, as a result of Article 4, does not apply.

Regulations and orders

34. A reference in this Schedule to regulations or an order (other than an Order in Council) is to regulations or an order made for the purposes of this Schedule by the Lord Chancellor.

Commencement

35. The following provisions of this Schedule have effect only if the Convention is in force in accordance with Article 57 –

    (a) paragraph 8,

    (b) paragraph 9,

    (c) paragraph 19(2) and (5),

    (d) Part 5,

    (e) paragraph 30.

Schedule 4 (section 66(3))

Provisions applying to existing Enduring Powers of Attorney

Part 1   Enduring powers of attorney

Enduring power of attorney to survive mental incapacity of donor

1. (1) Where an individual has created a power of attorney which is an enduring power within the meaning of this Schedule –

   (a) the power is not revoked by any subsequent mental incapacity of his,
   (b) upon such incapacity supervening, the donee of the power may not do anything under the authority of the power except as provided by sub-paragraph (2) unless or until the instrument creating the power is registered under paragraph 13, and
   (c) if and so long as paragraph (b) operates to suspend the donee's authority to act under the power, section 5 of the Powers of Attorney Act 1971 (c. 27) (protection of donee and third persons), so far as applicable, applies as if the power had been revoked by the donor's mental incapacity, and, accordingly, section 1 of this Act does not apply.

(2) Despite sub-paragraph (1)(b), where the attorney has made an application for registration of the instrument then, until it is registered, the attorney may take action under the power –

   (a) to maintain the donor or prevent loss to his estate, or
   (b) to maintain himself or other persons in so far as paragraph 3(2) permits him to do so.

(3) Where the attorney purports to act as provided by sub-paragraph (2) then, in favour of a person who deals with him without knowledge that the attorney is acting otherwise than in accordance with sub-paragraph (2)(a) or (b), the transaction between them is as valid as if the attorney were acting in accordance with sub-paragraph (2)(a) or (b).

Characteristics of an enduring power of attorney

2. (1) Subject to sub-paragraphs (5) and (6) and paragraph 20, a power of attorney is an enduring power within the meaning of this Schedule if the instrument which creates the power –

   (a) is in the prescribed form,
   (b) was executed in the prescribed manner by the donor and the attorney, and
   (c) incorporated at the time of execution by the donor the prescribed explanatory information.

(2) In this paragraph, 'prescribed' means prescribed by such of the following regulations as applied when the instrument was executed –

   (a) the Enduring Powers of Attorney (Prescribed Form) Regulations 1986 (S.I. 1986/126),

(b) the Enduring Powers of Attorney (Prescribed Form) Regulations 1987 (S.I. 1987/1612),

(c) the Enduring Powers of Attorney (Prescribed Form) Regulations 1990 (S.I. 1990/1376),

(d) the Enduring Powers of Attorney (Welsh Language Prescribed Form) Regulations 2000 (S.I. 2000/289).

(3) An instrument in the prescribed form purporting to have been executed in the prescribed manner is to be taken, in the absence of evidence to the contrary, to be a document which incorporated at the time of execution by the donor the prescribed explanatory information.

(4) If an instrument differs in an immaterial respect in form or mode of expression from the prescribed form it is to be treated as sufficient in point of form and expression.

(5) A power of attorney cannot be an enduring power unless, when he executes the instrument creating it, the attorney is –

(a) an individual who has reached 18 and is not bankrupt, or

(b) a trust corporation.

(6) A power of attorney which gives the attorney a right to appoint a substitute or successor cannot be an enduring power.

(7) An enduring power is revoked by the bankruptcy of the donor or attorney.

(8) But where the donor or attorney is bankrupt merely because an interim bankruptcy restrictions order has effect in respect of him, the power is suspended for so long as the order has effect.

(9) An enduring power is revoked if the court –

(a) exercises a power under sections 16 to 20 in relation to the donor, and

(b) directs that the enduring power is to be revoked.

(10) No disclaimer of an enduring power, whether by deed or otherwise, is valid unless and until the attorney gives notice of it to the donor or, where paragraph 4(6) or 15(1) applies, to the Public Guardian.

Scope of authority etc. of attorney under enduring power

3. (1) If the instrument which creates an enduring power of attorney is expressed to confer general authority on the attorney, the instrument operates to confer, subject to –

(a) the restriction imposed by sub-paragraph (3), and

(b) any conditions or restrictions contained in the instrument, authority to do on behalf of the donor anything which the donor could lawfully do by an attorney at the time when the donor executed the instrument.

(2) Subject to any conditions or restrictions contained in the instrument, an attorney under an enduring power, whether general or limited, may (without obtaining any consent) act under the power so as to benefit himself or other persons than the donor to the following extent but no further –

(a) he may so act in relation to himself or in relation to any other person if the donor might be expected to provide for his or that person's needs respectively, and

(b) he may do whatever the donor might be expected to do to meet those needs.

(3) Without prejudice to sub-paragraph (2) but subject to any conditions or restrictions contained in the instrument, an attorney under an enduring power, whether general or limited, may (without obtaining any consent) dispose of the property of the donor by way of gift to the following extent but no further –

(a) he may make gifts of a seasonal nature or at a time, or on an anniversary, of a birth, a marriage or the formation of a civil partnership, to persons (including himself) who are related to or connected with the donor, and

(b) he may make gifts to any charity to whom the donor made or might be expected to make gifts, provided that the value of each such gift is not unreasonable having regard to all the circumstances and in particular the size of the donor's estate.

Part 2   Action on actual or impending incapacity of donor

Duties of attorney in event of actual or impending incapacity of donor

4. (1) Sub-paragraphs (2) to (6) apply if the attorney under an enduring power has reason to believe that the donor is or is becoming mentally incapable.

(2) The attorney must, as soon as practicable, make an application to the Public Guardian for the registration of the instrument creating the power.

(3) Before making an application for registration the attorney must comply with the provisions as to notice set out in Part 3 of this Schedule.

(4) An application for registration –
   (a) must be made in the prescribed form, and
   (b) must contain such statements as may be prescribed.

(5) The attorney –
   (a) may, before making an application for the registration of the instrument, refer to the court for its determination any question as to the validity of the power, and
   (b) must comply with any direction given to him by the court on that determination.

(6) No disclaimer of the power is valid unless and until the attorney gives notice of it to the Public Guardian; and the Public Guardian must notify the donor if he receives a notice under this sub-paragraph.

(7) A person who, in an application for registration, makes a statement which he knows to be false in a material particular is guilty of an offence and is liable –
   (a) on summary conviction, to imprisonment for a term not exceeding 12 months or a fine not exceeding the statutory maximum or both;
   (b) on conviction on indictment, to imprisonment for a term not exceeding 2 years or a fine or both.

(8) In this paragraph, 'prescribed' means prescribed by regulations made for the purposes of this Schedule by the Lord Chancellor.

Part 3   Notification prior to registration

Duty to give notice to relatives

5. Subject to paragraph 7, before making an application for registration the attorney must give notice of his intention to do so to all those persons (if any) who are entitled to receive notice by virtue of paragraph 6.

6. (1) Subject to sub-paragraphs (2) to (4), persons of the following classes ('relatives') are entitled to receive notice under paragraph 5 –

    (a) the donor's spouse or civil partner,

    (b) the donor's children,

    (c) the donor's parents,

    (d) the donor's brothers and sisters, whether of the whole or half blood,

    (e) the widow, widower or surviving civil partner of a child of the donor,

    (f) the donor's grandchildren,

    (g) the children of the donor's brothers and sisters of the whole blood,

    (h) the children of the donor's brothers and sisters of the half blood,

    (i) the donor's uncles and aunts of the whole blood,

    (j) the children of the donor's uncles and aunts of the whole blood.

(2) A person is not entitled to receive notice under paragraph 5 if –

    (a) his name or address is not known to the attorney and cannot be reasonably ascertained by him, or

    (b) the attorney has reason to believe that he has not reached 18 or is mentally incapable.

(3) Except where sub-paragraph (4) applies –

    (a) no more than 3 persons are entitled to receive notice under paragraph 5, and

    (b) in determining the persons who are so entitled, persons falling within the class in sub-paragraph (1)(a) are to be preferred to persons falling within the class in sub-paragraph (1)(b), those falling within the class in sub-paragraph (1)(b) are to be preferred to those falling within the class in sub-paragraph (1)(c), and so on.

(4) Despite the limit of 3 specified in sub-paragraph (3), where –

    (a) there is more than one person falling within any of classes (a) to (j) of sub-paragraph (1), and

    (b) at least one of those persons would be entitled to receive notice under paragraph 5, then, subject to sub-paragraph (2), all the persons falling within that class are entitled to receive notice under paragraph 5.

7. (1) An attorney is not required to give notice under paragraph 5 –

    (a) to himself, or

    (b) to any other attorney under the power who is joining in making the application, even though he or, as the case may be, the other attorney is entitled to receive notice by virtue of paragraph 6.

(2) In the case of any person who is entitled to receive notice by virtue of paragraph 6, the attorney, before applying for registration, may make an application to the court to be dispensed from the requirement to give him notice; and the court must grant the application if it is satisfied –

    (a) that it would be undesirable or impracticable for the attorney to give him notice, or

    (b) that no useful purpose is likely to be served by giving him notice.

Duty to give notice to donor

8. (1) Subject to sub-paragraph (2), before making an application for registration the attorney must give notice of his intention to do so to the donor.

(2) Paragraph 7(2) applies in relation to the donor as it applies in relation to a person who is entitled to receive notice under paragraph 5.

Contents of notices

9. A notice to relatives under this Part of this Schedule must –
   (a) be in the prescribed form,
   (b) state that the attorney proposes to make an application to the Public Guardian for the registration of the instrument creating the enduring power in question,
   (c) inform the person to whom it is given of his right to object to the registration under paragraph 13(4), and
   (d) specify, as the grounds on which an objection to registration may be made, the grounds set out in paragraph 13(9).

10. A notice to the donor under this Part of this Schedule –
   (a) must be in the prescribed form,
   (b) must contain the statement mentioned in paragraph 9(b), and
   (c) must inform the donor that, while the instrument remains registered, any revocation of the power by him will be ineffective unless and until the revocation is confirmed by the court.

Duty to give notice to other attorneys

11. (1)   Subject to sub-paragraph (2), before making an application for registration an attorney under a joint and several power must give notice of his intention to do so to any other attorney under the power who is not joining in making the application; and paragraphs 7(2) and 9 apply in relation to attorneys entitled to receive notice by virtue of this paragraph as they apply in relation to persons entitled to receive notice by virtue of paragraph 6.

(2)   An attorney is not entitled to receive notice by virtue of this paragraph if –
   (a) his address is not known to the applying attorney and cannot reasonably be ascertained by him, or
   (b) the applying attorney has reason to believe that he has not reached 18 or is mentally incapable.

Supplementary

12. Despite section 7 of the Interpretation Act 1978 (c. 30) (construction of references to service by post), for the purposes of this Part of this Schedule a notice given by post is to be regarded as given on the date on which it was posted.

Part 4   Registration

Registration of instrument creating power

13. (1)   If an application is made in accordance with paragraph 4(3) and (4) the Public Guardian must, subject to the provisions of this paragraph, register the instrument to which the application relates.

(2)   If it appears to the Public Guardian that –
   (a) there is a deputy appointed for the donor of the power created by the instrument, and
   (b) the powers conferred on the deputy would, if the instrument were registered, to any extent conflict with the powers conferred on the attorney, the Public Guardian must not register the instrument except in accordance with the court's directions.

(3) The court may, on the application of the attorney, direct the Public Guardian to register an instrument even though notice has not been given as required by paragraph 4(3) and Part 3 of this Schedule to a person entitled to receive it, if the court is satisfied –

   (a) that it was undesirable or impracticable for the attorney to give notice to that person, or
   (b) that no useful purpose is likely to be served by giving him notice.

(4) Sub-paragraph (5) applies if, before the end of the period of 5 weeks beginning with the date (or the latest date) on which the attorney gave notice under paragraph 5 of an application for registration, the Public Guardian receives a valid notice of objection to the registration from a person entitled to notice of the application.

(5) The Public Guardian must not register the instrument except in accordance with the court's directions.

(6) Sub-paragraph (7) applies if, in the case of an application for registration –

   (a) it appears from the application that there is no one to whom notice has been given under paragraph 5, or
   (b) the Public Guardian has reason to believe that appropriate inquiries might bring to light evidence on which he could be satisfied that one of the grounds of objection set out in sub-paragraph (9) was established.

(7) The Public Guardian –

   (a) must not register the instrument, and
   (b) must undertake such inquiries as he thinks appropriate in all the circumstances.

(8) If, having complied with sub-paragraph (7)(b), the Public Guardian is satisfied that one of the grounds of objection set out in sub-paragraph (9) is established –

   (a) the attorney may apply to the court for directions, and
   (b) the Public Guardian must not register the instrument except in accordance with the court's directions.

(9) A notice of objection under this paragraph is valid if made on one or more of the following grounds –

   (a) that the power purported to have been created by the instrument was not valid as an enduring power of attorney,
   (b) that the power created by the instrument no longer subsists,
   (c) that the application is premature because the donor is not yet becoming mentally incapable,
   (d) that fraud or undue pressure was used to induce the donor to create the power,
   (e) that, having regard to all the circumstances and in particular the attorney's relationship to or connection with the donor, the attorney is unsuitable to be the donor's attorney.

(10) If any of those grounds is established to the satisfaction of the court it must direct the Public Guardian not to register the instrument, but if not so satisfied it must direct its registration.

(11) If the court directs the Public Guardian not to register an instrument because it is satisfied that the ground in sub-paragraph (9)(d) or (e) is established, it must by order revoke the power created by the instrument.

(12) If the court directs the Public Guardian not to register an instrument because it is satisfied that any ground in sub-paragraph (9) except that in paragraph (c) is established, the instrument must be delivered up to be cancelled unless the court otherwise directs.

Register of enduring powers

14. The Public Guardian has the function of establishing and maintaining a register of enduring powers for the purposes of this Schedule.

Part 5   Legal position after registration

Effect and proof of registration

15. (1)   The effect of the registration of an instrument under paragraph 13 is that –

(a) no revocation of the power by the donor is valid unless and until the court confirms the revocation under paragraph 16(3);

(b) no disclaimer of the power is valid unless and until the attorney gives notice of it to the Public Guardian;

(c) the donor may not extend or restrict the scope of the authority conferred by the instrument and no instruction or consent given by him after registration, in the case of a consent, confers any right and, in the case of an instruction, imposes or confers any obligation or right on or creates any liability of the attorney or other persons having notice of the instruction or consent.

(2) Sub-paragraph (1) applies for so long as the instrument is registered under paragraph 13 whether or not the donor is for the time being mentally incapable.

(3) A document purporting to be an office copy of an instrument registered under this Schedule is, in any part of the United Kingdom, evidence of –

(a) the contents of the instrument, and

(b) the fact that it has been so registered.

(4) Sub-paragraph (3) is without prejudice to section 3 of the Powers of Attorney Act 1971 (c. 27) (proof by certified copies) and to any other method of proof authorised by law.

Functions of court with regard to registered power

16. (1)   Where an instrument has been registered under paragraph 13, the court has the following functions with respect to the power and the donor of and the attorney appointed to act under the power.

(2) The court may –

(a) determine any question as to the meaning or effect of the instrument;

(b) give directions with respect to –

(i) the management or disposal by the attorney of the property and affairs of the donor;

(ii) the rendering of accounts by the attorney and the production of the records kept by him for the purpose;

(iii) the remuneration or expenses of the attorney whether or not in default of or in accordance with any provision made by the instrument, including directions for the repayment of excessive or the payment of additional remuneration;

(c) require the attorney to supply information or produce documents or things in his possession as attorney;

(d) give any consent or authorisation to act which the attorney would have to obtain from a mentally capable donor;

(e) authorise the attorney to act so as to benefit himself or other persons than the donor otherwise than in accordance with paragraph 3(2) and (3) (but subject to any conditions or restrictions contained in the instrument);

(f) relieve the attorney wholly or partly from any liability which he has or may have incurred on account of a breach of his duties as attorney.

(3) On application made for the purpose by or on behalf of the donor, the court must confirm the revocation of the power if satisfied that the donor –

(a) has done whatever is necessary in law to effect an express revocation of the power, and

(b) was mentally capable of revoking a power of attorney when he did so (whether or not he is so when the court considers the application).

(4) The court must direct the Public Guardian to cancel the registration of an instrument registered under paragraph 13 in any of the following circumstances –

(a) on confirming the revocation of the power under sub-paragraph (3),

(b) on directing under paragraph 2(9)(b) that the power is to be revoked,

(c) on being satisfied that the donor is and is likely to remain mentally capable,

(d) on being satisfied that the power has expired or has been revoked by the mental incapacity of the attorney,

(e) on being satisfied that the power was not a valid and subsisting enduring power when registration was effected,

(f) on being satisfied that fraud or undue pressure was used to induce the donor to create the power,

(g) on being satisfied that, having regard to all the circumstances and in particular the attorney's relationship to or connection with the donor, the attorney is unsuitable to be the donor's attorney.

(5) If the court directs the Public Guardian to cancel the registration of an instrument on being satisfied of the matters specified in sub-paragraph (4)(f) or (g) it must by order revoke the power created by the instrument.

(6) If the court directs the cancellation of the registration of an instrument under sub-paragraph (4) except paragraph (c) the instrument must be delivered up to the Public Guardian to be cancelled, unless the court otherwise directs.

Cancellation of registration by Public Guardian

17. The Public Guardian must cancel the registration of an instrument creating an enduring power of attorney –

(a) on receipt of a disclaimer signed by the attorney;

(b) if satisfied that the power has been revoked by the death or bankruptcy of the donor or attorney or, if the attorney is a body corporate, by its winding up or dissolution;

(c) on receipt of notification from the court that the court has revoked the power;

(d) on confirmation from the court that the donor has revoked the power.

Part 6   Protection of attorney and third parties

Protection of attorney and third persons where power is invalid or revoked

18. (1) Sub-paragraphs (2) and (3) apply where an instrument which did not create a valid power of attorney has been registered under paragraph 13 (whether or not the registration has been cancelled at the time of the act or transaction in question).

(2) An attorney who acts in pursuance of the power does not incur any liability (either to the donor or to any other person) because of the non-existence of the power unless at the time of acting he knows –
- (a) that the instrument did not create a valid enduring power,
- (b) that an event has occurred which, if the instrument had created a valid enduring power, would have had the effect of revoking the power, or
- (c) that, if the instrument had created a valid enduring power, the power would have expired before that time.

(3) Any transaction between the attorney and another person is, in favour of that person, as valid as if the power had then been in existence, unless at the time of the transaction that person has knowledge of any of the matters mentioned in sub-paragraph (2).

(4) If the interest of a purchaser depends on whether a transaction between the attorney and another person was valid by virtue of sub-paragraph (3), it is conclusively presumed in favour of the purchaser that the transaction was valid if –
- (a) the transaction between that person and the attorney was completed within 12 months of the date on which the instrument was registered, or
- (b) that person makes a statutory declaration, before or within 3 months after the completion of the purchase, that he had no reason at the time of the transaction to doubt that the attorney had authority to dispose of the property which was the subject of the transaction.

(5) For the purposes of section 5 of the Powers of Attorney Act 1971 (c. 27) (protection where power is revoked) in its application to an enduring power the revocation of which by the donor is by virtue of paragraph 15 invalid unless and until confirmed by the court under paragraph 16 –
- (a) knowledge of the confirmation of the revocation is knowledge of the revocation of the power, but
- (b) knowledge of the unconfirmed revocation is not.

Further protection of attorney and third persons

19. (1) If –
- (a) an instrument framed in a form prescribed as mentioned in paragraph 2(2) creates a power which is not a valid enduring power, and
- (b) the power is revoked by the mental incapacity of the donor, sub-paragraphs (2) and (3) apply, whether or not the instrument has been registered.

(2) An attorney who acts in pursuance of the power does not, by reason of the revocation, incur any liability (either to the donor or to any other person) unless at the time of acting he knows –
- (a) that the instrument did not create a valid enduring power, and
- (b) that the donor has become mentally incapable.

(3) Any transaction between the attorney and another person is, in favour of that person, as valid as if the power had then been in existence, unless at the time of the transaction that person knows –
- (a) that the instrument did not create a valid enduring power, and
- (b) that the donor has become mentally incapable.

(4) Paragraph 18(4) applies for the purpose of determining whether a transaction was valid by virtue of sub-paragraph (3) as it applies for the purpose or determining whether a transaction was valid by virtue of paragraph 18(3).

Part 7   Joint and joint and several attorneys

Application to joint and joint and several attorneys

20. (1)   An instrument which appoints more than one person to be an attorney cannot create an enduring power unless the attorneys are appointed to act –

    (a) jointly, or

    (b) jointly and severally.

(2) This Schedule, in its application to joint attorneys, applies to them collectively as it applies to a single attorney but subject to the modifications specified in paragraph 21.

(3) This Schedule, in its application to joint and several attorneys, applies with the modifications specified in sub-paragraphs (4) to (7) and in paragraph 22.

(4) A failure, as respects any one attorney, to comply with the requirements for the creation of enduring powers –

    (a) prevents the instrument from creating such a power in his case, but

    (b) does not affect its efficacy for that purpose as respects the other or others or its efficacy in his case for the purpose of creating a power of attorney which is not an enduring power.

(5) If one or more but not both or all the attorneys makes or joins in making an application for registration of the instrument –

    (a) an attorney who is not an applicant as well as one who is may act pending the registration of the instrument as provided in paragraph 1(2),

    (b) notice of the application must also be given under Part 3 of this Schedule to the other attorney or attorneys, and

    (c) objection may validly be taken to the registration on a ground relating to an attorney or to the power of an attorney who is not an applicant as well as to one or the power of one who is an applicant.

(6) The Public Guardian is not precluded by paragraph 13(5) or (8) from registering an instrument and the court must not direct him not to do so under paragraph 13(10) if an enduring power subsists as respects some attorney who is not affected by the ground or grounds of the objection in question; and where the Public Guardian registers an instrument in that case, he must make against the registration an entry in the prescribed form.

(7) Sub-paragraph (6) does not preclude the court from revoking a power in so far as it confers a power on any other attorney in respect of whom the ground in paragraph 13(9) (d) or (e) is established; and where any ground in paragraph 13(9) affecting any other attorney is established the court must direct the Public Guardian to make against the registration an entry in the prescribed form.

(8) In sub-paragraph (4), 'the requirements for the creation of enduring powers' means the provisions of –

    (a) paragraph 2 other than sub-paragraphs (8) and (9), and

    (b) the regulations mentioned in paragraph 2.

Joint attorneys

21. (1) In paragraph 2(5), the reference to the time when the attorney executes the instrument is to be read as a reference to the time when the second or last attorney executes the instrument.

(2) In paragraph 2(6) to (8), the reference to the attorney is to be read as a reference to any attorney under the power.

(3) Paragraph 13 has effect as if the ground of objection to the registration of the instrument specified in sub-paragraph (9)(e) applied to any attorney under the power.

(4) In paragraph 16(2), references to the attorney are to be read as including references to any attorney under the power.

(5) In paragraph 16(4), references to the attorney are to be read as including references to any attorney under the power.

(6) In paragraph 17, references to the attorney are to be read as including references to any attorney under the power.

Joint and several attorneys

22. (1) In paragraph 2(7), the reference to the bankruptcy of the attorney is to be read as a reference to the bankruptcy of the last remaining attorney under the power; and the bankruptcy of any other attorney under the power causes that person to cease to be an attorney under the power.

(2) In paragraph 2(8), the reference to the suspension of the power is to be read as a reference to its suspension in so far as it relates to the attorney in respect of whom the interim bankruptcy restrictions order has effect.

(3) The restriction upon disclaimer imposed by paragraph 4(6) applies only to those attorneys who have reason to believe that the donor is or is becoming mentally incapable.

Part 8   Interpretation

23. (1) In this Schedule –

'enduring power' is to be construed in accordance with paragraph 2,

'mentally incapable' or 'mental incapacity', except where it refers to revocation at common law, means in relation to any person, that he is incapable by reason of mental disorder (within the meaning of the Mental Health Act) of managing and administering his property and affairs and 'mentally capable' and 'mental capacity' are to be construed accordingly,

'notice' means notice in writing, and

'prescribed', except for the purposes of paragraph 2, means prescribed by regulations made for the purposes of this Schedule by the Lord Chancellor.

(1A)   In sub-paragraph (1), 'mental disorder' has the same meaning as in the Mental Health Act but disregarding the amendments made to that Act by the Mental Health Act 2007.

(2) Any question arising under or for the purposes of this Schedule as to what the donor of the power might at any time be expected to do is to be determined by assuming that he had full mental capacity at the time but otherwise by reference to the circumstances existing at that time.

Schedule 5 (section 66(4))

Transitional provisions and savings

Part 1   Repeal of Part 7 of the Mental Health Act 1983

Existing receivers

1. (1) This paragraph applies where, immediately before the commencement day, there is a receiver ('R') for a person ('P') appointed under section 99 of the Mental Health Act.

(2) On and after that day –

   (a) this Act applies as if R were a deputy appointed for P by the court, but with the functions that R had as receiver immediately before that day, and

   (b) a reference in any other enactment to a deputy appointed by the court includes a person appointed as a deputy as a result of paragraph (a).

(3) On any application to it by R, the court may end R's appointment as P's deputy.

(4) Where, as a result of section 20(1), R may not make a decision on behalf of P in relation to a relevant matter, R must apply to the court.

(5) If, on the application, the court is satisfied that P is capable of managing his property and affairs in relation to the relevant matter –

   (a) it must make an order ending R's appointment as P's deputy in relation to that matter, but

   (b) it may, in relation to any other matter, exercise in relation to P any of the powers which it has under sections 15 to 19.

(6) If it is not satisfied, the court may exercise in relation to P any of the powers which it has under sections 15 to 19.

(7) R's appointment as P's deputy ceases to have effect if P dies.

(8) 'Relevant matter' means a matter in relation to which, immediately before the commencement day, R was authorised to act as P's receiver.

(9) In sub-paragraph (1), the reference to a receiver appointed under section 99 of the Mental Health Act includes a reference to a person who by virtue of Schedule 5 to that Act was deemed to be a receiver appointed under that section.

Orders, appointments etc.

2. (1) Any order or appointment made, direction or authority given or other thing done which has, or by virtue of Schedule 5 to the Mental Health Act was deemed to have, effect under Part 7 of the Act immediately before the commencement day is to continue to have effect despite the repeal of Part 7.

(2) In so far as any such order, appointment, direction, authority or thing could have been made, given or done under sections 15 to 20 if those sections had then been in force –

(a) it is to be treated as made, given or done under those sections, and

(b) the powers of variation and discharge conferred by section 16(7) apply accordingly.

(3) Sub-paragraph (1) –

(a) does not apply to nominations under section 93(1) or (4) of the Mental Health Act, and

(b) as respects receivers, has effect subject to paragraph 1.

(4) This Act does not affect the operation of section 109 of the Mental Health Act (effect and proof of orders etc.) in relation to orders made and directions given under Part 7 of that Act.

(5) This paragraph is without prejudice to section 16 of the Interpretation Act 1978 (c. 30) (general savings on repeal).

Pending proceedings

3. (1) Any application for the exercise of a power under Part 7 of the Mental Health Act which is pending immediately before the commencement day is to be treated, in so far as a corresponding power is exercisable under sections 16 to 20, as an application for the exercise of that power.

(2) For the purposes of sub-paragraph (1) an application for the appointment of a receiver is to be treated as an application for the appointment of a deputy.

Appeals

4. (1) Part 7 of the Mental Health Act and the rules made under it are to continue to apply to any appeal brought by virtue of section 105 of that Act which has not been determined before the commencement day.

(2) If in the case of an appeal brought by virtue of section 105(1) (appeal to nominated judge) the judge nominated under section 93 of the Mental Health Act has begun to hear the appeal, he is to continue to do so but otherwise it is to be heard by a puisne judge of the High Court nominated under section 46.

Fees

5. All fees and other payments which, having become due, have not been paid to the former Court of Protection before the commencement day, are to be paid to the new Court of Protection.

Court records

6. (1) The records of the former Court of Protection are to be treated, on and after the commencement day, as records of the new Court of Protection and are to be dealt with accordingly under the Public Records Act 1958 (c. 51).

(2) On and after the commencement day, the Public Guardian is, for the purpose of exercising any of his functions, to be given such access as he may require to such of the records mentioned in sub-paragraph (1) as relate to the appointment of receivers under section 99 of the Mental Health Act.

Existing charges

7. This Act does not affect the operation in relation to a charge created before the commencement day of –

  (a) so much of section 101(6) of the Mental Health Act as precludes a charge created under section 101(5) from conferring a right of sale or foreclosure during the lifetime of the patient, or

  (b) section 106(6) of the Mental Health Act (charge created by virtue of section 106(5) not to cause interest to fail etc.).

Preservation of interests on disposal of property

8. Paragraph 8(1) of Schedule 2 applies in relation to any disposal of property (within the meaning of that provision) by a person living on 1st November 1960, being a disposal effected under the Lunacy Act 1890 (c. 5) as it applies in relation to the disposal of property effected under sections 16 to 20.

Accounts

9. Court of Protection Rules may provide that, in a case where paragraph 1 applies, R is to have a duty to render accounts –

  (a) while he is receiver;

  (b) after he is discharged.

Interpretation

10. In this Part of this Schedule –

  (a) 'the commencement day' means the day on which section 66(1)(a) (repeal of Part 7 of the Mental Health Act) comes into force,

  (b) 'the former Court of Protection' means the office abolished by section 45, and

  (c) 'the new Court of Protection' means the court established by that section.

Part 2   Repeal of the Enduring Powers of Attorney Act 1985

Orders, determinations, etc.

11. (1) Any order or determination made, or other thing done, under the 1985 Act which has effect immediately before the commencement day continues to have effect despite the repeal of that Act.

(2) In so far as any such order, determination or thing could have been made or done under Schedule 4 if it had then been in force –

  (a) it is to be treated as made or done under that Schedule, and

  (b) the powers of variation and discharge exercisable by the court apply accordingly.

(3) Any instrument registered under the 1985 Act is to be treated as having been registered by the Public Guardian under Schedule 4.

(4) This paragraph is without prejudice to section 16 of the Interpretation Act 1978 (c. 30) (general savings on repeal).

Pending proceedings

12. (1)   An application for the exercise of a power under the 1985 Act which is pending immediately before the commencement day is to be treated, in so far as a corresponding power is exercisable under Schedule 4, as an application for the exercise of that power.

(2) For the purposes of sub-paragraph (1) –

(a) a pending application under section 4(2) of the 1985 Act for the registration of an instrument is to be treated as an application to the Public Guardian under paragraph 4 of Schedule 4 and any notice given in connection with that application under Schedule 1 to the 1985 Act is to be treated as given under Part 3 of Schedule 4,

(b) a notice of objection to the registration of an instrument is to be treated as a notice of objection under paragraph 13 of Schedule 4, and

(c) pending proceedings under section 5 of the 1985 Act are to be treated as proceedings on an application for the exercise by the court of a power which would become exercisable in relation to an instrument under paragraph 16(2) of Schedule 4 on its registration.

Appeals

13. (1)   The 1985 Act and, so far as relevant, the provisions of Part 7 of the Mental Health Act and the rules made under it as applied by section 10 of the 1985 Act are to continue to have effect in relation to any appeal brought by virtue of section 10(1)(c) of the 1985 Act which has not been determined before the commencement day.

(2) If, in the case of an appeal brought by virtue of section 105(1) of the Mental Health Act as applied by section 10(1)(c) of the 1985 Act (appeal to nominated judge), the judge nominated under section 93 of the Mental Health Act has begun to hear the appeal, he is to continue to do so but otherwise the appeal is to be heard by a puisne judge of the High Court nominated under section 46.

Exercise of powers of donor as trustee

14. (1)   Section 2(8) of the 1985 Act (which prevents a power of attorney under section 25 of the Trustee Act 1925 (c. 19) as enacted from being an enduring power) is to continue to apply to any enduring power –

(a) created before 1 March 2000, and

(b) having effect immediately before the commencement day.

(2) Section 3(3) of the 1985 Act (which entitles the donee of an enduring power to exercise the donor's powers as trustee) is to continue to apply to any enduring power to which, as a result of the provision mentioned in sub-paragraph (3), it applies immediately before the commencement day.

(3) The provision is section 4(3)(a) of the Trustee Delegation Act 1999 (c. 15) (which provides for section 3(3) of the 1985 Act to cease to apply to an enduring power when its registration is cancelled, if it was registered in response to an application made before 1st March 2001).

(4) Even though section 4 of the 1999 Act is repealed by this Act, that section is to continue to apply in relation to an enduring power –

(a) to which section 3(3) of the 1985 Act applies as a result of sub-paragraph (2), or

(b) to which, immediately before the repeal of section 4 of the 1999 Act, section 1 of that Act applies as a result of section 4 of it.

(5) The reference in section 1(9) of the 1999 Act to section 4(6) of that Act is to be read with sub-paragraphs (2) to (4).

Interpretation

15. In this Part of this Schedule, 'the commencement day' means the day on which section 66(1)(b) (repeal of the 1985 Act) comes into force.

Schedule 6

Minor and consequential amendments

(not reproduced here)

Schedule 7

Repeals

(not reproduced here)

Appendix 1A DOLS Regulations on Representative

The Mental Capacity (Deprivation of Liberty: Appointment of Relevant Person's Representative) Regulations 2008. SI 2008/1315
The Secretary of State for Health makes these Regulations in exercise of the powers conferred by section 65(1) of, and paragraphs 138(1), 142 to 145, 148, 149 and 151 of Schedule A1 to, the Mental Capacity Act 2005.

Citation, commencement and application
1. (1) These Regulations may be cited as the Mental Capacity (Deprivation of Liberty: Appointment of Relevant Person's Representative) Regulations 2008 and shall come into force on 3rd November 2008.

(2) These Regulations apply in relation to England only.

Interpretation
2. In these Regulations –

'best interests assessor' means a person selected to carry out a best interests assessment under paragraph 38 of Schedule A1 to the Act;

'donee' is a person who has a lasting power of attorney conferred on them by the relevant person, giving that donee the authority to make decisions about the relevant person's personal welfare;

'the Act' means the Mental Capacity Act 2005; and

'the relevant person's managing authority' means the managing authority that has made the application for a standard authorisation in respect of the relevant person.

Part 1 Selection of representatives

Selection of a person to be a representative – general
3. (1) In addition to any requirements in regulations 6 to 9 and 11, a person can only be selected to be a representative if they are –

(a) 18 years of age or over;
(b) able to keep in contact with the relevant person;
(c) willing to be the relevant person's representative;
(d) not financially interested in the relevant person's managing authority;
(e) not a relative of a person who is financially interested in the managing authority;
(f) not employed by, or providing services to, the relevant person's managing authority, where the relevant person's managing authority is a care home;

    (g) not employed to work in the relevant person's managing authority in a role that is, or could be, related to the relevant person's case, where the relevant person's managing authority is a hospital; and

    (h) not employed to work in the supervisory body that is appointing the representative in a role that is, or could be, related to the relevant person's case.

(2) For the purposes of this regulation a 'relative' means –

    (a) a spouse, ex-spouse, civil partner or ex-civil partner;

    (b) a person living with the relevant person as if they were a spouse or a civil partner;

    (c) a parent or child;

    (d) a brother or sister;

    (e) a child of a person falling within sub-paragraphs (a), (b) or (d);

    (f) a grandparent or grandchild;

    (g) a grandparent-in-law or grandchild-in-law;

    (h) an uncle or aunt;

    (i) a brother-in-law or sister-in-law;

    (j) a son-in-law or daughter-in-law;

    (k) a first cousin; or

    (l) a half-brother or half-sister.

(3) For the purposes of this regulation –

    (a) the relationships in paragraph (2)(c) to (k) include step relationships;

    (b) references to step relationships and in-laws in paragraph (2) are to be read in accordance with section 246 of the Civil Partnership Act 2004;

    (c) a person has a financial interest in a managing authority where –

      (i) that person is a partner, director, other office-holder or major shareholder of the managing authority that has made the application for a standard authorisation, and

      (ii) the managing authority is a care home or independent hospital; and

    (d) a major shareholder means –

      (i) any person holding one tenth or more of the issued shares in the managing authority, where the managing authority is a company limited by shares, and

      (ii) in all other cases, any of the owners of the managing authority.

Determination of capacity

4. The best interests assessor must determine whether the relevant person has capacity to select a representative.

Selection by the relevant person

5. (1) Where the best interests assessor determines that the relevant person has capacity, the relevant person may select a family member, friend or carer.

(2) Where the relevant person does not wish to make a selection under paragraph (1), regulation 8 applies.

Selection by a donee or deputy

6. (1) Where –

    (a) the best interests assessor determines that the relevant person lacks capacity to select a representative; and

(b) the relevant person has a donee or deputy and the donee's or deputy's scope of authority permits the selection of a family member, friend or carer of the relevant person, the donee or deputy may select such a person.

(2) A donee or deputy may select himself or herself to be the relevant person's representative.

(3) Where a donee or deputy does not wish to make a selection under paragraph (1) or (2), regulation 8 applies.

Confirmation of eligibility of family member, friend or carer and recommendation to the supervisory body

7. (1) The best interests assessor must confirm that a person selected under regulation 5(1) or 6(1) or (2) is eligible to be a representative.

(2) Where the best interests assessor confirms the selected person's eligibility under paragraph (1), the assessor must recommend the appointment of that person as a representative to the supervisory body.

(3) Where the best interests assessor is unable to confirm the selected person's eligibility under paragraph (1), the assessor must –

(a) advise the person who made the selection of that decision and give the reasons for it; and

(b) invite them to make a further selection.

Selection by the best interests assessor

8. (1) The best interests assessor may select a family member, friend or carer as a representative where paragraph (2) applies.

(2) The best interests assessor may make a selection where –

(a) the relevant person has the capacity to make a selection under regulation 5(1) but does not wish to do so;

(b) the relevant person's donee or deputy does not wish to make a selection under regulation 6(1) or (2); or

(c) the relevant person lacks the capacity to make a selection and –

(i) does not have a donee or deputy, or

(ii) has a donee or deputy but the donee's or deputy's scope of authority does not permit the selection of a representative.

(3) Where the best interests assessor selects a person in accordance with paragraph (2), the assessor must recommend that person for appointment as a representative to the supervisory body.

(4) But the best interests assessor must not select a person under paragraph (2) where the relevant person, donee or deputy objects to that selection.

(5) The best interests assessor must notify the supervisory body if they do not select a person who is eligible to be a representative.

Selection by the supervisory body

9. (1) Where a supervisory body is given notice under regulation 8(5), it may select a person to be the representative, who –

(a) would be performing the role in a professional capacity;

(b) has satisfactory skills and experience to perform the role;

(c) is not a family member, friend or carer of the relevant person;

(d) is not employed by, or providing services to, the relevant person's managing authority, where the relevant person's managing authority is a care home;

(e) is not employed to work in the relevant person's managing authority in a role that is, or could be, related to the relevant person's case, where the relevant person's managing authority is a hospital; and

(f) is not employed to work in the supervisory body that is appointing the representative in a role that is, or could be, related to the relevant person's case.

(2) The supervisory body must be satisfied that there is in respect of the person –

(a) an enhanced criminal record certificate issued pursuant to section 113B of the Police Act 1997 (enhanced criminal record certificates); or

(b) if the purpose for which the certificate is required is not one prescribed under subsection (2) of that section, a criminal record certificate issued pursuant to section 113A of that Act (criminal record certificates).

Part 2   Appointment of representatives

Commencement of appointment procedure

10. The procedure for appointing a representative must begin as soon as –

(a) a best interests assessor is selected by the supervisory body for the purposes of a request for a standard authorisation; or

(b) a relevant person's representative's appointment terminates, or is to be terminated, under regulation 14 and the relevant person remains subject to a standard authorisation.

Appointment of representative

11. Except where regulation 9 applies, a supervisory body may not appoint a representative unless the person is recommended to it under regulations 7 or 8.

Formalities of appointing a representative

12. (1) The offer of an appointment to a representative must be made in writing and state –

(a) the duties of a representative to –

(i) maintain contact with the relevant person,

(ii) represent the relevant person in matters relating to, or connected with, the deprivation of liberty, and

(iii) support the relevant person in matters relating to, or connected with, the deprivation of liberty; and

(b) the length of the period of the appointment.

(2) The representative must inform the supervisory body in writing that they are willing to accept the appointment and that they have understood the duties set out in sub-paragraph (1)(a).

(3) The appointment must be made for the period of the standard authorisation.

(4) The supervisory body must send copies of the written appointment to –

(a) the appointed person;

(b) the relevant person;

(c) the relevant person's managing authority;

(d) any donee or deputy of the relevant person;

(e) any independent mental capacity advocate appointed in accordance with sections 37 to 39D of the Act, involved in the relevant person's case; and

(f) every interested person named by the best interests assessor in their report as somebody the assessor has consulted in carrying out the assessment.

Termination of representative's appointment

13. A person ceases to be a representative if –

(a) the person dies;

(b) the person informs the supervisory body that they are no longer willing to continue as representative;

(c) the period of the appointment ends;

(d) a relevant person who has selected a family member, friend or carer under regulation 5(1) who has been appointed as their representative informs the supervisory body that they object to the person continuing to be a representative;

(e) a donee or deputy who has selected a family member, friend or carer of the relevant person under regulation 6(1) who has been appointed as a representative informs the supervisory body that they object to the person continuing to be a representative;

(f) the supervisory body terminates the appointment because it is satisfied that the representative is not maintaining sufficient contact with the relevant person in order to support and represent them;

(g) the supervisory body terminates the appointment because it is satisfied that the representative is not acting in the best interests of the relevant person; or

(h) the supervisory body terminates the appointment because it is satisfied that the person is no longer eligible or was not eligible at the time of appointment, to be a representative.

Formalities of termination of representative's appointment

14. (1) Where a representative's appointment is to be terminated for a reason specified in paragraphs (c) to (h) of regulation 13, the supervisory body must inform the representative of –

(a) the pending termination of the appointment;

(b) the reasons for the termination of the appointment; and

(c) the date on which the appointment terminates.

(2) The supervisory body must send copies of the termination of the appointment to –

(a) the relevant person;

(b) the relevant person's managing authority;

(c) any donee or deputy of the relevant person;

(d) any independent mental capacity advocate appointed in accordance with sections 37 to 39D of the Act, involved in the relevant person's case; and

(e) every interested person named by the best interests assessor in their report as somebody the assessor has consulted in carrying out the assessment.

Payment to a representative

15. A supervisory body may make payments to a representative appointed following a selection under regulation 9.

Appendix 1B DOLS Assessment Regulations

The Mental Capacity (Deprivation of Liberty: Standard Authorisations, Assessments and Ordinary Residence) Regulations 2008. SI 2008/1858

The Secretary of State for Health makes these Regulations in exercise of the powers conferred by section 65(1) of, and paragraphs 31, 33(4), 47, 70, 129(3), 130 and 183(6) and (7) of Schedule A1 to, the Mental Capacity Act 2005.

Part 1 Preliminary

Citation, commencement and application

1. (1) These Regulations may be cited as the Mental Capacity (Deprivation of Liberty: Standard Authorisations, Assessments and Ordinary Residence) Regulations 2008 and shall come into force on 3rd November 2008.

(2) These Regulations apply in relation to England only.

Interpretation

2. In these Regulations –

'approved mental health professional' means a person approved under section 114(1) of the Mental Health Act 1983 to act as an approved mental health professional for the purposes of that Act;

'best interests assessor' means a person selected to carry out a best interests assessment under paragraph 38 of Schedule A1 to the Act;

'General Social Care Council' has the meaning given by section 54(1) of the Care Standards Act 2000; and

'the Act' means the Mental Capacity Act 2005.

Part 2 Eligibility to carry out assessments

Eligibility – general

3. (1) In addition to any requirement in regulations 4 to 9, a person is eligible to carry out an assessment where paragraphs (2) to (4) are met.

(2) The person must –
- (a) be insured in respect of any liabilities that might arise in connection with carrying out the assessment; and
- (b) satisfy the supervisory body that he or she has such insurance.

(3) The supervisory body must be satisfied that the person has the skills and experience appropriate to the assessment to be carried out which must include, but are not limited to, the following –

(a) an applied knowledge of the Mental Capacity Act 2005 and related Code of Practice; and

(b) the ability to keep appropriate records and to provide clear and reasoned reports in accordance with legal requirements and good practice.

(4) The supervisory body must be satisfied that there is in respect of the person –

(a) an enhanced criminal record certificate issued under section 113B of the Police Act 1997 (enhanced criminal record certificates); or

(b) if the purpose for which the certificate is required is not one prescribed under subsection (2) of that section, a criminal record certificate issued pursuant to section 113A of that Act (criminal record certificates).

Eligibility to carry out a mental health assessment

4. (1) A person is eligible to carry out a mental health assessment if paragraphs (2) and (3) are met.

(2) The person must be –

(a) approved under section 12 of the Mental Health Act 1983; or

(b) a registered medical practitioner who the supervisory body is satisfied has at least three years post registration experience in the diagnosis or treatment of mental disorder.

(3) The supervisory body must be satisfied that the person has successfully completed the Deprivation of Liberty Safeguards Mental Health Assessors training programme made available by the Royal College of Psychiatrists.

(4) Except in the 12 month period beginning with the date the person has successfully completed the programme referred to in paragraph (3), the supervisory body must be satisfied that the person has, in the 12 months prior to selection, completed further training relevant to their role as a mental health assessor.

Eligibility to carry out a best interests assessment

5. (1) A person is eligible to carry out a best interests assessment if paragraphs (2) and (3) are met.

(2) The person must be one of the following –

(a) an approved mental health professional;

(b) a social worker registered with the General Social Care Council;

(c) a first level nurse, registered in Sub-Part 1 of the Nurses' Part of the Register maintained under article 5 of the Nursing and Midwifery Order 2001;

(d) an occupational therapist registered in Part 6 of the register maintained under article 5 of the Health Professions Order 2001; or

(e) a chartered psychologist who is listed in the British Psychological Society's Register of Chartered Psychologists and who holds a relevant practising certificate issued by that Society.

(3) The supervisory body must be satisfied that the person –

(a) is not suspended from the register or list relevant to the person's profession mentioned in paragraph (2);

(b) has at least two years post registration experience in one of the professions mentioned in paragraph (2);

(c) has successfully completed training that has been approved by the Secretary of State to be a best interests assessor;

(d) except in the 12 month period beginning with the date the person has successfully completed the training referred to in sub-paragraph (c), the supervisory body must be satisfied that the person has, in the 12 months prior to selection, completed further training relevant to their role as a best interests assessor; and

(e) has the skills necessary to obtain, evaluate and analyse complex evidence and differing views and to weigh them appropriately in decision making.

Eligibility to carry out a mental capacity assessment

6. A person is eligible to carry out a mental capacity assessment if that person is eligible to carry out –

(a) a mental health assessment; or

(b) a best interests assessment.

Eligibility to carry out an eligibility assessment

7. A person is eligible to carry out an eligibility assessment if that person is –

(a) approved under section 12 of the Mental Health Act 1983 and is eligible to carry out a mental health assessment; or

(b) an approved mental health professional and is eligible to carry out a best interests assessment.

Eligibility to carry out an age assessment

8. A person is eligible to carry out an age assessment if that person is eligible to carry out a best interests assessment.

Eligibility to carry out a no refusals assessment

9. A person is eligible to carry out a no refusals assessment if that person is eligible to carry out a best interests assessment.

Part 3   Selection of assessors

Selection of assessors – relatives

10. (1)   A supervisory body must not select a person to carry out an assessment if the person is –

(a) a relative of the relevant person; or

(b) a relative of a person who is financially interested in the care of the relevant person.

(2) For the purposes of this regulation a 'relative' means –

(a) a spouse, ex-spouse, civil partner or ex-civil partner;

(b) a person living with the relevant person as if they were a spouse or a civil partner;

(c) a parent or child;

(d) a brother or sister;

(e) a child of a person falling within sub-paragraphs (a), (b) or (d);

(f) a grandparent or grandchild;

(g) a grandparent-in-law or grandchild-in-law;

(h) an uncle or aunt;

(i) a brother-in-law or sister-in-law;

    (j) a son-in-law or daughter-in-law;

    (k) a first cousin; or

    (l) a half-brother or half-sister.

(3) For the purposes of this regulation

    (a) the relationships in paragraph (2)(c) to (k) include step relationships;

    (b) references to step relationships and in-laws in paragraph (2) are to be read in accordance with section 246 of the Civil Partnership Act 2004; and

    (c) financial interest has the meaning given in regulation 11.

Selection of assessors – financial interest

11. (1) A supervisory body must not select a person to carry out an assessment where the person has a financial interest in the case.

(2) A person has a financial interest in a case where –

    (a) that person is a partner, director, other office-holder or major shareholder of the managing authority that has made the application for a standard authorisation; and

    (b) the managing authority is a care home or independent hospital.

(3) A major shareholder means –

    (a) any person holding one tenth or more of the issued shares in the managing authority, where the managing authority is a company limited by shares; and

    (b) in all other cases, any of the owners of the managing authority.

Selection of best interests assessors

12. (1) A supervisory body must not select a person to carry out a best interests assessment if that person is involved in the care, or making decisions about the care, of the relevant person.

(2) Where the managing authority and supervisory body are both the same body, the supervisory body must not select a person to carry out a best interests assessment who is employed by it or who is providing services to it.

Part 4 Assessments

Time frame for assessments

13. (1) Except as provided in paragraph (2), all assessments required for a standard authorisation must be completed within the period of 21 days beginning with the date that the supervisory body receives a request for such an authorisation.

(2) Where a supervisory body receives a request for a standard authorisation and the managing authority has given an urgent authorisation under paragraph 76 of Schedule A1 to the Act, the assessments required for that standard authorisation must be completed within the period during which the urgent authorisation is in force.

Time limit for carrying out an assessment to decide whether or not there is an unauthorised deprivation of liberty

14. Subject to paragraph 69(3) to (5) of Schedule A1 to the Act, an assessment required under that paragraph must be completed within the period of 7 days beginning with the date that the supervisory body receives the request from an eligible person.

Relevant eligibility information

15. (1)   This regulation applies where an individual is being assessed and the eligibility assessor and the best interests assessor are not the same person.

(2) The eligibility assessor must request that the best interests assessor provides any relevant eligibility information that the best interests assessor may have.

(3) The best interests assessor must comply with any request made under this regulation.

(4) In this regulation 'eligibility assessor' means a person selected to carry out the eligibility assessment under paragraph 46 of Schedule A1 to the Act.

Part 5   Requests for a standard authorisation

Information to be provided in a request for a standard authorisation

16. (1)   A request for a standard authorisation must include the following information –
   (a) the name and gender of the relevant person;
   (b) the age of the relevant person or, where this is not known, whether the managing authority believes that the relevant person is aged 18 years or older;
   (c) the address and telephone number where the relevant person is currently located;
   (d) the name, address and telephone number of the managing authority and the name of the person within the managing authority who is dealing with the request;
   (e) the purpose for which the authorisation is requested;
   (f) the date from which the standard authorisation is sought; and
   (g) whether the managing authority has given an urgent authorisation under paragraph 76 of Schedule A1 to the Act and, if so, the date on which it expires.

(2) Except as provided for in paragraph (3), a request for a standard authorisation must include the following information if it is available or could reasonably be obtained by the managing authority –
   (a) any medical information relating to the relevant person's health that the managing authority considers to be relevant to the proposed restrictions to the relevant person's liberty;
   (b) the diagnosis of the mental disorder (within the meaning of the Mental Health Act 1983 but disregarding any exclusion for persons with learning disability) that the relevant person is suffering from;
   (c) any relevant care plans and relevant needs assessments;
   (d) the racial, ethnic or national origins of the relevant person;
   (e) whether the relevant person has any special communication needs;
   (f) details of the proposed restrictions on the relevant person's liberty;
   (g) whether section 39A of the Act (person becomes subject to Schedule A1)(b) applies;
   (h) where the purpose of the proposed restrictions to the relevant person's liberty is to give treatment, whether the relevant person has made an advance decision that may be valid and applicable to some or all of that treatment;
   (i) whether the relevant person is subject to –

        (i) the hospital treatment regime,

        (ii) the community treatment regime, or

        (iii) the guardianship regime;

    (j) the name, address and telephone number of –

        (i) anyone named by the relevant person as someone to be consulted about his welfare,

        (ii) anyone engaged in caring for the person or interested in his welfare,

        (iii) any donee of a lasting power of attorney granted by the person,

        (iv) any deputy appointed for the person by the court, and

        (v) any independent mental capacity advocate appointed in accordance with sections 37 to 39D of the Act; and

    (k) whether there is an existing authorisation in relation to the detention of the relevant person and, if so, the date of the expiry of that authorisation.

(3) Where –

    (a) there is an existing authorisation in force in relation to the detention of the relevant person; and

    (b) the managing authority makes a request in accordance with paragraph 30 of Schedule A1 to the Act for a further standard authorisation in relation to the same relevant person, the request need not include any of the information mentioned in paragraph (2)(a) to (j) if that information remains the same as that supplied in relation to the request for the existing authorisation.

(4) In this regulation 'existing authorisation' has the same meaning as in paragraph 29 of Schedule A1 to the Act.

Part 6   Supervisory bodies: care homes

Disputes about the Place of Ordinary Residence

Application and Interpretation of Part 6

17. (1) This Part applies where –

    (a) a local authority ('local authority A') receives a request from –

        (i) a care home for a standard authorisation under paragraph 24, 25 or 30 of Schedule A1 to the Act, or

        (ii) an eligible person to decide whether or not there is an unauthorised deprivation of liberty in a care home under paragraph 68 of Schedule A1 to the Act;

    (b) local authority A wishes to dispute that it is the supervisory body; and

    (c) a question as to the ordinary residence of the relevant person is to be determined by the Secretary of State under paragraph 183 of Schedule A1 to the Act.

(2) In this Part –

    (a) 'local authority A' has the meaning given in paragraph (1); and

    (b) 'local authority C' has the meaning given in regulation 18(2).

Arrangements where there is a question as to the ordinary residence

18. (1) Local authority A must act as supervisory body in relation to a request mentioned in regulation 17(1)(a) until the determination of the question as to the ordinary residence of the relevant person.

(2) But where another local authority ('local authority C') agrees to act as the supervisory body in place of local authority A, that local authority shall become the supervisory body until the determination of the question as to the ordinary residence of the relevant person.

(3) When the question about the ordinary residence of the relevant person has been determined, the local authority which has been identified as the supervisory body shall become the supervisory body.

Effect of change in supervisory body following determination of any question about ordinary residence

19. (1)   Where the question of ordinary residence of the relevant person is determined in accordance with paragraph 183(3) of Schedule A1 to the Act, and another local authority ('local authority B') becomes the supervisory body in place of local authority A or local authority C, as the case may be, paragraphs (3) to (6) shall apply.

(2) Where the question of ordinary residence of the relevant person is determined in accordance with paragraph 183(3) of Schedule A1 to the Act and local authority C remains the supervisory body, paragraphs (7) to (9) shall apply.

(3) Local authority B shall be treated as the supervisory body that received the request mentioned in regulation 17(1)(a) and must comply with the time limits specified in –

  (a) regulation 13 for carrying out the assessments required for a standard authorisation; or

  (b) regulation 14 for carrying out an assessment required under paragraph 69 of Schedule A1 to the Act, as the case may be, where the assessments have still to be completed.

(4) Anything done by or in relation to local authority A or local authority C in connection with the authorisation or request, as the case may be, has effect, so far as is necessary for continuing its effect after the change, as if done by or in relation to local authority B.

(5) Anything which relates to the authorisation or request and which is in the process of being done by or in relation to local authority A or local authority C at the time of the change may be continued by or in relation to local authority B.

(6) But –

  (a) local authority A or local authority C does not, by virtue of this regulation, cease to be liable for anything done by it in connection with the authorisation or request before the change; and

  (b) local authority B does not, by virtue of this regulation, become liable for any such thing.

(7) Local authority C shall be treated as the supervisory body that received the request mentioned in regulation 17(1)(a) and must comply with the time limits specified in –

  (a) regulation 13 for carrying out the assessments required for a standard authorisation; or

  (b) regulation 14 for carrying out an assessment required under paragraph 69 of Schedule A1 to the Act, as the case may be, where the assessments have still to be completed.

(8) Anything done by or in relation to local authority A in connection with the authorisation or request, as the case may be, has effect, so far as is necessary for continuing its effect after the change, as if done by or in relation to local authority C.

(9) Anything which relates to the authorisation or request and which is in the process of being done by or in relation to local authority A at the time of the change may be continued by or in relation to local authority C.

(10)   But –

  (a) local authority A does not, by virtue of this regulation, cease to be liable for anything done by it in connection with the authorisation or request before the change; and

  (b) local authority C does not, by virtue of this regulation, become liable for any such thing.

Appendix 2
Helping people to make their own decisions

2A   A quick summary as set out in Chapter 3 of the Code of Practice to the Mental Capacity Act 2005

To help someone make a decision for themselves, check the following points:

Providing relevant information

- Does the person have all the relevant information they need to make a particular decision?
- If they have a choice, have they been given information on all the alternatives?

Communicating in an appropriate way

- Could information be explained or presented in a way that is easier for the person to understand (for example, by using simple language or visual aids)?
- Have different methods of communication been explored if required, including non-verbal communication?
- Could anyone else help with communication (for example, a family member, support worker, interpreter, speech and language therapist or advocate)?

Making the person feel at ease

- Are there particular times of day when the person's understanding is better?
- Are there particular locations where they may feel more at ease?
- Could the decision be put off to see whether the person can make the decision at a later time when circumstances are right for them?

Supporting the person

- Can anyone else help or support the person to make choices or express a view?

2B

If the person is still unable to make the decision and you have to act under s 5:

Key checks for decision-makers

1. What is the act or decision?
2. Why does it need to be performed now?
3. Do you have a reasonable belief that the person lacks capacity in relation to the matter at the particular time of intervention (see Appendix 3)? And finally
4. Can you confirm that it will be in the person's best interests and that you have followed the checklist (see Appendix 4).

Appendix 3
Assessing capacity

The quick summary at the beginning of Chapter 4 of the Code of Practice provides a useful checklist.

Assessing capacity

This checklist is a summary of points to consider when assessing a person's capacity to make a specific decision:

Presuming someone has capacity

- The starting assumption must always be that a person has the capacity to make a decision, unless it can be established that they lack capacity.

Understanding what is meant by capacity and lack of capacity

- A person's capacity must be assessed specifically in terms of their capacity to make a particular decision at the time it needs to be made.

Treating everyone equally

- A person's capacity must not be judged simply on the basis of their age, appearance, condition or an aspect of their behaviour.

Supporting the person to make the decision for themselves

- It is important to take all possible steps to try to help people make a decision for themselves.

Assessing capacity

- Anyone assessing someone's capacity to make a decision for themselves should use the two-stage test of capacity.
- Does the person have an impairment of the mind or brain, or is there some sort of disturbance affecting the way their brain or mind works? (It doesn't matter whether the impairment or disturbance is temporary or permanent.)
- If so, does that impairment or disturbance mean that the person is unable to make the decision in question at the time it needs to be made?

Assessing ability to make a decision

- Does the person have a general understanding of what decision they need to make and why they need to make it?
- Does the person have a general understanding of the likely consequences of making, or not making, this decision?
- Is the person able to understand, retain, use and weigh up the information relevant to this decision?
- Can the person communicate their decision (by talking, using sign language or any other means)? Would the services of a professional (such as a speech and language therapist) be helpful?

Assessing capacity to make more complex or serious decisions

- Is there a need for a more thorough assessment (perhaps by involving a doctor or other professional expert)?

Appendix 4
Best interests checklist

From the quick summary in Chapter 5 of the Code of Practice to the Mental Capacity Act 2005

A person trying to work out the best interests of a person who lacks capacity to make a particular decision ('lacks capacity') should:

Encourage participation

- Do whatever is possible to permit and encourage the person to take part, or to improve their ability to take part, in making the decision.

Identify all relevant circumstances

- Try to identify all the things that the person who lacks capacity would take into account if they were making the decision or acting for themselves

Find out the person's views

- Try to find out the views of the person who lacks capacity, including:
  - the person's past and present wishes and feelings – these may have been expressed verbally, in writing or through behaviour or habits
  - any beliefs and values (e.g. religious, cultural, moral or political) that would be likely to influence the decision in question
  - any other factors the person themselves would be likely to consider if they were making the decision or acting for themselves.

Avoid discrimination

- Not make assumptions about someone's best interests simply on the basis of the person's age, appearance, condition or behaviour.

Assess whether the person might regain capacity

- Consider whether the person is likely to regain capacity (e.g. after receiving medical treatment). If so, can the decision wait until then?

If the decision concerns life-sustaining treatment

- Not be motivated in any way by a desire to bring about the person's death. They should not make assumptions about the person's quality of life.

Consult others

- If it is practical and appropriate to do so, consult other people for their views about the person's best interests and to see if they have any information about the person's wishes and feelings, beliefs and values. In particular, try to consult:
  - anyone previously named by the person as someone to be consulted on either the decision in question or on similar issues
  - anyone engaged in caring for the person
  - close relatives, friends or others who take an interest in the person's welfare
  - any attorney appointed under a Lasting Power of Attorney or Enduring Power of Attorney made by the person
  - any deputy appointed by the Court of Protection to make decisions for the person.
- For decisions about major medical treatment or where the person should live and where there is no-one who fits into any of the above categories, an Independent Mental Capacity Advocate (IMCA) must be consulted (see Code, Chapter 10 for more information about IMCAs).
- When consulting, remember that the person who lacks the capacity to make the decision or act for themselves still has a right to keep their affairs private – so it would not be right to share every piece of information with everyone.

Avoid restricting the person's rights

- See if there are other options that may be less restrictive of the person's rights.

Take all of this into account

- Weigh up all of these factors in order to work out what is in the person's best interests.

Appendix 5
Multiple choice answers

This appendix gives the answers to the questions that appear at the end of some chapters. The first number gives the chapter number, so 2.1 is the first question at the end of Chapter 2. If the reasons for the answers are not clear, return to the body of the chapter for an explanation.

2.1 The Mental Capacity Act 2005:
   (a) Places advance decisions relating to treatment on a statutory footing ✓
   (b) Defines incapacity ✓
   (c) Retains the current common law test for capacity to consent to treatment, without change ☐
   (d) Introduces substituted decision-making in relation to healthcare matters ✓
   (e) Regulates research relating to incapacitated persons ✓
   (f) Fills the 'Bournewood Gap' by allowing deputies to authorise deprivation of liberty ☐

2.2 The Mental Capacity Act contains a checklist which determines who should be the decision-maker in any specified situation:
   (a) True ☐
   (b) False ✓

2.3 Under the Mental Capacity Act someone may be appointed under a Lasting Power of Attorney to make healthcare decisions for a person when he/she becomes incapacitated:
   (a) True ✓
   (b) False ☐

2.4 To be protected when doing anything under s 5 of the Act a person must:
   (a) Establish that the person lacks capacity in relation to the matter in question ✓
   (b) Notify the Public Guardian of the decision if it incurs significant costs ☐
   (c) Believe that the action will be in the person's best interests ✓
   (d) Obtain medical evidence of mental incapacity ☐
   (e) Inform the nearest relative of any action taken ☐

3.1 The Code of Practice to the Mental Capacity Act 2005 provides guidance for:

    (a) People assessing capacity ✓

    (b) People appointed as attorneys under Lasting Powers of Attorney ✓

    (c) People appointed as guardians under the Mental Health Act 1983 ☐

    (d) Deputies appointed by the Court of Protection ✓

    (e) Independent Mental Capacity Advocates ✓

    (f) Independent Mental Health Advocates ☐

3.2 Under the Mental Capacity Act a failure to follow the Code of Practice would always lead to court proceedings if reported to the relevant authority:

    (a) True ☐

    (b) False ✓

3.3 Principles for the Mental Capacity Act are set out in the Code of Practice and not in the Act itself:

    (a) True ☐

    (b) False ✓

4.1 Key principles of the Mental Capacity Act include:

    (a) A presumption of capacity exists for all those aged 16 or over ✓

    (b) All practicable steps are to be taken to help a person make the decision before they're considered incapable ✓

    (c) An unwise decision implies a lack of capacity ☐

    (d) Acts done on behalf of an incapacitated person must be in his/her best interests ✓

    (e) All decisions made on behalf of an incapacitated person must be registered with the Court of Protection ☐

    (f) Decisions should be the least expensive available in terms of cost to the person ☐

    (g) Decisions should seek to be less restrictive in terms of the person's rights and freedom of action ✓

4.2 The Court of Protection is not covered by the principles as they only apply to other decision-makers under the Act:

    (a) True ☐

    (b) False ✓

5.1 A decision on a person's mental capacity needs to be made in relation to the particular matter at the time when the decision has to be made:

    (a) True ✓

    (b) False ☐

5.2 The test for capacity under the Mental Capacity Act is whether the person can:
   (a) Understand the relevant information ✓
   (b) Retain the relevant information ✓
   (c) Believe the relevant information ☐
   (d) Use or weigh the relevant information as part of the decision-making process ✓
   (e) Communicate the decision ✓
   (f) Read and sign a consent form ☐

5.3 The fact that a person is able to retain the information relevant to a decision for a short period only will prevent him from being regarded as able to make the decision:
   (a) True ☐
   (b) False ✓

6.1 According to the Mental Capacity Act decisions made in relation to an incapacitated person must be in that person's best interests but the list of points to consider are in the Code rather than being set out in the statute:
   (a) True ✓
   (b) False ☐

6.2 Following best interests could lead to the withdrawal of life-sustaining treatment:
   (a) True ✓
   (b) False ☐

6.3 The best interests checklist includes:
   (a) Decisions should not be based on a person's appearance ✓
   (b) Waiting where possible for the person to regain capacity ✓
   (c) Never going against the incapacitated person's current views ☐
   (d) Consulting anyone who has been named by the person ✓
   (e) Seeking to incur minimal expense for the person themselves ☐
   (f) Identifying all relevant circumstances ✓

11.1 The IMCA service:
   (a) Is based on a statutory requirement ✓
   (b) Uses only qualified solicitors ☐
   (c) Aims to represent and support people for particular acts ✓
   (d) Provides substituted decision-making in relation to healthcare matters ☐
   (e) May be involved in vulnerable adult procedures ✓
   (f) Has the right to interview certain people in private ✓

11.2 IMCAs provide a form of non-instructional advocacy:
    (a) True   ✓
    (b) False

11.3 An IMCA has the power to veto any decision made by a local authority
    or NHS Trust:
    (a) True
    (b) False   ✓

12.1 The following would be typical situations where the Court of Protection
    would be involved:
    (a) It was felt that there might be the need for a deputy to be appointed ✓
    (b) A person was appealing against detention under the Mental Health Act
    (c) A person wished to challenge a decision that he or she lacked capacity
         in relation to a matter ✓
    (d) A nearest relative wanted to make an application for guardianship
    (e) Someone alleged that an attorney was not applying the best
         interests checklist ✓
    (f) An IMCA believed a decision-maker was failing to take into account
         his or her submissions as to what was in the best interests of a person
         lacking capacity ✓

12.2 The Court of Protection can only intervene if the person in question
    has a mental disorder as defined by the Mental Health Act 1983:
    (a) True
    (b) False   ✓

12.3 The Public Guardian is responsible for:
    (a) Establishing and maintaining registers of LPAs ✓
    (b) Establishing and maintaining registers of guardianships under
         the Mental Health Act
    (c) Supervising court-appointed deputies ✓
    (d) Supervising nearest relatives appointed by the County Court
    (e) Directing Court of Protection Visitors to visit and report on persons
         lacking capacity ✓
    (f) Receiving reports from deputies or attorneys ✓

15.1 'An impairment of, or a disturbance in the functioning of, the mind or
    brain' is a key phrase to be found in **BOTH** the Mental Health Act 2007
    and the Mental Capacity Act 2005:
    (a) True
    (b) False   ✓

15.2 In *HL v UK* the European Court ruled that there had been breaches of:

(a) Article 3 – prohibition of torture ☐

(b) Article 5.1 – right to liberty and security of person ✓

(c) Article 5.4 – right to a speedy review of detention ✓

(d) Article 8.1 – right to respect for private and family life ☐

(e) Article 12 – right to marry and found a family ☐

(f) Article 14 – prohibition of discrimination ☐

15.3 The Mental Capacity Act limits the following areas to people of 18 or over:

(a) Making an advance decision ✓

(b) Any intervention under s 5 on the basis of mental incapacity ☐

(c) Making a Lasting Power of Attorney ✓

(d) Being a named person for consultation as part of the best interests checklist ☐

(e) Becoming an attorney under a Lasting Power of Attorney ✓

(f) Use of the new Bournewood safeguards when implemented ✓

16.1 The Government has introduced measures to close the 'Bournewood Gap'. For relevant cases supervisory bodies will commission which of the following assessments:

(a) Best interests ✓

(b) No refusals (e.g. from LPA) ✓

(c) Age ✓

(d) Financial ☐

(e) Eligibility ✓

(f) Whether receiving MHA s 117 after-care ☐

(g) Mental capacity ✓

(h) Abnormally aggressive or seriously irresponsible conduct ☐

(i) Mental health ✓

16.2 Under the new DOLS measures one professional could carry out all of the required assessments:

(a) True ☐

(b) False ✓

16.3 Under the new DOLS measures a representative will be appointed for the individual after deprivation of liberty has been authorised:

(a) True ✓

(b) False ☐

Appendix 6

Lasting Powers of Attorney and advance decisions

This appendix summarises some key points and questions relating to Lasting Powers of Attorney (LPAs) and to advance decisions. Details on the LPA points are contained in Chapter 8 and details on advance decisions are in Chapter 10.

Key points and questions relating to Lasting Powers of Attorney

- What area of decision-making does the person wish to cover?
- Does the LPA cover this area of decision-making?
- Have the formal requirements been met if the LPA covers life-sustaining treatment?
- Did the donor understand what was included in life-sustaining treatment?
- How old is the donor/attorney? They must both be at least 18.
- The LPA does not bypass best interests checklist and s 1 principles.
- Has the donor of a personal welfare LPA become incapacitated?
- Can the donor make the relevant decision for himself?
- Does the LPA cover the same ground as an advance decision?
- Is the attorney failing to act in the best interests of the donor, or abusing him?

Key points and questions relating to advance decisions

- If the advance decision is to refuse life-sustaining treatment, does it meet the formal requirements?
- Did the person have capacity when making the advance decision?
- Is there any evidence of a change of mind or of withdrawal?
- Is there a change of circumstances which may have affected the person's decision?
- Does the advance decision clearly cover the treatment in question?
- Did the person mean the advance decision to apply in these circumstances?
- If not meeting the requirements for an advance decision it may still be a statement of wishes to be considered under s 4
- An advance decision trumps the best interests checklist
- An advance decision does not cover treatment regulated by Part 4 of the Mental Health Act 1983
- Is there an LPA covering the same circumstances?

Appendix 7
Identifying a deprivation of liberty

For a deprivation of liberty to be occurring the following must be met:

Are the following present?	*Guidance*
Deprivation of liberty (continuous/ complete supervision *and* control *and* not free to leave) . . .	Ask whether the person(s) or body responsible for the individual have a plan which means that they need always broadly to know:
	• where the individual is; and
	• what they are doing at any one time.
	If 'yes' to both this is a strong pointer to continuous/complete supervision, and control (Law Society, 2015, page 26).
	See below in relation to those aged under 18.
	In relation to 'not free to leave', focus on the actions or potential actions of those providing care, not the individual. For example, what would those providing care do should the person or the person supported by a member of their family leave the place of residence? If attempts would be made to return the person, this is a strong indicator that the person is not free to leave.
for a not negligible length of time	This is difficult to define. In the case of *HL v UK* three months was considered too long in the absence of an authority; in the case of *Sessay* (2011), 12 hours of detention in a psychiatric hospital amounted to a deprivation of liberty; and in the case of *ZH* (2013) 40 minutes of police intervention and restraint amounted to deprivation of liberty.
a lack of valid consent	Is the person unable to make a decision because of an impairment of, or disturbance in, the functioning of the mind or brain? See Chapter 5 for more information in relation to the test for incapacity, and below for information in relation to the relevant information that the person may need to know to make the decision.

(Continued)

285

(Continued)

Are the following present?	Guidance
responsibility to the state	This is not clearly defined, but will include involvement of a public authority, and may include those self-funding, and utilising direct payments for residential accommodation in an establishment inspected by the state. See the Law Society's *Identifying a Deprivation of Liberty: A Practical Guide* (2015) for more information.

Establishing whether the person can give a valid consent

It can be difficult for decision-makers to decide what information an individual needs to be able to understand and weight as part of the process of making a decision. Often the courts refer to the 'salient details'; this, however, offers little guidance to those in practice. The following cases have outlined relevant information in relation to being accommodated in a hospital for the purpose of receiving care and treatment for mental disorder, and capacity to decide on residence, care and contact with others. Decision-makers should be cautious in relying upon these factors as a template when faced with similar decisions, as all cases differ, and therefore the facts of one case cannot be simply transposed to another.

In the case of *A PCT v LDV, CC and B Healthcare Group* (2013), the following salient details were considered relevant to L's decision to being accommodated in a hospital for the purpose of receiving care and treatment for mental disorder:

- *that she is in hospital to receive care and treatment for a mental disorder;*
- *that the care and treatment will include varying levels of supervision (including supervision in the community), use of physical restraint and the prescription and administration of medication to control her mood;*
- *that staff at the hospital will be entitled to carry out property and personal searches;*
- *that she must seek permission of the nursing staff to leave the hospital, and, until the staff at the hospital decide otherwise, will only be allowed to leave under supervision;*
- *that if she left the hospital without permission and without supervision, the staff would take steps to find and return her, including contacting the police.*

These points can be found at paragraph 39 of the above judgment, but it is important to note that the judge was *not seeking to set any sort of precedent, either as to the process to be followed or as to the type of information which is likely to be relevant in such cases, but merely to assist the parties in this case* (para 38); decision-makers must therefore consider the case before them, and decide what details are relevant to that decision.

The case of *LBX v K, L, M* (2013) considered the information that was and was not relevant to capacity to decide on residence, care and contact with others.

In relation to capacity to decide as to residence the following information was considered relevant:

- *what the two options are, including information about what they are, what sort of property they are and what sort of facilities they have;*
- *in broad terms, what sort of area the properties are in (and any specific known risks beyond the usual risks faced by people living in an area if any such specific risks exist);*
- *the difference between living somewhere and visiting it;*
- *what activities L would be able to do if he lived in each place;*
- *whether and how he would be able to see his family and friends if he lived in each place;*
- *in relation to the proposed placement, that he would need to pay money to live there, which would be dealt with by his appointee, that he would need to pay bills, which would be dealt with by his appointee, and that there is an agreement that he has to comply with the relevant lists of 'do's and 'don't's, otherwise he will not be able to remain living at the placement;*
- *who he would be living with at each placement;*
- *what sort of care he would receive in each placement in broad terms, in other words, that he would receive similar support in the proposed placement to the support he currently receives, and any differences if he were to live at home; and*
- *the risk that his father might not want to see him if L chooses to live in the new placement.*

And the following information was considered not relevant:

- *the cost of the placements and the value of money;*
- *the legal nature of the tenancy agreement or licence; and,*
- *what his relationship with his father might be in 10 or 20 years' time if L chooses to live independently now.*

In relation to capacity to decide as to contact with others the following information was considered relevant:

- *who they are and in broad terms the nature of his relationship with them; secondly,*
- *what sort of contact he could have with each of them, including different locations, differing durations and differing arrangements regarding the presence of a support worker; and*
- *the positive and negative aspects of having contact with each person. This will necessarily and inevitably be influenced by L's evaluations. His evaluations will only be irrelevant if they are based on demonstrably false beliefs. For example, if he believed that a person had assaulted him when they had not. But L's present evaluation of the positive and negative aspects of . . . contact will not be the only relevant information. His past pleasant experience of contact with his father will also be relevant and he may need to be reminded of them as part of the assessment of capacity.*

And the following information was considered not relevant:

- *abstract notions, like the nature of friendship and the importance of family ties,*
- *the long-term possible effects of contact decisions,*
- *risks which are not in issue, for example, risk of financial abuse.*

In relation to capacity to decide on care the following information was considered relevant:

- *what areas he needs support with,*
- *what sort of support he needs,*
- *who will be providing him with support,*
- *what would happen if he did not have any support or he refused it, and,*
- *that carers might not always treat him properly and that he can complain if he is not happy about his care.*

And the following information was considered not relevant:

- *that is how his care will be funded, and*
- *how the overarching arrangements for monitoring and appointing care staff work.*

As outlined above, these factors cannot be relied upon in all similar cases; decision-makers must consider the relevant information in relation to each individual case and take all practicable steps to help the person decide.

Appendix 8
The DOLS procedures

The managing authority (e.g. a hospital or care home) will apply to the supervisory authority (i.e. the PCT or National Assembly or local authority) for authorisation of deprivation of liberty. The supervisory authority then commissions six assessments: age; mental health; mental capacity; best interests; eligibility; and no refusals.

1. *Age.* The person must be 18 or older.
2. *Mental health.* The person needs to have a mental disorder as defined by the Mental Health Act 1983. People with no mental disorder could not be deprived of their liberty under this provision and application would have to be made to the Court of Protection.
3. *Mental capacity.* The person must lack capacity to make a decision to be accommodated in the hospital, nursing home or care home.
4. *Best Interests.* This test includes the following conditions: the person is, or is to be, a detained resident; it is in their best interests to be a detained resident; in order to prevent harm to that person it is necessary for him to be a detained resident. It also needs to be a proportionate response to the likelihood of the relevant person suffering harm, and the seriousness of that harm, for him to be a detained resident.
5. *Eligibility.* The person must not be subject to Mental Health Act compulsion which conflicts with the proposal. This will require a check that there is no conflicting guardianship order, community treatment order, or s 17 leave based on a liability to be detained under the Mental Health Act.
6. *No refusals.* There must be no valid refusal to the decision concerning the person's residence from someone in a position of authority such as a donee of a lasting Power of Attorney or a deputy appointed by the Court of Protection. For someone being treated in a hospital there must be no objection from the person themselves. In these circumstances there should be an assessment carried out under the Mental Health Act.

Authorisation of deprivation of liberty

If all six conditions are met the following points apply:

- Authorisation must be in writing and include the purpose of the deprivation of liberty, the time period (max. one year), any conditions recommended by the best interests assessor, and the reasons that each of the assessment criteria are met.
- The supervisory body appoints a representative for the person (usually on the recommendation of the best interests assessor).
- Any appeals are to the Court of Protection.

References

Publications

Allen, N (2009) Restricting movement or depriving liberty? *Journal of Mental Health, Law*, 19: 105–210.

Ashton, G, Letts, P, Oates, L and Terrell, M (2006) *Mental Capacity: The New Law*. Bristol: Jordans.

Barber, P, Brown, R and Martin, D (2012) *Mental Health Law in England and Wales* (2nd edition). London: Sage/Learning Matters.

Brown, R (2013) *The Approved Mental Health Professional's Guide to Mental Health Law*. London: Sage/Learning Matters.

Brown, R, Adshead, G and Pollard, A (2012) *The Approved Social Worker's Guide to Psychiatry and Medication*. London: Sage/Learning Matters.

Council of Europe (1950) *The European Convention on Human Rights*.

Department for Constitutional Affairs (2007) *Mental Capacity Act 2005: Code of Practice*. London: HMSO.

Department of Health (2004) *Advice on the Decision of the European Court of Human Rights in the Case of HL v UK (the 'Bournewood' case)* (gateway reference 4269).

Department of Health (2007) *Adult Protection, Care Reviews and Independent Mental Capacity Advocates (IMCA): Guidance on Interpreting the Regulations Extending the IMCA Role*.

Department of Health (2015) *Mental Health Act 1983: Code of Practice*. London: HMSO.

Department of Health and Welsh Office (1997) *Mental Health Act 1983: Code of Practice*. London: HMSO.

Harbour, A (2008) *Mentally Disordered Children and the Law*. London: Jessica Kingsley.

Jones, R (ed) (2008) *Mental Health Act Manual* (11th edition). London: Sweet and Maxwell.

Law Commission (1991) *Mentally Incapacitated Adults and Decision-Making: An Overview*. Consultation Paper No. 119. London: HMSO.

Law Commission (1995) *Mental Incapacity*. Law Com No. 231. London: HMSO.

Law Society (1989) *Decision-Making and Mental Incapacity: A Discussion Document*. Memorandum by the Law Society's Mental Health Sub-Committee.

Law Society (2015) *Identifying a Deprivation of Liberty: A Practical Guide*.

Lord Chancellor's Department (1997) *Who Decides? Making Decisions on Behalf of Mentally Incapacitated Adults.* Cm 3803.

Lord Chancellor's Department (1999) *Making Decisions.* Cm 4465.

Martin, E and Law, J (eds) (2006) *Oxford Dictionary of Law.* Oxford: Oxford University Press.

Ministry of Justice (2008) *Mental Capacity Act 2005: Deprivation of Liberty Safeguards. Supplement to the Main Code of Practice.* London: HMSO.

Montgomery, J (2002) *Health Care Law.* Oxford: Oxford University Press.

Puri, B, Brown, R, McKee, H and Treasaden, I (2005) *Mental Health Law.* London: Hodder Arnold.

Statutes

1948 National Assistance Act

1969 Family Law Reform Act

1976 and 2000 Race Relations Acts

1977 National Health Service Act

1983 Mental Health Act

1984 Police and Criminal Evidence Act

1985 Enduring Powers of Attorney Act 1985

1989 Children Act

1990 National Health Service and Community Care Act

1998 Human Rights Act

1999 Health Act

2004 Human Tissue Act

2005 Mental Capacity Act

2006 NHS Act

2007 Mental Health Act

2012 Health and Social Care Act

Regulations and statutory instruments

The Court of Protection Rules (SI 2007, No. 1744)

The Court of Protection Fees Order (SI 2007, No. 1745)

Lasting Powers of Attorney, Enduring Powers of Attorney and Public Guardian Regulations (SI 2007, No. 1253)

Medicines for Human Use (Clinical Trials) Regulations (SI 2004, No. 1031)

The Mental Capacity Act 2005 (Independent Mental Capacity Advocates) (General) Regulations (SI 2006, No. 1832)

The Mental Capacity Act 2005 (Independent Mental Capacity Advocates) (Expansion of Role) Regulations (SI 2006, No. 2883)

The Mental Capacity Act 2005 Loss of Capacity during Research Project (England) Regulations (SI 2007, No. 679)

The Mental Capacity Act 2005 (Transitional and Consequential Provisions) Order 2007 (SI 2007, No. 1898)

The Mental Capacity Act 2005 (Transfer of Proceedings) Order (SI 2007, No. 1899)

The Mental Capacity (Deprivation of Liberty: Standard Authorisations, Assessment and Ordinary Residence) Regulations (SI 2008, No. 1858)

The Public Guardian (Fees, etc.) Regulations (SI 2007, No. 2051)

Case law

Airedale NHS Trust v Bland (1993) 2 WLR 316

AJ v A Local Authority (2015) EWCOP5

A Local Authority v E (2012) EWHC 1639 (COP)

AM v SLAM (2013) UKUT 0365

An NHS Trust v Dr A (2013) EWHC 2409 (COP)

A PCT v LDV, CC and B Healthcare Group (2013) EWHC 272

B v Croydon Health Authority (1995) 2 WLR 294

Bird v Luckie (1850) 8 Hare 301

C (Adult: Refusal of Medical Treatment) (1994)

C v Blackburn with Darwen BC (2011) EWHC 3321 (COP)

CC v KK (2012) EWHC (COP)

GJ (2009) EWHC 2972

Hillingdon v Neary (2011) EWHC 1377

HL v UK (2005) EHRR 32 (the Bournewood case)

HM v Switzerland (2002) ECHR 157

JE v DE (1) Surrey CC (2) (2006) EWHC 3549 (Fam) (Deprivation of liberty)

LB Redbridge v G (2014) EWHC 485

LBX v K, L, M (2013) EWHC 3230

LLBC v TG (2007) EWHC 2640

Newcastle Foundation Trust v LM (2014) EWHC 454 (COP)

Nielsen v Denmark (2000) ECHR 81

NL v Hampshire County Council (2014) UKUT 475

Nottinghamshire Healthcare NHS Trust v RC (2014) EWHC 1317 (COP)

P v Cheshire West and Chester Council

P & Q v Surrey County Council (2014) UKSC 19

PC v City of York (2013) EWCA Civ 478

R v Ashworth Hospital (now Mersey Care NHS Trust), ex p *Munjaz* (2005) 3 WLR 793

R v Dunn (2010) EWCA Crim 2935

R(Munjaz) v Mersey Care NHS Trust (2005) UKHL 58

Re F (2009) MHLR 196

Re SA (Vulnerable Adult with Capacity: Marriage) (2006) 1FLR 867

Re T (Adult: Refusal of Medical Treatment) (1992) 4 All ER 649

Sessay v South London & Maudsley NHS Foundation Trust and the Commissioner of Police for the Metropolis (2011) EWHC 2617

Storck v Germany (2005) 43 EHRR 96

Trust A and X, A local authority, Y and Z (2015)

Winterwerp v Netherlands (1979) 2 EHHR 387

ZH v Commissioner of the Police for the Metropolis (2013) EWCA Civ 69

Some useful websites

Office of the Public Guardian	**www.gov.uk/government/organisations/ office-of-the-public-guardian**
Ministry of Justice	**www.justice.gov.uk**

(this used to be the Department of Constitutional Affairs on **www.dca.gov.uk**) and booklets are at **www.dca.gov.uk/legal-policy/mental-capacity/publications.htm**

Department of Health	**www.dh.gov.uk**
Welsh Assembly	**www.wales.gov.uk**
Care Quality Commission	**www.cqc.org.uk**
Dave Sheppard	**www.mhaandmca.co.uk**

Index